The Media Teacher's Handbook

The Media Teacher's Handbook is an indispensable guide for all teachers, both specialist and non-specialist, delivering Media Studies and media education in secondary schools and colleges.

It is the first text to draw together the three key elements of secondary sector teaching in relation to media study – the *theoretical*, the *practical* and the *professional* – in order to support media teachers throughout their careers:

- Section one: *Contexts* explores the history of, rationale for, and justification of studying the Media from 1900 to the present day, and considers the tensions implicit in the subject caused by opposing views of culture.
- Section two: *Curriculum* comprises seven chapters that focus on studying the media from Key Stages 3 and 4 in English, through GCSE and A level Media Studies. It also explores approaches to teaching the Creative and Media Diploma, media and citizenship, and practical media production.
- Section three: *Career development* is designed to support those establishing and leading Media Studies departments and those who are charged with the initial preparation and professional development of teachers.

Written by experts involved in the teaching, training and examination of Media Studies, this one-stop resource is packed with illustrative case studies and exemplar schemes of work that can be easily adapted for your own needs. *Further reading* and *recommended resources* sections at the end of each chapter list additional books, films, DVDs, groups, agencies, organisations, contact details, websites and other materials that will support your teaching even further.

The Media Teacher's Handbook is an essential guide to the theory, pedagogy and practice of media education that will enable you to teach your subject expertly and with confidence.

Elaine Scarratt was founding Chair of the Media Education Association and is a freelance media adviser, teacher-trainer and writer.

Jon Davison has been Professor of teacher education in four universities including the Institute of Education, University of London, where he was also Dean.

The Me
Handbo

Edited by
Elaine Sc

Routledge
Taylor & Francis Group

LONDON AND NEW YORK

First published 2012
by Routledge
2 Park Square, Milton Park, Abingdon, Oxon OX14 4RN

Simultaneously published in the USA and Canada
by Routledge
711 Third Avenue, New York, NY 10017

Routledge is an imprint of the Taylor & Francis Group, an informa business

British Library Cataloguing in Publication Data
A catalogue record for this book is available from the British Library

Library of Congress Cataloging in Publication Data
Scarratt, Elaine.
   The media teacher's handbook/Elaine Scarratt and Jon Davison.
   p. cm.
   Includes bibliographical references and index.
   1. Mass media (Study and teaching) – United States. 2. Education, Higher – United
States. 3. Educational technology. 4. Digital media. I. Davison, Jon. II. Title.
   P91.5.U5S34 2012
   302.23071'1—dc23
   2011018385

ISBN: 978–0–415–49993–4 (hbk)
ISBN: 978–0–415–49994–1 (pbk)
ISBN: 978–0–203–22221–8 (ebk)

Typeset in Galliard
by Florence Production Ltd, Stoodleigh, Devon

MIX
Paper from
responsible sources
FSC   FSC® C004839
www.fsc.org

Printed and bound in Great Britain by
TJ International Ltd, Padstow, Cornwall

Contents

Illustrations

Figures

Schemes of Work

Table

Worksheets

Contributors

Christine Bell has taught Media Studies for 23 years at a large city comprehensive school of 2,000+ pupils in northeast England, where the school offers GCSE and A level Media Studies. Christine has been Director of Media for 15 years. She is a coursework moderator and Principal Examiner for the MS1 A level paper for the Welsh Joint Education Committee and a key deliverer at the Media Education Wales conference.

Jon Davison has been a Professor of teacher education in four UK universities including the Institute of Education, University of London where he was also Dean. His research interests include sociolinguistics, the teaching and learning of English and Media, citizenship education and the professional formation of teachers. Prior to working in universities he had been head of English and Media Studies in a large London comprehensive. He became an advisory teacher at the English and Media Centre, London, where he co-authored and edited two award-winning media study publications. He has published extensively on the teaching and learning of English and Media and on teacher education – most recently, *Professional Values and Practice* (Routledge 2005) and *Learning to Teach English in the Secondary School* 3rd edition (Routledge 2009), *Debates in English Teaching* (Routledge 2010). He is fellow of the Royal Society of Arts, the Higher Education Academy and the College of Teachers and Chair of the Society for Educational Studies.

Kate Domaille trained to be a teacher of English and Media in 1989 at the Institute of Education, University of London. She taught for 12 years in Camden and Islington building GCSE and A level Media courses in the schools and colleges in which she worked. She was a British Board of Film Classification Examiner and became a freelance writer and trainer in media education. Since 2002, Kate has worked as PGCE Tutor on the Secondary English course at Southampton University. Currently, she also provides Masters-level teaching support on the Institute of Education/BFI distance-learning programme and is an executive member of the Media Education Association. She has authored media teaching and learning materials on the MEA website to support the Training and Development Agency funded Teacher Training Resource Bank.

Jenny Grahame taught Sociology, English and Media Studies in Inner London comprehensive schools from 1974–1987. Since 1987 she has worked as Advisory Teacher and Consultant for Media Education at the English and Media Centre, London, where she runs courses in all aspects of media education and Media Studies, writes teaching resources and publications, and is Editor of *MediaMagazine*. She has been an examiner for Media Studies at GCSE and A level, and has developed a variety of CPD courses in Media Education, from PGCE to M Level, for many local authorities, Birkbeck College and the Institute of Education, London University. She has published extensively for the English and Media Centre: most recently, *Doing News, Doing TV Drama* and *Doing Ads*, which won the ERA Best Secondary Resource award. She is currently contributing to a major research project undertaken by the Centre for the Study of Children, Youth and the Media, investigating progression in the development of media literacy across the key stages. She is a founder member and Vice Chair of the Media Education Association.

Elaine Homer is Advanced Skills Teacher for Media at a large comprehensive school with specialist Arts College status in southeast London and she provides INSET for teachers across the borough. She is an ex-head of department with 13 years successful experience of course development and teaching across a range of media courses in three different London schools. She has published articles for the *MEA Magazine* and *Point of View*, the journal for the Media Education Association.

Rob McInnes is Head of Film and Media Studies at a large inner London comprehensive school that has run film and media courses for over 40 years. He has taught and examined on a range of Media Studies and English courses and has contributed to the development of several resources for secondary teachers (including *Screening Shorts*, BFI). He is the author of a number of articles, books and teaching materials on film and media including, most recently, *Teen Movies; A Teacher's Guide* and *Classroom Resources* (Auteur 2008).

Adam Ranson undertook a Masters degree in Media and Cultural Studies and has over 20 years' experience of teaching Media. Currently, he is BTEC Media Production Course leader at a college in southwest England. He is an assistant examiner for A level Media Studies and moderator for Broadcast Media Awards. He is an educational consultant and freelance writer for Available Light TV Productions/Channel 4. He has considerable experience running Media INSET courses for teachers including, for example, teaching E-Media and Web 2.0. He has a number of publications that have been published by the Higher Education Funding Council for England, the Department for Children, Schools and Families and Channel 4.

Elaine Scarratt is a freelance media adviser, teacher-trainer and writer. She is a member of the national Executive of the Media Education Association, of which she was the founding Chair from 2007–2009. She is an experienced media teacher who has worked in several large comprehensive schools, and was formerly Head of Media at Christ the King VI Form College. She is an Associate Tutor of the British Film Institute and Visiting Lecturer for London Metropolitan University's Secondary PGCE in English, Media and Drama. Elaine delivers INSET for teachers throughout the UK – BFI, Keynote Education, Philip Allan Associates; events for students – BFI, Belfast *Cinemagic* International Film Festival and writes resources for use in the classroom. She has contributed chapters on teaching media in the three editions of *Learning to Teach English in the Secondary School* (Routledge 1997, 2005, 2009) and her recent publications include *The Science Fiction Genre: A Teacher's Guide* (Auteur 2001), *The Science Fiction Genre: Classroom Resources* (Auteur 2001) and *Studying The Alien Quadrilogy* (Auteur 2010).

Roy Stafford worked on curriculum development in vocational media education as an FE lecturer in the 1970s and 1980s. He also started teaching film in adult education at this time and that continues today. After two years in teacher education he became a freelance lecturer, writer and examiner for various Awarding Bodies in 1991. Since then, Roy has travelled widely visiting many schools and colleges, examining and delivering events for students and teachers. He has co-written *The Media Student's Book* with Gill Branston (5th edition, Routledge 2010) and also written *Understanding Audiences and the Film Industry* (BFI 2007) as well as a range of other guides and teaching materials. Between 1991 and 2008 he edited the media education magazine *in the picture* and in 2009 helped launch *PoV* for the Media Education Association. His current work is mainly in cinema-based film education with an emphasis on film from outside Hollywood. Much of this work is collected on the blog 'The Case for Global Film' at itpworld.wordpress.com.

Emma Walters completed a BA in Broadcasting at Falmouth College of Art, Cornwall in 1996, after which she worked in the television industry for a variety of companies including Live TV, M.I.D.A (Moving Image Development Agency), Mersey TV, Red Productions, Rapture TV and Granada in a range of production roles including research, journalism, script and scheduling departments. While working in industry she completed a PgDip in Script Editing at John Moore's University in 1999. Since 2002, Emma has taught in Further Education in northwest England.

Jon Wardle is the Director of The Centre for Excellence in Media Practice at the only HEFCE Centre for Excellence in Media area in a UK university. He is chair of the annual Media Education Summit and is on the editorial board of the *Media Education Research Journal*. Jon is course leader of MA in Creative and Media Education and is a member of the *Skillset* 14–19 Diploma in Creative and Media development partnership. Alongside his media education research interests, he is active in the area of Media Business. In 2008 the National Association of Television Production Executives (NATPE) awarded him Educational Fellow status. Jon has led sessions as part of tailored training/consultancy for Al Jazeera, Fremantle, News Corp and Endemol UK. He completed an MBA at Southampton University and is currently working towards his Doctorate at Bristol University.

Introduction

Elaine Scarratt and Jon Davison

> Media Studies has challenged curricula, even though there are still schools and colleges where the subject option is still unavailable.
>
> (Alvarado, Gutch and Wollen, 1987: 5)

> I didn't realise until I did a film unit in my English degree that you could study film as part of education; it was brilliant. We filmed critical responses to one of our English texts as characters in the *Big Brother* house.
>
> (Aidan Thompson, doctoral student, University of Birmingham, 2011)

Both quotations that open this book sketch the frustrating contradictions in the contemporary media education landscape. At first glance media education appears to be flourishing and characterised by cross-curricular innovation, active pedagogy, creative use of technology for critical analysis, collaborative peer-to-peer learning and enthusiastic student engagement. There are over 40 specialist media arts schools, a number of which are producing inspiring curriculum innovations and Media Studies courses involve a greater number of students than ever before. However, while there are pockets of excellence across the UK, provision is patchy, and of variable quality, despite study of the Media being a statutory National Curriculum requirement.

As we shall explore in this book there are substantial contemporary and historical reasons for this apparently contradictory state of affairs that include cultural prejudices and entrenched views about cultural worth enacted in government education policies, and expressed by some social commentators and educationists, press antipathy and defensiveness, and diverse views of some media education advocates about the purposes and practices of media education.

The increasing and varied repertoire of academic and pre-vocational qualifications is an indication of students' interest in studying the Media. In addition to Media Studies, the range of courses includes Film Studies, Moving Image Media, Communication and Culture, iMedia, Applied Media, Communication and Production, Cultural and Media Diploma, BTEC Nationals Media, OCR Nationals Extended Diploma, NFCE Animation, NFCE Interactive Media, and so on. All these areas have or require fuller treatment elsewhere to do them justice. This book focuses on Media Studies, as it is currently the most common specialist media qualification studied in secondary schools and so likely to be tackled by teachers new to the media education field.

With such a wide array of media qualifications and curriculum practices that cross over into other subject areas, and confused and ill-informed public debate about culture and media, there can be an understandable lack of clarity as to what exactly the term 'Media Studies' means. In the same way that opportunities for learning about the Media are available but still 'hidden' for some students as the second opening quotation illustrates, opportunities for learning to teach about the Media (though typically fragmented, limited in scope and transitory), are not readily identifiable. It is a situation for too long compounded by the fact that there is no tradition of systemic formal professional preparation to teach the subject.

The Media Teacher's Handbook is the first book to draw together the three key elements of secondary sector teaching in relation to media study – the *theoretical*, the *practical* and the *professional* in order to support media teachers throughout their careers. Therefore, the book is divided into three broad sections: *Contexts, Curriculum* and *Career development* as it is intended to support teachers at all stages of their careers: from student- and newly-qualified teachers to experienced media teachers intending to become, or recently appointed, head of department. It will also support tutors and mentors working with inexperienced teachers during professional preparation and induction and those with responsibility for continuing professional development in schools, universities and local authorities. As well as providing practical advice on curricula and pedagogy, the book will support PGCE students, NQTs and colleagues following Masters-level courses in universities and schools.

Section One: *Contexts*

The first section of *The Media Teacher's Handbook* explores the history of, rationale for and justification of studying the Media from 1900 to the present day, and considers the tensions implicit in the subject that have resulted from opposing views of culture. Chapters 1 and 2 serve as an introduction to the field. The first chapter, *Media education: politics and policy*, provides a broad cultural and historical context for the uneven provision of media education, by exploring traditional and contemporary debates related to assumed hierarchies of cultural worth and the purposes of education. Chapter 2, *What is media education?*, aims broadly to orientate those new to teaching Media Studies with outlines of its key features and the conceptual framework of enquiry and characteristic pedagogy that informs specialist practice. It also considers issues raised in a number of current debates circulating in media education and Media Studies, for example: 'What is meant by media literacy and creativity?' Chapter 3, *Internet, computer games and media learning*, makes the case that in responding to the evolution of media technology and its new generations of users, media study should correspondingly evolve its own analytic discourse from 'Media 1.0' towards 'Media 2.0'. Chapter 4, *Global and local in media education*, the last chapter in this section, addresses the National Curriculum cross-curricular dimensions of 'Global dimension and sustainable development' with a focus on the global, and 'Identity and cultural diversity'. It shows how media texts, concepts and active pedagogy can shape and enhance cross-curricular enquiry into the dimensions' themes.

Section Two: *Curriculum*

The second, and largest, section of the book comprises seven chapters that focus on studying the Media from Key Stages 3 and 4 in English, through GCSE and A level Media Studies. The section also explores approaches to teaching the Creative and Media Diploma, media and citizenship, and practical media production.

Chapter 5, *Media and English in KS3 and KS4*, offers a broad overview of the state of play for media education for students aged 11–16 in the English curriculum, explores the new opportunities opening up for media study, and provides practical strategies for exploiting them to develop media skills both within, and despite, the constraints of the National Curriculum English Programmes of Study.

Chapters 6 and 7 focus on the teaching and learning of GCSE Media Studies.

Chapter 6, *Media Studies GCSE (1): possibilities and practice*, includes a comprehensive account of the Awarding Bodies' key specification requirements and issues to consider for planning schemes of work and preparing students for external assessment. It provides an exemplar course plan, advice on managing practical work and details of the technical resources needed for teaching the subject. Chapter 6 provides a context for Chapter 7, *Media Studies GCSE (2): schemes of work*, which is a comprehensive guide to constructing Unit 2, the controlled assessment section of a GCSE Media Studies course, with detailed schemes of work and case studies. The scheme of work is for the AQA Awarding Body specification, but the suggested texts and approaches can be easily adapted for OCR and WJEC.

Chapter 8, *Media Studies A level: an introduction*, outlines the key features of Awarding Body Specifications, offers some approaches to teaching and managing their delivery, and guidance to the wide range of supporting materials and sources of advice. Awarding Bodies provide a wealth of advice and guidance to support the many enthusiastic, but currently non-specialist, teachers in addressing the required high levels of practical and theoretical knowledge. Through indicating the Awarding Bodies' shared and divergent interpretations of the A level Media Studies course structures, the chapter aims to substantiate understanding of the pedagogy and educational philosophy that have shaped the specifications' content in this transitional phase of media education prompted by digital communication technologies.

Chapter 9, *Creative and Media Diploma*, argues that students' understanding of the discipline is closely aligned to the teaching and learning strategies employed, not simply the material covered through the curriculum and that the Diploma offers an opportunity for rethinking the media educator's role. The following chapter, *Media and citizenship*, is designed to support both Media Studies teachers with limited knowledge of the citizenship curriculum and teachers of citizenship with little experience of media teaching. It considers approaches to teaching about the news and provides a media case study related to identity and cultural diversity.

Chapter 11, *Practical media production*, examines the now inevitable centrality of media and information and communications technology (ICT) to the development of students' media literacy through not only viewing, listening to, and reading of, a wide range of mass media forms, but also through 'writing' their own media texts. This chapter provides approaches to 'low-tech' and 'high-tech' pre-production, production and editing activities in a range of media including desktop production (DTP), video, photography, website design, radio and video games.

Section Three: *Career development*

The final section of the book is designed to support colleagues in establishing and leading Media Studies departments and those who are charged with the initial preparation and professional development of teachers. Chapter 12, *Setting up, resourcing and managing a media department* contains support and advice for any media teacher setting up and managing a Media Studies department not only in relation to curriculum, equipment and resources, but also including a variety of departmental aspects such as staffing, timetabling, managing a budget, cross-curricular and extra-curricular links, links with outside agencies, monitoring, standardisation and assessment. Chapter 13 considers the *Professional preparation, progression and development of media teachers*. It explores the professional preparation of teachers for teaching media, drawing on approaches in Initial Teacher Education as well as post-qualification and Continuing Professional Development.

Reading and resources

As appropriate, chapters in this book outline key information and knowledge, rationales, issues and debates related to the area under consideration. Those with a curriculum focus introduce key learning areas and illustrative activities and pedagogy. The case studies included in chapters are ones that have worked well consistently; however their main purpose is illustrative since the best teaching and learning comes from teachers developing their own versions to suit their practice and their particular students.

Suggested *Further reading* texts at the ends of chapters will provide the reader with further insights and in-depth analysis of topics under consideration. Additionally, lists of *Recommended resources* at the ends of chapters include information on additional recommended books, films, dvds, groups, agencies, organisations, addresses, contact details, websites and other materials that will further support the reader. While every care has been taken to ensure that the recommendations listed are fully available at the time of publication and that websites have been selected for relative longevity and institutional reliability, as well as usefulness, with a change of government and an attendant recession economic policy axe there can be no definitive guarantees. Nevertheless, it is also likely that the websites for organisations thus affected will remain extant for some time.

Elaine Scarratt and Jon Davison

Recommended resources

Books

Fiske, J. (2010) *Introduction to Communication Studies* (3rd edition), London: Routledge.
Fiske, J. (2010) *Understanding Popular Culture* (2nd edition), London: Routledge.

Media educators' organisations

Association for Media Education in Scotland (AMES): the subject association for Scotland, contact d@murphy47.freeserve.co.uk. The *MEJ (Media Education Journal)* is available by subscription from rpreece@onetel.com.
Media Education Association (MEA): the subject association for England, Wales, N. Ireland and overseas: www.themea.org. Free membership, annual conference with cutting edge debates and classroom support, range of online information and materials including *PoV* the MEA journal. Teacher education materials also accessed via the TTRB.
Media Education Wales (MEW): strong focus on practical projects in Wales, and practical work resources www.mediaedwales.org.uk. Tom Barrance, Director of MEW, blogspot http://tombarrance.blogspot.com/.

Industry regulators

Advertising Standards Authority (ASA): independent regulator for all media, the site includes latest adjudications, and a hotlink to the Committee of Advertising Practice (CAP) codes, http://bcap.org.uk/.

British Board of Film Classification (BBFC): the film and video game regulator has a very good education site and will visit schools, www.sbbfc.co.uk/.

Ofcom: independent regulator and competition authority for UK communications industries, www.ofcom.org.uk/. Remit to Ofcom also has a remit for public (digital) media literacy; research findings and a monthly media literacy e-bulletin are at http://stakeholders.ofcom.org.uk/market-data-research/media-literacy/.

Press Complaints Commission (PCC): independent self-regulators, site includes Editors' Code of Practice and archive of cases, www.pcc.org.uk/index.html.

Contexts

Chapter 1

Media education
Politics and policy

Elaine Scarratt and Jon Davison

> Widespread media literacy is essential if all citizens are to wield power, make rational decisions, become effective change agents and have an active involvement with the media. It is in this much wider sense of 'education for democracy' that media education can play the most significant role of all.
>
> (Masterman 1985: 11–13)

> The media are undoubtedly the major contemporary means of cultural expression and communication: to become an active participant in public life necessarily involves making use of the modern media.
>
> (Buckingham 2003: 5)

Introduction

In many ways media education can be perceived as established and even flourishing. It has had a presence in teaching and learning activities for over 50 years, an expanding portfolio of formal qualifications for over 30 years, it has been a core curriculum element in subject English for over 20 years, and specialist Media Arts schools are now part of education's institutional landscape. If education is preparation for fruitful adult citizenship in a mass communication society, then arguments for studying media in the school curriculum were long ago self-evident – the Media's significance as a quantifiable existence in people's lives, forms of cultural expression and communication, and its industrial and economic value.

Media education as a grassroots movement of classroom teachers and other stakeholder advocates has had a long, patchy and disparate evolution. The main impetus has been to ensure that it does happen and characteristic contents, academic underpinnings and pedagogies have emerged. However, there has not been overarching agreement or sustained philosophy about its purpose.

> We spend very little time discussing what we are trying to achieve and what the measures of success might be.
>
> (Fraser and Wardle, 2011)

This is a concern, particularly given the speed of changes in communication technology and its uses, which is now being illustrated and addressed by media educators via the Manifesto for Media Education website set up by Fraser and Wardle: www.manifesto formediaeducation.co.uk/why-a-manifesto/.

The strength of such a grassroots movement, however, is in its sense of ownership and therefore sustained commitment. Generations of education practitioners have been committed to valuing the Media as 'the important and concrete' (Masterman 1980: 12) in young people's lives. Here Masterman is referring to television, but as digital technologies rapidly increase reception opportunities and creative possibilities the Media has become even more widely embedded in daily life. While social and economic 'digital divides' must be acknowledged, such technologies are increasingly integral to young people's daily entertainment, information gathering and social networking. In school they offer immediate relevance to stimulate students' general engagement in education. It is not unreasonable to expect that an education curriculum in tune with such contemporary developments should enthusiastically embrace media education.

While these arguments are 'disarmingly obvious' (Alvarado and Boyd-Barrett 1992: 94) and repeated by media education advocates to the point of 'banality' (Buckingham 2011), they are still current and yet to be fully realised. Media education, like any other subject area, is ever vulnerable to political whim: more so given its often-negative public profile. Education is political, and education policy is one of the early ways in which new governments establish their ideological intentions – the current Conservative/Liberal coalition being no exception. While media education embraces change, successive governments' responses to media education have ranged from active antipathy to circumspection and partial endorsement. Overall:

> the case has not been listened to ... and despite occasional signs of commitment to the field, policy-makers still appear to be ill-informed about its basic aims and methods.
>
> (Buckingham 2003: ix)

The purpose of this chapter is not to bemoan the past – indeed there have been several constructive public policy initiatives – but to provide a broad cultural and historical context for the uneven provision of media education, and its positioning in the mainstream secondary curriculum within another subject: English. The focus is on media in relation to English, as many student teachers are likely to be experiencing media education, perhaps for the first time, via English Initial Teacher Education (ITE) courses. This chapter can be read in conjunction with Chapter 5, which develops the advent of the 1988 National Curriculum and its subsequent versions, and demonstrates how the limited manifestation of media as 'multimodality' in the core English curriculum can be imaginatively and purposefully adapted. A chapter this length can only offer a snapshot of key moments in the complex interplay of stakeholder advocates and contemporary political, social and cultural conditions; readers are referred to the detailed chronicles noted in 'Recommended reading' below.

A (very) brief cultural and educational history

Diverse agencies in the secondary and Higher Education (HE) sectors aided the formation of secondary media education. Not least were individuals and groups of schoolteachers, and university and art college lecturers. Supportive organisations included subject associations – the National Association of Teachers of English (NATE), especially its regional London branch LATE, and the Association for Media Education in Scotland (AMES). There were also volunteer collectives of teachers and lecturers such as the Society for Education in Film and Television (SEFT); government-funded cultural agencies such as the British Film Institute (BFI); and local education professional development centres, most notably the English and Media Centre in London.

There have been several approaches to unpicking this complex yet patchy media education history. Bolas (2009) provides an in-depth forensic analysis of SEFT's pivotal role. Buckingham (2003) selects three historical paradigm shifts to 'trace different rationales and motivations' for teaching media education, which he summarises into three 'tendencies': democratisation, defensiveness and preparation (Buckingham 2003: 5–17). It is also challenging to match direct links to types of media education being practiced. Broadly speaking, media education today could be characterised by those who see the field as predominantly technology led to explore new media practices and forms; the centrality of creative production skills as intrinsically valid and the main means to developing both academic understanding and pre-vocational skills; and a Cultural Studies tradition of engaging analytically with meanings. On the other hand, Alvarado *et al.* (1987), looking back to developments up to that point, organised the field into 'histories' of four media education strands: cultural, political, sociological and skills.

The terms, apart from 'skills', are useful to delineate the field's overlapping areas of historical development. 'Skills' charts the emergence of government-initiated vocational and pre-vocational courses as well as critically reflective production work. However, the term 'skills' now has more specific connotations so the term 'production work' will be used. The 'sociological' strand came from early twentieth-century America's version of mass communication laboratory research based largely on psychology, which assumes that the Media has strong influential power over a passive audience. It is now regarded as an outdated effects model, but it was widely adopted, informed much educational policy documentation, and has prevailing public influence today. The 'political' promotes media education as a means of social empowerment and transformation illustrated by the Masterman quotation above that could now also be seen as a citizenship position.

The focus in this chapter is on the 'cultural' strand, which charts how formal media education emerged out of or despite contemporary education, political and cultural contexts, and broadly produced the current mainstream academic versions of media education in KS3–KS5. The central story is a simplistic battle between defenders of 'high culture' against the invasion of worthless 'popular culture'. It is a binary *cul de sac* that is still at play in some quarters. However, Bazalgette (1991: 2–7) offers a starting point for a more productive consideration and questioning of culture as 'a whole complex web of ways in which we share understandings about the world' and 'everyone's creative and communicative experience', which may be anything from 'established art forms' to 'gestures, jokes and hairstyles'.

While acknowledging that study of the Media evolved from several subjects the chapter now considers its core curriculum location in English: the area where it tends to be located in ITE. English is also the subject area in much government documentation to which media education is both most closely linked and set in opposition; and shared experiences in these areas are instructive about the constructed nature of approved knowledge. While the two subjects overall remain distinct, for instance through 'the theoretical engagement with digital technologies' and 'attention to commercial context' (McDougall 2006: 3), they have shared histories of perceived questionable cultural worth, responses to changing technology, and being a means of social engineering policies.

The heritage model of English literature implies a long 'natural' place in education, but English as a discrete school subject appeared only at the beginning of the twentieth century:

the Oxford School of English having been established in 1894 amid strong opposition from Classicists such as Professor Sanday who declared 'English is a subject suitable for women and the second- and third-rate men who are to become schoolmasters' (Davison 1997: 20). State education was premised upon the need for a trained, obedient and literate workforce, and many of the debates about, and enquiries into, education have been in response to perceived economic and industrial needs. The advent of English was in response to the growth of Victorian technology that required workers to read instructions, and to clearly understand and give information. This utilitarian approach to reading and writing was later supplemented by encouragement to give pupils 'some power over language as an instrument of thought and expression' (Board of Education (BoE) 1904, in Davison 2009: 22). Ongoing fierce debates about the nature and purpose of English persisted in its progress from new to established subject, especially in the 1980s (see below).

Some key issues

A facet of the cultural conflict set up between media and English has been the assumed cultural superiority of the word over the visual.

> In the Middle Ages visual communication was, for the masses, more important than writing. But Chartres cathedral was not culturally inferior to the *Imago Mundi* of Honorius of Autun. Cathedrals were the TV of those times.
>
> (Eco 1997)

Bazalgette (2008/09: 13) has cogently argued that most people's communicative and expressive experience of the world has long been and continues to be richly 'multimodal', incorporating images, writing, design features, symbolic figures, pattern, scale and so on. 'To define "traditional" texts as though they always just consisted of writing is to adopt the historical perspective of the powerful: the minorities who could read and write.' This is not an argument against literacy but to stress the long existence of ordinary people having always had their own means of cultural expression. 'Traditionally' this has been albeit in ephemeral forms such as storytelling, drama, music, song, dance accessible to all, and much of this expression and exchange impetus can be seen on the social networking sites.

In 1871, poet and Her Majesty's Inspector (HMI) Matthew Arnold believed that English literature was 'the greatest power available in education': an assertion that has informed English studies ever since. However, in other countries, the educational and cultural agenda embraced then new media. In Russia Lenin declared, 'Of all the arts, for us cinema is the most important.' Lenin not only acknowledged the power of cinema, but he also used film as a central agent in his drive to dramatically increase levels of literacy. The first 20 years of the twentieth century saw unprecedented growth in the film industry in much the same way that the last 30 years of the twentieth century saw the growth of television, video, satellite and cable, and the twenty-first century is seeing rapid expansion of digital technology. But whereas Lenin saw cinema as an important tool for education, educationists in England were openly hostile to its supposed effects. *Children and the Cinematograph*, a Lancashire Education Committee report:

> found that, with one exception, all the head teachers who were consulted agreed that cinematograph shows were physically detrimental to scholars in consequence

of the late hours, loss of sleep, and the bad atmosphere, and that the mental effect upon the children was to make them more fond of noise, ostentatious display, self-advertisement, and change. The pictures excited their minds and created a love of pleasure and disinclination for steady work and effort.

(*TES* 1915)

One can only admire the lone, unnamed, far-sighted head teacher who dissented from these sentiments. Such arguments above have been well rehearsed in subsequent decades decrying the supposed effects of comics, television, video games, mobile phones, internet social networking sites and so on. Perhaps what is most significant here is the phrase 'more fond of . . . change'. A view of culture as somehow great, fixed and therefore complete can only be threatened by a developing popular culture – in this case, cinema. Conversely, it may be inferred that education was not to be enjoyed, its purpose was to create a hatred of 'pleasure' and develop an inclination for 'steady work and effort' that would not 'excite their minds'.

Such views about popular culture also reflected deep-seated prejudice and fears of the working class. Arnold's *Culture and Anarchy* (1869) dehumanised representation of 'it' as 'raw and half-developed . . . half hidden among poverty and squalour' resonated into the early decades of the twentieth century. Memories of nineteenth-century turbulence, and fears of further social unrest, were revived as left wing philosophies gained ground via the Labour Party (founded 1893). Contemporary education documents reiterate an English-as-a-civilising-agent philosophy in which 'great works' were assumed to have 'formative influences over character' (BoE 1910). Popular novels, however, were 'only of transitory interest', involved 'little or no mental effort' (BoE 1910), and so were unsuitable for reading in school though occasionally useful to stimulate points for discussion.

Throughout the 1920s and 1930s questions of power and control underpinned English teaching policy. A supposedly powerful disturbing popular culture threatened not only the dominant culture but also the control teachers had over pupils. If educationists were to retain their control of the cultural agenda and pupils, it was vital that popular culture be denigrated and dismissed. The first major investigation into English teaching, The Newbolt Report (1921), expressed concerns that established cultural norms were being rejected:

We were told that the working classes, especially those belonging to organised labour movements were antagonistic to, and contemptuous of, literature, that they regard it merely as an ornament, a polite accomplishment, a subject to be despised by really virile men . . . Literature, in fact, seems to be classed by a large number of thinking working men with antimacassars, fish knives and other unintelligible and futile trivialities of middle class culture and to sidetrack the working class movement.

(BoE 1921: para. 233)

The fear here is of '*thinking* working men' rejecting the dominant cultural values of society: much more dangerous, of course, than mindless rejection by *unthinking* working men. Elsewhere 'evil habits of speech contracted in home and street' caused teachers to 'struggle' not with working class 'ignorance' but with the 'perverted power' such speech symbolised. The duty of the teacher, therefore, was not to empower pupils but to control and somehow disempower them.

1930s

The 1920s and 1930s saw great expansion of the popular press, publishing houses, BBC television (1932) followed radio, and the global expansion of Hollywood cinema. The 'pleasures' of popular culture flourished amid a volatile political background and harsh social conditions of the General Strike (1926), the Great Depression, the continuing spread of communism, and the arrival and swift dismissal of the first Labour government. Educationists maintained a high-cultural agenda submitting pupils 'to the influences of the great tradition . . . to learn to do fine things in a fine way' and become proud of the 'unequalled literary heritage' (Spens Report 1938). Typical of such documents, the report reiterated a health of the nation metaphor that viewed popular culture as a disease that exposure to high culture would automatically cure. It railed against:

> the popularisation of the infectious accents of Hollywood. The pervading influences of the hoarding, the cinema, and a large section of the public press, are (in this respect as in others) subtly corrupting the taste and habits of the rising generation.
>
> (BoE 1938: 222–3)

Through the language of disease, corruption and perversion, the mass media were linked with the working class, and positioned as corrupting a 'generation' of children.

Phrases such as 'the great tradition' and 'literary heritage' invite reference to F.R. Leavis who, with Denys Thompson in their book *Culture and the Environment: The Training of Critical Awareness* (1933), provided 'the first systematic set of proposals for teaching about the mass media in schools' (Buckingham 2003: 6). Leavis's mission, though, was concerned with the plight of the arts in an industrial civilisation characterised by media mass production. Teaching about journalism, popular fiction, radio and advertisements alongside English literature was intended for students to 'discriminate' between the self-evident authentic values and standards of the literary heritage, and the mass media's commercialisation, standardisation, manipulation and false superficial pleasures, 'resistance' to which would automatically follow. Leavis's prime purpose was 'inoculation' against the virulent infection of popular culture, and this version of critical awareness – discernment, and cultivation of good taste – became the dominant cultural education discourse from the 1930s to 1950s and, for some, continues to be so. There was an ironic convergence of concern and method in that both Leavis and the then paternalistic and equally anti-American mass broadcaster, the BBC, introduced popular culture in order to lead the way to a healthier cultural diet.

1950s–1970s

> We live in an expanding culture, yet we spend much of our energy regretting the fact, rather than seeking to understand its nature and conditions.
>
> (Williams 1958: 12)

The first two decades of this era were significant in bringing the working class a new confidence about their place in society, and a measure of social mobility. The relative prosperity of the 1950s brought more disposable income and a novel consumer culture. Benefiting from free secondary education for all in the 1944 Education Act, regional working class artistes were becoming culturally prominent. The new, commercially funded, ITV television station met popular demands for more entertainment programming than the BBC's 'knowing what was good for you' schedules. A 'generation-gap' emerged as young people absorbed American media, and found a new cultural confidence in glamorous professions such as pop music, fashion and photography in the swinging sixties. The political landscape changed as left-wing politics (notably trade unions and university students) challenged the old order of unfair social divisions and the war mongering of previous generations.

In the academic world, the British Cultural Studies movement challenged Leavisite elitism and divisive notions of culture. Two early key figures proposed a more inclusive version: Richard Hoggart in *The Uses of Literacy* (1959), and Raymond Williams, in *Culture and Society* (1958) who argued for an anthropological account of culture as 'a whole way of life'. Rather than comprising set canons of privileged artefacts, culture was seen as a process 'concerned with the production and exchange of meaning between the members of a society or group' (Hall 1997: 2). Stuart Hall followed Hoggart as director of the Centre for Contemporary Cultural Studies (CCCS) at the University of Birmingham, and was one of the many influential theorists there whose ideas were absorbed into media education, including his decoding theory of reading, and ideas about culture and identity formation – particularly race. The focus of meaning making was shifted to both producers and consumers rather than being the preserve of the former. Popular culture was treated as a valid area of serious academic enquiry and attracted radical left wing analysis that applied theories such as Marxism, feminism, critical race and post-structuralist theories. Much CCCS thinking was disseminated into secondary education and its theoretical influence is most directly evident today in A level Media Studies. *The Popular Arts* (1964) by Stuart Hall and Paddy Whannel (then Head of the BFI Education Department) contained extensive suggestions for thematic and textual teaching about a range of media – pop music, magazines, advertising, television, cinema.

Overall motivations for media education were multifaceted but decidedly anti-American.

All display 'cultural defensiveness' (Buckingham 2003). Film study in Hall's and Whannel's terms meant *appreciation* aimed at discerning worthiness, preferably in British or European texts. This version of discrimination, they argued, shifted the discussion within the mass media rather than against it. Hostility to the mass media was common to both Leavisite traditionalists and theorists on the Left. Hoggart was hostile to the mass media as a 'processed' consumer culture largely derived from America; and wanted to prevent it corrupting the 'living' heritage of collective working class culture. It is a perspective illustrated in the social realist film *Saturday Night and Sunday Morning* (1960) by Arthur Seaton's anger at his father watching television with his back to the family kitchen table.

The 1944 Education Act had set up a tripartite secondary system with an academic hierarchy of grammar, technical and secondary modern schools, and comprehensives. The academically conservative grammar schools' curricula were seen as defining valid knowledge, a rigidity that continues today in some parts of today's equivalents of the sector, hampering the development of media education there. Other aspects of secondary education saw 'progressive' pedagogies evolve with child-centred approaches 'as part of a wider move towards *democratization*' that validated students' out-of-school cultures as valid and worthy of consideration in the school curriculum' and aimed to 'build connections between the cultures of the school and those of the home and the peer group' (Buckingham 2003: 9). In English, progressive pedagogies involved writing about personal experiences, studying pop music lyrics and so on. It was typically younger progressive English teachers who were genuinely in tune with the new times who saw the benefits of using media forms, especially films that had 'no built in hierarchy of values' and 'children enjoyed spontaneously' (Bolas 2009: 3). Although there were instances of 'anything goes' and directionless 'busy work', 'child-centredness' as educational, such progressive practice was not mere indulgence. The validation of children's experience made them more amenable to learning than alienating 'improving' texts, and open to broader more challenging knowledge beyond their immediate horizons. Media texts made such processes even easier because:

> consumption of television, radio, press, or cinema has its abstract features, and involves the acquisition and understanding of knowledge outside 'daily life and common experience'.
>
> (Collins 1992: 58)

This early positioning in progressive English, through both teacher motivation and strategic targeting by the BFI, eventually 'naturalised' English as the core subject host for media in the newly implemented National Curriculum in 1988. While such subject roots have been richly productive, it also later developed several substantial subject 'relationship' and teacher pedagogy issues (see Chapter 5). The shift away from humanities also heavily coloured media education as text-based to the detriment of its essential production and consumption components.

Half our future

The Newsom Report (DES, 1963) acknowledged that 'television is now part of our culture and therefore a legitimate study for schools' and although 'a discriminating approach' should be aimed for, 'it is equally important that children should learn to appreciate the positive values and the variety of experiences the medium can provide' (DES 1963: 22.14). Discrimination was needed because of the potential 'seriously depressed class of pupils' on teachers' hands due to 'the culture provided by all the mass media, but particularly film and television' (DES 1963: 251). Though patchy nationally, the foundations of a range of film pedagogy were laid – production work, analysis of how cinema communicated was used to develop critical awareness and independent judgment. Much happened in the margins of or outside the school timetable, such as film production workshops and film clubs (the antecedents perhaps to today's CineClub and Film Club). Activities were limited by pre-video technology, especially for watching a whole film, as was television study. The main approach was thematic – viewing film extracts via 16mm projectors that could be viewed only once, to prompt discussions about personal and social topics. Such approaches were also typically used to occupy early school leavers not taking exam courses, which had an adverse effect on the perceived status of film/media study.

Alvarado *et al.* identify 'relevance' as the key advocacy word for media education in the 1960s. They further propose it as 'the most prevalent rationale today' (DES 1963: 21) – Awarding Body specifications, for example, all include this notion in their learning aims. For Newsom, relevance referred to both using media in the curriculum and using society's increasingly ubiquitous media technologies as educational tools in the classroom. Then, as now, 'children do the majority of their learning through the media' (Alvarado and Boyd-Barrett 1992: 24). Such use of media of course raises questions about their apparent 'neutrality', and makes demands on and expands the potential of teachers' pedagogy. Then, as now, with digital technologies, there were issues about students' higher expectations of, and blurring of boundaries between, teaching, learning and entertainment.

A Language for Life

The Bullock Report (DES 1975) was considered groundbreaking in promoting proper study of the Media. However, the authors encountered little media study in practice, and demonstrated how the substance of such reports can be the product of belief rather than considered judgment based upon evidence:

> Though the experimental evidence is limited we believe that the general effect of television watching has been to reduce the amount of time spent in private reading.
>
> (DES 1975: para. 2.7)

Rhetoric was resurrected to continue the negative effects discourse, and to position teachers in opposition to popular culture:

> Another charge laid against television is that it develops a mass culture, sometimes dreary to the point of mindlessness. Many of our correspondents claimed that it not only reduced interest in the written language but debased the spoken language as well. Radio was held at least as guilty in this. Between them radio and television spread the catch-phrase, the advertising jingle, and the frenetic trivia of the disc-jockey . . . it is clear that the content and form of much radio and television utterance makes the teacher's job a great deal more difficult.
>
> (DES 1975: para 2.8)

Nevertheless, the Bullock Report added weight to the Newsom Report's validation of moving image study at a time of 'real intellectual ferment' (Mottershead 2009: 27). The 1950s were a time of growing interest in media education, the 1960s were typically defensive, but the 1970s produced major development. There were few classroom resources, but more urgently a 'body of theoretical work was a pre-requisite to better critical and educational practice' (Alvarado *et al.* 1987: 27). The CCCS had located meta-narrative theories, and there was formidable critical film literature available, but it was primarily the work of volunteer teachers and lecturers who set up SEFT, a grass roots movement of 'committed and gifted "amateurs"' who identified the key analytical approaches, then dubbed '*Screen* theory'. Bolas (2009) chronicles this time of educator creativity extensively, for which Mottershead (2009) provides a useful introduction.

SEFT's journals *Screen* and *Screen Education* conveyed the theories of Barthes, Althusser, Metz and Lacan in post-1968 'social revolution' France. Semiotics, structuralism, psychoanalytic theory, post-structuralism and Marxist theories of ideology focused on meaning, construction and values through the broader perspectives of industrial systems of construction and consumption. Ironically, cinema declined with the rise of video technology and television became the hegemonic medium but the new approaches, initially primarily applied to film, were also applied to television – as well as newspapers, magazines, comics and advertising.

Meanwhile, the first Level 2 equivalent qualifications appeared: CSE TV Studies (1971), and O level Film Studies (1972). These were Mode 3 courses developed locally by teacher consortia and validated by examination boards. Media qualifications blossomed rapidly with almost continually expanding candidate entries, becoming a demand-led option particularly following the advent of film and media GCSEs and A levels in the mid to late 1980s. Conversely, national expansion shifted creative and administrative control to the examination boards to construct common standards and accountability. Such institutional issues introduce the successes and confrontations of the 1980s. Media education proponents had been privileged to operate in 'a flexible institutional apparatus' (Bolas 2009: 2) on the margins of the curriculum, but although teacher expertise informs examination specification construction, Awarding Bodies may now have ownership of shaping media education, undermining educator ownership.

The 1980s and 1990s

Much of the 1980s was politically volatile and, for media education, a contradictory time of rapid expansion for qualifications while space in the central curriculum was squeezed (see Chapter 5). In 1979 the Conservative government implemented an American influenced free market philosophy that encouraged an aggressive capitalist culture. It sought to curb trade union power especially in the mines and the newspaper industry. Over the next two decades, teachers were engineered into a more biddable workforce through 'a pincer movement' of a new, huge, centralised curriculum and bureaucratic systems of accountability: a pedagogical model founded on 'delivery', coupled to an inspection regime to ensure compliance. Second, Local Education Authorities (LEAs) were virtually eliminated. The loss of LEA advisers was a serious setback for media education. Stafford (2009: 24), in recounting these highly political moves in the 1980s feared contemporary parallels: 'History records that in times of cutbacks, the curriculum narrows to focus on the basics and instrumental', a prescient notion given the new Minister for Education, Michael Gove's enthusiasm for the educational philosophy of Matthew Arnold (Buckingham 2011).

However, the 1980s initially continued the previous decade's impetus for media education. The BFI, Film Education and the English Centre (now English and Media Centre [EMC]) produced stimulating academically focused classroom resources that promoted active critical learning. They were often produced out of extended reflective teacher Continuing Professional Development (CPD) and targeted a wide range of media teaching in specialist and cross-media contexts. Adapting esoteric Screen Theory for classroom practice was a formidable challenge met by Masterman's highly influential *Teaching about Television* (1980), and *Teaching the Media* (1985). A disparate field of content and rationale led by subjective teacher tastes and judgments, and advocacy led by theorists' and practitioners' assumptions and agendas, was given intellectual coherence (Jones 2000). Semiological analysis of texts and study of the economics of their industrial contexts were used to focus on language and representation to expose the text's 'hidden' ideologies. In this way students could protect themselves from such false beliefs through awareness of how dominant groups in society, including media corporations, reinforced those ideologies for their own purposes.

However, Masterman's work was inflected by his own agenda. Buckingham (2003: 10) dubs this aim of exposing how the Media worked '*demystification*', and sees it as a variation of the defensive motive for media education, that is 'political defensiveness'. It was particularly suited to the era's clearly defined political stances and clashes, and for some continues to inform discussions such as corporate globalisation of the media industries (see Chapter 4). The political dramas of the day invited news analysis. Apparent anti-trade union bias detected by the Glasgow University Media Group using content analysis research was a significant reference academic point, but infuriated the BBC. Other vivid social issues invited student engagement such as the 'identity politics' of race and gender constructed by 'negative' and 'positive' media representations. Masterman's second main contribution was to provide academic validity to 'practical work', though his emphasis on this as the main purpose has since been questioned. He was concerned by the educational paucity of making (inevitably) amateurish versions of, and comparisons with, professional products. Practical exercises were only educational if they served critical understanding through interrogating dominant television practices and the ideological meanings thus produced.

Production work

Production work had featured intermittently with varying degrees of academic focus and student autonomy, but the arrival of video technology in the 1970s boosted its presence and democratic practices in media education – off-air recording, instant replay, student accessibility to production equipment, the power to edit moving images and represent experiences. Such availability also coincided with a major reinvigoration of the skills for employment agenda initiated by Labour's Great Debate launched in 1976 demanding educators pay more attention to the needs of industry. The Conservatives, however, anxious about social instability added a measure of social control to their motives by aiming to lower employment expectations: 'people must be educated to once more know their place' (Ranson 1984). The Conservative government's Department of Employment met the skills imperative by funding the Manpower Services Commission to create Further Education (FE) vocational courses and secondary pre-vocational courses. They have been characterised by short-term permutations ever since, and added yet more courses to the media qualifications paradigm. The troubling broad educational vocational/academic separation and hierarchy set up complicated divisions in a media education curriculum endeavouring to integrate critical and production practice. More recent versions of the skills for industry strand appeared when New Labour (1997) recognised the flourishing media industries engendered by digital technology and saw media skills as emblematic in the new youth oriented enterprise culture of 'Cool Britannia'. A similar process was played out when Skillset, the media industry skills training body, contributed to developing the Cultural and Media Diploma (see Chapter 9) in the first wave of interdisciplinary Diplomas.

A new hope?

Accumulated developments had encouraged advocates to push for media to have a central curriculum place as the National Curriculum emerged. It is fair to say that the 1980s saw the blooming of media education internationally; media education philosophy was moving apace in Europe:

> The school and the family share the responsibility of preparing the young person living in a world of powerful images, words and sounds. Children and adults need to be literate in all three of these symbolic systems, and this will require some reassessment of educational priorities. Such reassessment might well result in an integrated approach to the teaching of language and communication.
>
> (UNESCO Declaration on Media Education, 22 January 1982)

In Scotland media education modules were established, and media elements included in subjects such as Art and Modern Studies. Indicators seemed to be positive for the English and Welsh system. *Popular TV and Schoolchildren: The Report of a Group of Teachers* (DES 1983) was commissioned and accepted by the then Secretary of State for Education, Keith Joseph. It 'was a model of sensible evaluation and did much to establish the principle of media education as an entitlement for all children' and proposed that 'all teachers should be involved in examining and discussing television programmes with young people' (Davison 1997: 39). However, the Report's subtitle hinted at a significant qualification that shifted its discourse away from government policy.

Debate raged over various HMI consultative '5–16' curriculum documents in the process of establishing England's first National Curriculum, and brought Conservative anti-media education sentiment out into the public domain. The government set about ending progressive practices in English and thereby the potential for an equal mutually reinforcing relationship with media. Education Secretary Kenneth Baker asked Brian Cox, co-author of the right-wing 1970s Black Papers to produce proposals for how the Media could be incorporated in the curriculum. He concluded that 'The kinds of questions routinely asked in media education can be fruitfully applied to literature' (DES and Welsh Office 1989: para. 7.23).

The Cox Report defined five lucid models for the English practice they observed (see Moss in Davison and Dowson 2009: 4–5 for more detail). The 'cultural analysis' version acknowledged the range of social, cultural and historical factors in interactions between producers, audiences and texts. It strongly accommodated media in characterising English as helping children to critically understand the world and their cultural environment, and stated they should '. . . know about the processes by which meanings are conveyed and about the ways in which print and other media carry values' (DES and Welsh Office 1989: para. 2.25).

The conceptual tools employed in media analysis (see Chapter 2) include representation, which considers what is selected and rendered 'visible' for publication and what is therefore consigned to 'invisibility'. Choosing a 'cultural heritage' model, with its emphasis on appreciating the finest in English literature, for the 1988 National Curriculum pointedly rejected the opportunity for a 'cultural analysis' approach. This representation of English selected thereby revealed the government's underlying anti-media agenda.

Ultimately, it is important to be aware of media education, even in the most recent incarnation of the National Curriculum, it is not as a fixed natural entity. Chapter 5 charts the ingenuity needed to include worthwhile media teaching in this and regularly appearing subsequent versions of the National Curriculum, though the inclusion in 1990 of media as a basic statutory entitlement was welcomed simply for its presence.

Government speeches and documents illustrate ambivalent attitudes. Speaking at a public conference in 1989, Angela Rumbold, Kenneth Baker's junior minister for education, stated:

> we at the DES think it is important that all children are helped to develop their critical faculties, in the best sense of the word 'critical', so that they can assess and evaluate the presentation of both fact and fiction in the media. The ability to 'read' media texts – that is, to see them in the light of such a critical awareness and evaluation, and to have some understanding of the processes that produce them – is an important skill for contemporary and future citizens.
>
> (Bazalgette 1991)

There is a shift in discourse, despite the Leavisite undertone, to the British Cultural Studies philosophy of culture as dynamic and growing:

> the emphasis of the idea of culture is right when it reminds us that a culture, essentially, is unplannable. We have to ensure the means of life, and the means of community. But what will then be lived, we cannot know or say.
>
> (Williams 1958)

However, while Ms Rumbold's speech marked a change in attitude at the DES, her words accorded with views in Europe, they were not part of an official government document.

The 1990s saw the ascendancy of support for media education in Europe in an unprecedented way and this was encapsulated in the Council of Europe's Education Ministers' 1989 declaration that:

> Given the major role that media such as television, cinema, radio and the press play in children's cultural experience, media education should begin as early as possible and continue throughout compulsory schooling.
>
> (Bazalgette 1991)

The UK Government signed the declaration, but its abiding attitude to media education was quickly demonstrated in 1990. The BFI's planned first national/international conference for media educators, supported by the United Nations International Cultural and Education Fund, was held in Toulouse, France. It had not been allowed to take place on British soil because the Thatcher government regarded UNESCO as a proscribed organisation – the IRA being another such example with this status at the time. In a speech to the Conservative Party Conference on 7 October 1992, the then Secretary of State for Education, John Patten, delivered a carefully constructed case against media education:

> We believe in greater choice and diversity, in ensuring every child is equipped for adult life. We want the best education system in order to benefit all – not just a few. To achieve the best, we must raise standards. There are no short cuts to good education . . . But all too often, the problems of education lie – not with the parents, not with the teachers – but with the 1960s theorists, with the trendy left, and with the teachers' union bosses.

Children and parents are positioned with the government in wanting and needing 'the basics' of a 'good education' with 'standards' – while the examination boards are lined up oppositionally with '1960s theorists', 'the trendy left', and 'teachers' union bosses' aiming to destroy 'our great literary heritage'. Patten concluded, They'd give us chips with Chaucer. Milton with mayonnaise. Mr Chairman, I want William Shakespeare in our classrooms, not Ronald McDonald! The speech also employs advertising techniques '. . . the art of advertising involves the invention of persuasive arguments which are neither true nor false' (Boorstein 1971: 94).

Such self-fulfilling prophecies become inarguable truths and are rendered true by assertion – wanting the 'best education system', to 'raise standards' are aligned with the government. In *The Guardian*, 16 April 1993, John Patten praised the challenges to the imagination of literature compared to 'television, films or video'. However, although a Jesuit-educated Catholic, he overlooked the Education Secretariat of the Jesuit Curia's 1987 statement: 'Jesuit education includes programmes which enable pupils to understand and critically evaluate the influences of the mass media. Through proper education, these instruments of modern life can help men and women become more, not less, human.'

2000s

Increasingly there have been moments of accord in the statements of policy makers and media education advocates. In line with Bazalgette's typically broad perspectives, she has long argued for literacy to encompass all media, not just words:

> you cannot be literate in the 21st Century unless you are literate in all the Media that are used to communicate.
>
> (Bazalgette in Duffy 2008)

> I believe that in the modern world media literacy will become as important a skill as maths or science. Decoding our media will be as important to our lives as citizens as understanding great literature is to our cultural lives.
>
> (Tessa Jowell, Culture Secretary, UK Film Council
> press release, January 2004)

Jowell's statement seemed to be an explicit endorsement of the central importance of media education in schools, but without systemic teacher training and significant curriculum changes, for instance the inclusion of assessment criteria for media, the onus has remained on individual teachers, pioneering schools, high quality media education publishers and, increasingly, Media Studies Awarding Bodies to continue paving the way in meeting such aspirations. The Labour government also retained the service of the Conservative government-appointed Chief HMI Chris Woodhead, who continued throughout the decade to be vociferous in his opposition to Media Studies even after retirement: 'The best schools struggle to outdo the influence of peer pressure, and the teenage culture created by the pop and fashion industries, but struggle they must' (Woodhead 2000). His opposition expanded to accord with the prejudiced hierarchy of traditional 'hard' and new 'soft' subjects (including Media Studies despite its longevity) identified by Russell Group universities:

> Media Studies is a subject with little intellectual coherence and meagre relevance to the world of work. Its popularity says a great deal about our current education system. With the notable exception of religious studies, few if any GCSE and A level subjects with the word 'studies' in the title have real credibility.
>
> (*The Sunday Times* 8 March 2009)

While there are still major shortcomings from educational policy makers, and for media education in the mainstream curriculum, the 'Noughties' brought 'media literacy', if not media education, into the public domain in relatively constructive, if limited, ways. The media regulator Ofcom was 'tasked' in 2003 to engender national media literacy. This was predominantly a functional literacy exercise prompted at the time by Labour's drive to digitise Britain. It also operates as a protectionist agenda for people to learn to protect themselves from 'harmful' content, whereas media education has moved on to viewing media literacy as a democratising and critical tool to '*prepare*' (Buckingham 2003) young people for autonomous citizenship in the digital age.

The government, however, recognised the quality of work at the Centre for the Study of Children, Youth and Media, and appointed its director, a long time media education pioneer, David Buckingham, to lead the literature research in the Byron review into children and the digital world – *Safer Children in a Digital World* (DCSF 2008). Its conclusions were carefully balanced to reassure the government and its 'Every Child Matters' concern over child protection on the internet, but also advocated the importance of the informed use of the Media through critical autonomy. Buckingham was then appointed to lead the enquiry into another area of government concern: *The Impact of the Commercial World Children's Wellbeing* (DCSF 2009).

Several initiatives appeared within and on the peripheries of the school curriculum for instance the Diplomas with 'Creative and Media' in the first cycle, 'Find Your Talent', and Film Club indicating public recognition of the cultural and industrial value of the Media. Another national 'literacy strategy' with a specific focused emerged – the UK Film Council's *Film: 21st Literacy Strategy* (www.21stcenturyliteracy.org.uk/), aiming to develop a new generation of film literate audiences. The UK Film Council also hosted an eventually short-term combination of media education bodies and major media organisations – the Media Literacy Task Force. It at least served to produce a 'Charter for Media Literacy', which is now integrated into its parent European site at www.euromedialiteracy.eu/, led to the BBC's annual *School Report* project, and a more comprehensive characterisation of media literacy as the 'Three Cs' of Creative, Cultural and Critical understanding (see Chapter 2).

More directly for teachers, in 2006 the then DfES funded the creation of a subject association for all media educators – the Media Education Association (MEA) http://themea.org/. Free subscription includes an independent online forum providing support and participation in the development of media education, for instance by links to *A Manifesto for Media Education* and, importantly, collective representation of media education's interests. Further openness to education perspectives on media literacy were indicated by Ofcom funding the MEA's re-launched annual conference in November 2010 as an international event encompassing major media education debates and hands-on skills training.

Summary

The sustained commitment and talent of media educators, allied with informed elements of government and public bodies, has moved media study a long way in a hundred years. Education has to be relevant to life in the real world and move with the accelerating pace and opportunities offered, not least by new media technologies. For that reason alone, the importance of media education no longer needs to be established but much more systematically embedded in the school curriculum to prepare students for twenty-first-century citizenship. This chapter has contextualised the still dramatically varied conditions for teaching and learning about the Media in the secondary sector. Opportunities for media teacher training and development are similarly uneven, but practitioner generated support is using the Media itself to share good practice, effectively regain an independent voice, and combine efforts to formulate a coherent vision for the future of media education.

Recommended reading

These suggestions provide a thorough overview of the past to not only contextualise practice and issues in the present, but also to explore current debates for teachers to engage with development of the media education field.

Alvardo, M., Gutch, R. and Wollen, T. (1987) *Learning the Media: An Introduction to Media Teaching*, London: Macmillan.

Buckingham, D. (2003) *Media Education: Literacy, Learning and Contemporary Culture*, Cambridge: Polity Press.

Lusted, D. (1991) *The Media Studies Book: A Guide for Teachers*, London: Routledge.

Chapter 2

What is media education?

Elaine Scarratt

> What are teachers to make of the complex shifting world of warring definitions, half-realised policies and widely divergent practices?
>
> (Burn and Durran 2007: 21)

Introduction

If media education seems a complex and confusing field to the new media teacher, it is not entirely the dilemma of a sudden encounter with the unfamiliar. All subject fields evolve but media education is also characterised by having to 'grab a toehold' (Lusted 1991) wherever possible in the curriculum – raising questions not only of 'what' it is but 'where' it is. Chapter 1 outlined why the answer is, 'predominantly in the curriculum margins with a small central part in the core subject of English'. Any subject area is characterised by differing educational philosophies and influences, not least government policies: media education is even more so given its disparate evolution, curriculum manifestations and teachers' backgrounds. This chapter aims broadly to orientate those new to media education with outlines of its key features and the conceptual framework of enquiry that informs specialist practice. It also considers issues raised in some current debates circulating in media education: what is meant by media literacy and creativity? How far and in what ways will the current constitution of media study have to change in response to society's expanded access to and use of digital technologies? As a subject of the 'here and now' with change as a central characteristic, how will such rapid changes be managed?

Although there is cross-specification agreement on learning aims and assessment objectives in Media Studies specifications, there has yet to be an overarching statement of purpose for media education from its practitioners. 'Manifesto for Media Education' is an initiative set up by leading practitioners in an attempt 'to develop a shared understanding, (and) some shared reasons, for media education' (www.manifestoformediaeducation.co.uk). While engaging with such fundamental ideas may seem a little ahead of time for the early stages of a media teacher's career, it is important to begin reflection on one's own attitudes to the Media and motivations for teaching it.

A 'horizontal' view of culture that sees all kinds of media texts as worthy of study has long informed media education practice, rather than a 'high art'/'popular culture' hierarchical divide of educational validity. However, in society at large the latter notion persists, an example being the recent parental attempt to remove study of *The Simpsons* as not culturally worthwhile (BBC 2010). Media teachers therefore have to be prepared to argue their case, even with other teachers and school management:

if we are convinced of the importance and necessity of media education, then we shall need to be not simply teachers of, but *advocates for* our subject, *advancing* its cause whenever we can within our own institutions, amongst parents and with colleagues and policy makers. Our reasoning needs to be *compelling* and *persuasive*, as well as plain and intelligible.

(Masterman 1985:1)

What's in a name?

One of the confusions about media study in education is what to call it. 'Media education' is the generic term for the process of all media teaching and learning wherever it occurs in the curriculum and in practice is a cross-curricular enterprise. In the core subject of KS3 and KS4 English (see Chapter 5), study of the Media is a statutory entitlement for all students, and there are units in other National Curriculum subjects such as Citizenship (see Chapter 10), PSHE, RE and Design Technology. The non-statutory cross-curriculum dimensions offer explicit opportunities: 'Technology and the Media', and Chapter 4 demonstrates how to also exploit the indirect opportunities, for example in 'Global Dimension and Sustainable Development'.

Whereas 'Media Studies' comprises specialist courses with distinct content, concepts and modes of enquiry from other subject areas, it is taken as an option at 14+, for example at GCSE (see Chapters 6 and 7) and A level (see Chapter 8). Other specialist subject qualifications, such as Sociology and ICT, also include media units. The 14+ pre-vocational option Diploma in Creative and Media (see Chapter 9) combines specialist Media Studies and the multi-disciplinary interests characterising it and media education. The nature of media study inevitably has variations, for example, constructed in Media Studies by competing Awarding Body specifications, but is more significantly inflected in media elements across the curriculum by subject hosts. As media education has yet to have its own explicitly defined conceptual basis, progression markers and assessment criteria, it is vulnerable to unequal subject partnerships.

Terminology

Getting to grips with a new education field entails learning its discourse, including specialist terminology. Needless to say there are some minor variations. The explanations and 'definitions' here are starting points to be checked against other reading and Awarding Bodies' specific expectations. It is best to be consistent for your purposes. Two reliable books that clarify without losing complexity are: *Media and Film Studies Handbook*, Clark *et al.* (2007) – a comprehensive glossary of specialist media discourse and terminology with contemporary illustrations. Though originally targeted at a legacy A level specification, the title of *Key Concepts and Skills for Media Studies*, Clark *et al.* (2002) illustrates its content and implies its broad application for media education. Specialist technical terms and conventions organised with their particular media forms can be found in any of the GCSE and A level 'textbooks' at the end of Chapters 6–8.

The Media, texts, products and topics

There are two main notions of the 'the Media'. First, as a unified social institution such as 'the' church, politics, education, it is often used as an easy target, because of its ubiquity and high profile, to be held accountable for many of society's problems. For these reasons, it has significant potential in shaping perceptions and interactions with the world and, like the other social institutions is a secondary discourse (after family) in identity formation. However, believing that the Media is 'a singular set of ideologies and beliefs . . . is no longer easy to sustain' (Buckingham 2003: 12); nor can it single-handedly impose false values and have a 'uniformly harmful' influence on a passive populace (also see Gauntlett 1998).

The media, plural, are the many forms of modern communications and their products. In specialist media courses the products are organised into three groups characterised by their technological platforms:

- *Audio-visual*: cinema, television, radio, music videos, animation. Film and television are often categorised as 'moving image', however it misleadingly diverts attention from the importance of sound, and examiners' reports regularly note 'sound' as a weak area of analysis.
- *Print*: newspapers, magazines, comics.
- *E-media*: the internet, mobile phones, computer games, video games.

These separations are inevitably crude and, since they are based on pre-digital construc- tions they do not reflect cross-platform form modulations such as magazines, advertising and news. However, these groupings are a useful way into analysis through identifying characteristic media language conventions; and as a means to discuss the impacts of digital technology, such as convergence – electronic devices carrying multiple media forms, increased synergy, new forms (computer games), changing audience relationships with media.

Media education is about the production, circulation and reception of meaning. It has a dual concern as an academic field studying the Media, which is a set of industrial practices, so two collective terms are used for what the Media make. The term 'products' is used in the context of studying media industries. Removed from their industrial origin and reconfigured as objects of academic study in the classroom products become 'texts' in the way any object of investigation becomes a text – 'a haircut, hip hop lyrics, a dance, a film' (Branston and Stafford 2010: 11). Texts comprise textual, inter-textual, and extra-textual meanings, for which the main analytical tool is semiotics (Barthes 1973). Semiotic reading 'relates texts to their surrounding social orders'. Branston and Stafford (2010) usefully point to the Latin origin of text meaning 'tissue' and Barthes' notion of (narrative) texts weaving together 'different strands and processes'. Texts then are *polysemic*: a complex interplay of meanings created by producers (consciously or unconsciously), audiences, industrial processes and contemporary social contexts. Some meanings are internal to the text constructed by media language choices; some refer to other texts, others are 'extra-textual' (outside) influences, such as the expectations constructed by marketing; or interactivity such as audience votes in reality show contests. Therefore, the boundaries of a text can blur (see *Postmodernism* in Chapter 8, page 144):

- television soap storylines are previewed and soap star stories are run in newspapers;
- on TV programme websites, such as *Skins*, fans can download exclusive material not broadcast on TV, including mini episodes and characters' video blogs;
- elaborate simulated website worlds created pre-film release, such as *Super 8*'s (www.scariestthingieversaw.com/).

Especially in Media Studies specifications, the main emphasis is on contemporary texts: approximately from the preceding five years. The necessity to keep up to date is part of media education's stimulus and challenge to the teacher. However, earlier texts are also essential for their intrinsic worth, informative historical comparisons, and understanding how texts are formed by, and reflect, contemporary historical, political and economic conditions, and cultural values and attitudes. For example, early twentieth-century representations of race and gender in advertisements; or a long view of a genre to understand how it works as a process of repetition and variation, and re-booting and re-branding. Media topics (see Chapter 6) can focus recurring media content and the issues and debates they raise. Many can be discussed in the light of concepts such as representation and institution, such as: celebrity culture; reality TV; representations of social groups such as youth, immigrants; controversial films with 12A certifications; moral panics about digital technology.

Cross-curricular media: subject origins

Media education draws on 'aspects of literature studies, art, business studies . . . economics, politics and sociology' (Branston and Stafford 2010: 13), as well as history to provide contemporary contextualisation and, latterly, computer studies. It is academically informed and given unifying coherence by 'communications theory of many kinds, cultural studies, and so on' (Branston and Stafford 2010: 4). The subject area then is a rich, interdisciplinary brew that requires some breadth as well as depth of knowledge. The field's hybridity has been further influenced by the subject backgrounds of media teachers, for many of whom media education is a later, though often enthusiastic, subject addition to their primary specialism. It is a process that continues to be reinforced by the absence of nationally systemic specialist media ITE. In 2001 Stafford summarised the hybridity as generating 'creative tension' in the mix of a 'text-based approach derived from English and a more "people and process" approach derived from the social sciences'. Recent discussion on the OCR teachers' online messageboard highlighted the interesting challenges of amalgamating these disciplines at A2 (see Chapter 8), and reflected concerns earlier in media education's evolution of imposing, or moderating, theoretical understanding from disciplines, and sources, initially developed for Higher Education.

The 'text/people and processes' conundrum is part of current debates about how media education should develop. Whether it should be either/or, or both, is a consideration for new teachers to be alert to and a debate to engage in for their own choice of practice. Stafford (2009) revives a neglected ingredient in the mix by proposing a more business studies type approach. Focus on the two processes above overlooks the essential nature of the Media, which though many are 'creative' industries, they are industries nevertheless. Studying them via their business models would engender more comprehensive and realistic economic understanding of the Media as industries. A more streamlined version of Media Studies in particular may be helpful for other teachers to provide fair representations of the subject, and for students and parents to understand and make better informed subject choices. On the other hand, Media Studies/media education's diversity may be its strength, which needs to be better conveyed. There is an academic rigour, all too often unanticipated by students and of which too many public voices are unaware. As a whole package that includes production work, both individual and with others and subjected to critical self-evaluation, it provides a range of interpersonal and intellectual skills rooted in and transferable to the 'real' worlds of work, leisure and Higher Education.

All this has led to diverse but overlapping areas of media education identified in different ways historically (see Chapter 1) but recently by Bazalgette (2010) as three main strands. Cultural and Communication is the main manifestation but has its own 'creative tension' in the mix of a 'text-based approach derived from English and a more "people and process" approach derived from the social sciences' (Stafford 2001). The pedagogy is broadly characterised as the analytical tendency. The cultural and communication theories, which were adapted from Higher Education (HE) inform this analysis and though they structure media practice at all key stages, they are most explicitly encountered at KS5 and so are addressed in Chapter 8 (A level media studies).

Arts and aesthetics is a more recent development in, for instance, qualifications such as Moving Image Arts, Film Studies and the Creative and Media Diploma, which challenges the arbitrariness of academic boundaries. Focusing on ideological analysis and meanings of representations was and is a central media education project but was also a means of establishing media education by differentiating it from existing subjects such as Art and English. However, considerations of audience pleasure and undertaking creative work have reinstated this element as part of the media picture.

E-technologies (digital media) have prompted one of the major debates about the future of media education. Some, Gauntlett (2007b), believe the extent of their impact on society is so revolutionary – the interactivity of Web 2.0, new media forms such as computer games, user generated content, and extensive visible social interaction via such media – that the restructuring of Media Studies' conceptual framework to a 'Media Studies 2.0' version is essential. Digital technologies have boosted the variety and accessibility of opportunities for good quality production work for real audience responses, e.g. on YouTube, so teachers need to have 'an array of digital production skills – downloading, sharing, videoing, tagging, texting, ripping, burning, messaging, networking, playing, producing and building' (McDougall and Potamitis 2010: 27). Study activities also benefit by being more in tune with the real world, such as using blogs to reflect on and share work, PowerPoint presentations, mobile phones for digital photography and so on. These developments are currently more apparent, but not exclusively, at KS5 where logistical problems, such as internet filtering, storing information and so on can be more easily addressed.

Others question this technological determinist approach and believe the concepts by their nature have accommodating flexibility. Though digital technology is a highly significant development and can be highly stimulating and engaging for students when used well, the depth and breadth of its changes and benefits can be exaggerated. There is certainly a 'digital divide' between many young people's everyday practices in leisure time – 'playing games, surfing entertainment sites on the internet, instant messaging, social networking, and downloading and editing video and music' (Buckingham 2007b: 2), and the mainly limited functional technological learning in school. However, it is too easy to overestimate students' prior capabilities and outside school access to digital technology (Sefton Green 1999; Buckingham 2007a). Despite apparent social transformations the social factors that condition students' educational access, ability and engagement are unchanged, and in 2010 one million young people did not have access to a computer. Whatever the eventualities, there are emergent modifications to the key media concepts and these are also noted.

Cross-curricular media education

The multi-discipline nature of media education makes it ideal for cross-curricular education. However, it is vulnerable to co-option into other subject agendas because it has no independent curricular content, no National Curriculum assessment criteria or place in national tests, inspection frameworks or contribution to national league tables. Although this allows 'more freedom in terms of what is taught, how it is taught, and to whom [it] suffers from devaluation in the eyes of the establishment and in the eyes of students, because it is not identified, resourced, or given a means of accreditation' (Jenkins 1986: 6). Concerns about 'teaching in other spaces' are still valid in places, but can be dealt with. The benefits of 'moving image' work for other subjects are increasingly supported by classroom research (Marsh 2005) and even promoted, for instance by the AQA Awarding Body in their joint English Media Studies GCSE publicity. The more flexible conceptual structure of the National Curriculum (2008) means that the Media Studies' conceptual framework can be adapted to jointly plan equal status common and subject specific learning aims – and evaluation strategies linked to assessment criteria (see Chapter 5).

Burn and Durran (2007) demonstrate how specialist media arts schools are of course ideal for re-organising the curriculum in this way – in English, Dance, Maths, Science, Geography and Modern Languages (e.g. animations of volcanoes, a documentary about coastal erosion), but their detailed accounts and rationales make the case studies easily adaptable for any supportive institution. Connolly (2011), also in a Specialist Visual and Media Arts school but in a deprived area with attendant attitudes to education, provides an inspirational account of how senior management with media expertise and an educational vision placed media texts and pedagogy at the centre of a whole school and local community enterprise. Media education's transformative potential has been realised in the school with raised achievement across the ability range, ignited interest and aspirations in other subject areas and in active community interest through, for example, photography exhibitions with local disabled groups and video game workshops for the local youth service. Such local enhanced social inclusion brings its own political values. There are excellent published materials to guide media skills development in cross-curricular study such as reading film language strategies in the British Film Institute published *Moving Images in the Classroom* (2000). Film Education has many film case studies for use with cross-curricular schemes of work – both sets of materials are free to download, and English and Media Centre materials are noted in Chapter 5. The curriculum review for 2013 is likely to discourage inter-disciplinary opportunities, but there is increasing evidence for the benefits of such projects, and subject separation runs counter to the interplay of disciplines in cultural organisations, such as Tyneside Cinema Newcastle; National Media Museum Bradford, and Rich Mix and the BFI Southbank in London.

Media literacy

> Advancing media literacy is . . . a collaborative responsibility of government, the media industries, educators and cultural agencies, as well as citizens themselves.
> (Media Literacy Task Force, submission to the Byron Review, 2007)

A few individual media education advocates and organisations have an effective role in public media education policy making. However, a corollary to the absence of a collectively endorsed view on the purposes of media education by its teachers is that public discourse about media education can be colonised by particular agendas. In *UK Children's Media Literacy* Ofcom (2010), the independent broadcast media regulator given the remit for national media literacy by the Communications Act (2003), notes that 'there is no single agreed definition of media literacy', and aiming for a dynamic comprehensive formulation continues as a key debate within media education. Public policy debate has shifted from antagonistic and wholly protectionist stances to interest in individual informed decision-making. For instance, the government-commissioned Byron Review (2007) into media impacts on children and young people, particularly internet computer games, recommended this age group be 'empowered' to 'manage risks' in 'a risk-averse culture' through a 'shared culture of responsibility' to support them in 'developing critical evaluation skills' (Executive Summary); although school network filtering would suggest a contrary enactment. Ofcom endorses the aspiration to 'higher order critical thinking skills such as questioning, analysing and evaluating . . . information' and its extensive financially supported research programme (see online Ofcom bulletins) has included convening a 'Media Literacy Research Forum' (2008) for media education experts to develop a framework for media literacy, and in 2010 relaunching the Media Education Association's annual conferences. However, as a broadcast and online regulator its remit does not cover print media, so its responsibility is for public functional 'digital literacy' – and online protection. Cultural agencies such as the BFI and its working parties (1999), and the UK Film Council (2009), have also inevitably promoted selective, though worthy, interests for 'cineliteracy' or 'moving image literacy'.

The Communications Act (2003) adopted the term 'media literacy' from the United States and Canada, and it resonated with then New Labour government's educational policies that foregrounded 'literacy'. There is, however, uncertainty about how to conceptualise media literacy. Discourses surrounding subsequent initiatives appear to treat 'media literacy' as a subject area. The Center for Media Literacy, Canada (Boles 2011) for instance cites both media literacy and media education as processes. In British schools, however, 'media *education* . . . is the process of teaching and learning about media; media *literacy* is the outcome' (Buckingham 2003: 4), see also Burn and Durran (2007: 21). What is open to debate is the nature of the outcome.

Simple definitions of media literacy retain a metaphorical comparison with 'traditional literacy' of reading and writing but having the ability to 'read' and 'write audiovisual information rather than text' (Ofcom 2010). It has been a time of proliferating literacies: across cultural life – 'emotional literacy', and sub-literacies in subjects, especially so for media education given its rapidly increasing textual forms: 'television literacy', 'game literacy', 'network literacy' (computer navigation skills). McDougall and Potamitis (2010: 1–13) has a usefully informative overview of current educational versions, which could also be used for discussion prompts. Elsewhere, some argue that since so many texts can now be described as multimodal – websites games, advertisements and there are now electronic books being developed with embedded video, these literacy sub-divisions are unmanageable, arbitrary and ultimately meaningless. Further, it reinforces the view that there is a false division between English and media notions of 'reading' and 'writing', and that 'literacy' should be redefined to accommodate this comprehensiveness.

Bazalgette (2008/9: 14–15) considers how to corral the commonalities of diverse media forms into defining manageable literacy learning outcomes. She challenges the assumption that the multimodalities are integrated and proposes that 'the combination of text and moving image on the same page is often a convenient way of accessing both, but as an awkward hybrid it rarely constitutes a coherent text in is own right'. For example, in a Sky News bulletin the crawler at the bottom of the frame is read differently from the moving images and audio track. She therefore proposes two sets of skills – 'time-based' and 'page-based' texts, with the latter including but going beyond traditional printed pages of books, newspapers adverts to say 'web pages, SMS messages, DVD and games menus'.

This is a debate that can be part of a course, and certainly an issue for the (near) future in media education, but what of identifying literacy outcomes in current constructions of media education? The learning aims in Media Studies specifications were commonly agreed across the Awarding Body specifications but in effect have that limitation. In lieu, and in anticipation of a broadly endorsed 'manifesto', the '3Cs' of media literacy in the *European Charter for Media Literacy* (EuroMediaLiteracy 2009) is a useful interim model that 'includes but goes well beyond technical proficiency' (see *Recommended resources*, page 39). Burn and Durran (2007) has an extended discussion of media literacy and demonstrates how their version of the 3Cs model is applied in practice.

The 3Cs are three main areas of learning:

Cultural literacy: the key point here is media education validating students' media experiences and extending their access to culturally and stylistically diverse media products and technologies to enable breadth and depth of understanding. It is a 'horizontal' value model, rather than a hierarchy of high art and popular culture, that incorporates 'both extremes of the cultural spectrum and anything in between that suits our purposes' (Burn 2010). 'Quality' can be characterised as texts that are 'rich' in pedagogical value for enquiry informed by the key media concepts: it is 'the cultural process of education, how people explore attitudes and values and their own identity through interaction with cultural artefacts' (Lyng 2008).

Critical literacy: the confidence of informed judgments about taste and pleasure; assessing information, representations and relations of power. For some, particularly in the 1980s, the focus was on 'decoding the ideological dimensions of texts, institutions, social practices and cultural forms' to reveal 'selective interests' (Freire in McLaren 1988: 213), or 'demystification' (Masterman 1985).

"'I feel more suggestible already" the comedian Richard Blackwood said in Chris Morris' *Brass Eye* special, having sniffed a computer keyboard that supposedly emitted fumes designed to increase children's vulnerability to online paedophiles' (Walters 2010). Morris' work suggests the broader approach of critical questioning and intellectual rigour to create independent informed analysis. He has consistently satirised willful credulity, willingness to be beguiled by dramatic presentation (*The Day Today*), and not being critically alert to the substance and sources of information. His BAFTA award winning film, *Four Lions* (2010) based on extensive research into the realities of young jihadists' behaviour has been welcomed by British Muslims as it challenges the climate of fear perpetuated in some media quarters (though they are not the sole initiators) by notions of ever-ready highly trained soldiers on suicidal missions.

Creative literacy: students should have opportunities to make media products in a range of media. Media Studies courses must include use of digital media, but that does not mean it replaces all others. Students should choose technology appropriate to their intended meanings and product: 'it is necessary in creative practical work for students to reflect on the aesthetic characteristics of any given medium before they pitch into production for instance . . . to produce a fanzine or mini-comic using scissors, glue and a photocopier rather than Adobe InDesign' (McDougall and Potamitis 2010: 27), or say shoot a New Wave sequence with Super-8.

The 'Find Your Talent' initiative, which aimed to bring five hours of weekly culture to schools, was promoted by then Secretary of State for Education Margaret Hodge as enabling life-transforming epiphany moments from encounters with great art. Burn and Durran (2007) propose a more sustained developmental version of a 'transformative process'. It is rooted in creativity, which they propose is at work in both discursive responses and practical production. Both activities have their sources in students' reflections on the meanings garnered from media experiences, which process from inaccessible 'internal mental operations' to becoming externalised and articulated in different forms – words and media products respectively.

Creativity has 'common sense' assumptions about what it means, but closer scrutiny reveals it is a vague, romanticised, complex and ill-defined concept. Nevertheless it is in some Media Studies' assessment criteria for production work. For AQA GCSE 'creativity' is only in the higher level criteria, but it is not defined *per se*. The criteria to imply the high end aesthetic content qualities of originality, inventiveness, and fresh and unexpected connections outlined in the National Curriculum for say art and English, p. 62. Any Awarding Body training day discussions of exemplar student work will reveal the level of subjectivity in such judgments. Creativity is not just about content and 'art'.

While there are no easy answers, there are several useful sources to help itemise creativity in ways that make learning expectations clear to students, and can focus assessment whatever the educational context. *Creative Partnerships*, the organisation linking schools to the world of work, identify creative professionals as ranging from architects to scientists, to multimedia developers and artists. Science and art are differently realised expressions of the same creative processes of 'questioning, producing, making connections, and taking innovative and imaginative approaches to problem solving'. These attributes are echoed in the subject interpretations of the creativity, one of the concepts underpinning National Curriculum (2008), and which offer several docking points for multi-disciplinary media education. OCR's assessment criteria (GCSE and A level) delineate types and levels of technical skills – ones that it is too easy to assume students' arrive at school with. Readman's (2009) academic research adds substance to and extends the underlying principles noted above, and Stafford's proposals for a 'creative curriculum' in Buckingham (1995) propose, still relevant, working practices and personal qualities as part of the creative process. For instance, problem solving has diverse applications such as dealing with technological challenges and rigorously reworking ideas. Achievement in creative work entails inner resourcefulness, not taking the easy options, taking 'the initiative' and interpersonal skills of group work.

The key media concepts

Despite all this diversity there is a unifying method of educational strategy. Subjects can be defined in terms of a body of knowledge, or a skill set. Media Studies has a conceptual framework of enquiry and understanding. There is less certainty about how it may or even should work in the context of media education. Chapter 5 notes ways in which a particular version can be utilised within English but also concerns about the potential reductive effect on media study as an educational field. Burn (2010) suggests that it is more productive to 'muddle the boundaries, find common ground use tensions to challenge each field of study to move beyond its limitations and prejudices'.

For Media Studies the conceptual framework provides a coherent way to study what might otherwise appear to be an *ad hoc* succession of disparate texts, practices and interactions in different media forms. A concise repertoire of concepts makes this fragmented diversity manageable through recognising commonalities and contextualising differences.

This section outlines the most common model of four key concepts:

- media languages (including genre and narrative);
- representations (including ideologies, messages and values);
- audiences;
- institutions.

The concepts have been conceived, codified and clustered in different ways over time: 'Signpost Questions' (Grahame 1991, 1996), 'Key Aspects' (Bazalgette 1991). Variations persist across the curriculum, for instance in English (see Chapter 5) and in Media Studies, for example WJEC's 'Media Texts' and 'Media Organisations'. Nevertheless, all Awarding Body specifications have common broad structures and cover the same territory. It is useful to be aware of different approaches to analysis, but there is no need to be distracted by inconsistencies. Teachers should model a consistent discourse for students; predominantly informed by specification choice and, at times, compromised by other curriculum requirements.

The concepts then provide a sound way to organise planning, learning, assessment in a curriculum, and reflection on teaching and learning. They are an intellectual safety net to which students can be returned. Teachers originally trained in other discourses need to internalise them and while they may seem 'unnatural' at first, such a process will be useful for understanding students' initial difficulties. Not having to 'deliver' a body of knowledge gives freedom to choose content, change it to keep up to date and respond to students' interests. Although there may be recurring favourites, it also avoids the restrictions of a 'canon'. Strategically, in the broader education context, the concepts are a means to codify and demonstrate the academic content of critical media literacy.

The advantage of a conceptual framework is its flexibility and innate ability to absorb change – a characteristic feature of the Media. However, some argue that digital technology, especially the internet's second phase (Web 2.0) has brought fundamental changes: an array of interactive opportunities and creative activities; a rapid increase in and variety of content; the greater sharing of experiences and ideas, and changes to how media are distributed and exchanged. In short, to the extent that the conceptual framework of 'Media Studies 1' should be dismantled (Gauntlett 2007b), and reconceived as new Media Studies discourse foregrounding the 'changing nature of audience and representation' (McDougall and Potamitis 2010: 54). This is a major debate, prompted largely from Higher Education, about the future of media education with which teachers need to engage, for instance via the subject association (http://themea.org), which is also linked to *A Manifesto for Media Education*.

The chapter now outlines the current conceptual framework retained in its main manifestations in the revised Media Studies specifications (A level 2008, GCSE 2009), which include contemporary media technology and issues. The media concepts also support media education's active pedagogy as an investigative model of enquiry. The concepts are interrelated and not hierarchical. However, because of the factual subject knowledge involved, 'institution' can be perceived as more challenging for non-specialist teachers. Buckingham (2003: 62–67), using case studies adapted from Domaille and Grahame (2001), models how 'institution' can be incorporated in accessible and active ways so all four concepts can have equal treatment at KS3. Many media organisations now have informative websites, which are noted in *Recommended resources* (see page 39), and Awarding Body resources.

Media languages (including genre and narrative)

The current concepts were originally theoretically informed by structuralist philosophies such as linguistics. The use of semiotics in media language analysis owes much to Saussure's 'signs, system and arbitrariness', which is accessibly explained in Bouissac (2010). Media languages refers to the combinations of still and moving images, sound, verbal and written signs that comprise media texts. They can be perceived as languages because their codes and conventions are learned and their meanings are understood. Much media language learning is unconscious and textual analysis, as a process that involves the conscious taking apart of elements, makes the 'familiar strange' as a means to make implicit learning articulated. Signs are broadly divided into technical codes, meaning created directly from the technology of a form – close-up camera shots to convey characters' reactions, music to evoke particular emotions and to anticipate narrative developments, editing choices to construct narrative. Visual codes, or cultural codes, are mainly the mise-en-scène: settings, clothes, colour choices and so on that confer meaning from the cultural (extra-textual) context.

Media signs, amalgamated in combinations and sequences, in effect have grammatical rules that may be conventionally repeated, varied or even subverted. The notion of 'rules' is useful in identifying the effects of language choices in these processes. However, for understanding how media texts work it is rather rigid; whereas 'flexible guidelines' (Thompson 1999) flags up a preferred dynamic analytical approach that questions how texts *use* different forms of language, rather than as a means to seeing how text 'fit into' conventional forms.

Thompson proposed this phrase in relation to film genre but it can be generally applied. Genre is a commonly understood way to identify and categorise types of stories through familiar conventions and coded meanings. It is a conception expected up to KS4 (TV sitcom, disaster movies), and employed by industry and audiences. However, genre's origin in film has sat uneasily in other media forms; television also has formats for example, and at KS5 the 'how texts *use*' approach is expected. An earlier media concept of 'categories' points to genre as just one way to organise media texts – for instance by age (children's comics), industry sectors (independents), industry economic imperatives (franchises, branding), use of digital media technologies ('mashups', 'sweding'). Genre, then, has come under particular scrutiny in discussions about Media Studies 2.0 (Gauntlett 2007b).

Narrative considers how different forms and their texts are organised and convey their content, so it is applied to both fiction and non-fiction forms: television news programmes and their running order of 'stories', choice of technical codes and mise-en-scène, for example. Again structural theory can be a useful prompt, such as the anthropology sourced broad underlying structures of Todorov and Propp, but they are best used as a questioning device. An investigative approach asks how different forms tell their stories, by whom, how is the audience positioned; what are they told, what is kept back? As Chapter 3 elaborates, new media technologies and forms have brought new perspectives into ideas of narrative through, for instance, *ludology*.

Media representations

While the principle of conceptual equality stands, representation is central to the field in its current and potential manifestations (see McDougall and Potamitis above). For Buckingham (2003: 57), the 'notion of representation is one of the founding principles of media education. The Media do not offer us a transparent "window" on the world, but a mediated version of the world.' Becoming critically alert to the Media as indirect communication carrying selected and re-constructed meanings about the world 'forms the basis of the media education curriculum' Buckingham (2003: 3). Representation though is not about comparing 'truth' and deviation; it is about modality, the ways meanings are encoded and create a sense of authenticity within the codes and conventions of a text, or 'genre'. How close or not to the 'real' world those encodings are meant to be – in, say, fantasy films and documentaries. Representation, and media education, then looks at realisms, the reconstructed versions of 'reality'.

It looks at demographic groups: age, gender, race, ethnicity and so on. Considering people in and across media texts involves analysing how conventions influence the representation and 'typing' – the use of archetypes, genre types, stereotypes. Again the focus is on *use*. Noting stereotypes as part of power relations has some purpose, but criticism in the light of possible 'accuracy' elsewhere is redundant, whereas considering their functions for audiences and narrative is more productive. As reflections of the societies in which they are produced media texts act as social documents, and Chapter 4 examines the political dimensions of representation, from characters carrying burdens of representation, identity formation and personal politics to revealing unequal social structures. Representation also examines how events and issues are treated in the Media, raising issues of bias and professed objectivity, and questions of who is in control of the texts, whose ideas are excluded? Overall the surface representations are a means to ascertaining underlying themes of ideologies, messages and values.

Media audiences

The original and residual notion of audiences is as the end component of the production process, receivers of media products made by media industries. Study looks at how audiences are targeted as demographic groups, mass and niche markets, and constructed by marketing into psychographic profiles, and the ways in which products are constructed accordingly to appeal. Audience responses are measured quantifiably, circulation and box office figures, and the theory outcomes of qualitative audience research are used to discuss the meanings audiences make. There is a duality at the heart of audiences as being 'individual yet common' (Phillips 2001: 85) as *responses* are the former, but *audiences* are constructed as the latter.

Analysis has shifted away from discredited 'effects' models associated with protection agendas. However, the concept includes discussing the agendas of different participants in debates about media violence, commercialisation and sexualisation of childhood, and regulation. The main interest is in active audience theories exploring conditions of reception and what meanings audiences make. These reception theories include formula such as encoding/decoding models of reading (dominant, negotiated and oppositional). Interest in what people do with the media are formulated into, for example, Uses and Gratifications Theory characterising responses as information seeking, escapism, identification and socialisation.

The concept of media audiences comprises the main focus of attention for changes in reconfiguring Media Studies because of the increase in interactivity, computer games especially role playing and multi-player narrative construction formats, and creative activity (see Chapter 3). Terms such as 'prosumers' (producer/consumers) are appearing; in the meantime the term 'users' is gaining currency in specifications. Chapter 4 considers how digital technologies make the Media and its audiences both global and local audiences.

Media institutions

This concept by its nature is closely linked to audience. It looks at the organisations (another name for the concept) that produce, circulate and exhibit media products, and provide the platforms for audience/user media activity. Students learn about professional practice and the processes that make products and therefore affect their nature, such as media technologies, budgets and regulation. Also how distribution, and target audiences, shape texts, for instance type of TV channel, schedules and funding (commercial breaks, product placement). Ownership raises issues about marketplace domination and associated legislation, and plurality of provision. While there are imbalances to acknowledge, simplistic assertions about art *versus* commerce arguments should be avoided in preference for looking at how organisations survive in the marketplace and the connections between them, for instance large film corporations need, the fresh ideas of products from independent and alternative sectors. The changes digital technologies have brought is a key issue for new Media Studies such as the expanded opportunities through convergence and synergy to disseminate products and the repertoire of forms they can have. Consideration of the issues raised by democratisation of access include the challenges brought by 'pirate' activity – radio stations, illegal film copying and controlling new technologies, as Chapter 3 notes about the music industry.

Pedagogy

Finally, in this chapter, a brief word about pedagogy. The proposed three strands of media education above reflect another 'creative tension' in media teaching – between the practical and academic. While pedagogical practice varies, the preferred approach is diversity of strategies, especially 'learning by doing' (Chapter 13 outlines the education philosophy underpinning media enquiry). A distinctive feature of media education is the extent to which practical work, the equivalent of 'writing' in English, is equally central to analytical work. Undertaking and reflecting on creative processes also stimulates academic understanding: 'creative production can be a means of generating new and more profound critical insights' (Buckingham 2003: 22). Chapter 11 shows how this can be achieved through well-focused and purposeful activities ranging from 'low-tech' to major production work.

Active pedagogy also applies to academic work, including the more demanding theoretical challenges at A level. Students better retain knowledge, understanding and skills gained from learning by doing. It is more enjoyable and so makes them open to more learning. Direct teacher input of information is essential, but it is just one approach within an overall range of collaborative strategies that repositions the teaching emphasis from the didactic to a more facilitative role. Structured student discussions, simulations, research, textual analysis, presentations, sharing discovered information and opinions through a variety of student groupings prompts discursive exchanges and observations that arise organically and can then be reconstructed into formalised analysis and fed back with reference to students' own discoveries. The English and Media Centre materials are exemplary collections of active learning, and the BFI's *Moving Images in the Classroom* is another model of such techniques to break down learning about audio-visual language. Conceptually based, active pedagogy reinforces media education's spiral model of learning so that media forms and processes can be revisited and conceptually interrogated at increasingly theoretical levels and higher expectations of knowledge and understanding.

Summary

This chapter has outlined some of the complexities, tensions and unresolved issues that can make media education a confusing terrain. As a subject area committed to culture as a lived dynamic process it validates and extends young people's existing knowledge and experience of the Media. Accommodating the rapid changes that new technologies are bringing to media education has its challenges for all teachers. However, Media Studies is a well-focused but flexible mode of enquiry that gives teachers a secure framework and relative freedom to develop their pedagogical philosophy. Cross-curricular media education has its vulnerabilities, but realisation of its multi-disciplinary qualities through the benefits of projects created with specialist expertise and institutional support demonstrate the educational and social benefits it can bring. Following its disparate beginnings momentum is growing for a consensual view of the purposes of media education. Meanwhile, many students are benefiting from the initiative and drive of teachers who enable them to acquire the range of transferable cultural, creative and critical skills that prepare them for informed active participation in today's society.

Further reading

Branston, G. with Stafford, R. (2010) *The Media Student's Handbook* (5th edition), London: Routledge.
The regular new editions of this book are a testament to its value as a comprehensive source of subject knowledge. While particularly strong on media industries, it is comprehensive with thorough informative accounts of current media issues and debates supported by extended case studies.
Buckingham, D. (2003) *Media Education: Literacy, Learning and Contemporary Culture,* London: Polity Press.
David Buckingham's book provides beginning and experienced media teachers with a comprehensive overview of the debates, theories and principles underpinning the teaching of media. The book also develops a detailed and compelling rationale for a form of media education that is theoretically rigorous and manageable in practice.
Burn, A. and Durran, J. (2007) *Media Literacy in Schools: Practice, Production and Progression,* London: Paul Chapman Publishing.
Includes DVD of student work.
McDougall, J. and Potamitis, N. (2010) *The Media Teacher's Book* (2nd edition), London: Hodder Education.
This book provides an informed perspective on how digital technologies are refocusing media education. Targeted at sixth form teaching the book demonstrates how digital technologies can be used, forming the rationale for the companion website at www.hodderplus.co.uk/mediateacher (accessed 11 March 2011).

Recommended resources

Media glossaries

Clark, V., Jones, P., Malyszko, B. and Wharton, D. (2007) *Media and Film Studies Handbook*, London: Hodder Arnold. Very student friendly reference companion: brief, clear explanations and illustrative examples of a comprehensive range of terminology and theories.

Hayward, S. (2006) *Cinema Studies: The Key Concepts*, 3rd edition, London: Routledge. Covers a broad range of cultural theories as well as cinema issues. Contains thorough and comprehensive summaries of a broad range of cultural theories as well as cinema issues. Targeted at undergraduates, useful for teacher preparation and the very able.

Probert, D. (2005) *AS/A Level Media Studies Essential Word Dictionary*, London: Philip Allan.
A dictionary for AS and A2 students directly relevant to AS/A level Media Studies. Entries are cross-referenced to related terms and concepts and include guidance from David Probert, an experienced examiner.

School websites

There are many very good examples of school departments with resources and examples of student work; many examples of the latter can be found on *YouTube*. The selections here are well resourced institutions with long established departments, and are offered as inspirational models of good practice:

Hurtwood House: excellent examples of student work,
    www.hurtwoodhouse.com/creative/performingarts/media.
Long Road Sixth Form College: strong base for OCR A level and the CMD, hotlink to showreel on
    YouTube, www.longroadmedia.com/; also see English & Media Centre.
The Parkside Federation, formerly Parkside Community College: the first Specialist Media Arts college.
    Excellent teacher support and resources particularly KS3 cross-media schemes of work and media
    assessment guidance, Level 2 CMD, practical work guides, www.parksidemedia.net/parkside_media.

Chapter 3

Internet, computer games and media learning

Adam Ranson

Introduction

This chapter aims to provide a brief set of 'pointers for the perplexed' in three areas: *technicity, manageability* and *teachability*. 'New Media' is a term that has lost some of its meaning in over-generalised application, but it refers to an object of study that has very particular challenges for the media educator. The first challenge is *technicity*. Many teachers are confident users of games and Web 2.0 applications, but others are tentative or even technophobic. Media educators and the institutions that they work within, need to make decisions about the amount of time and resources they are willing to put aside to 'keep on top' of the technology as it develops.

Closely allied to this issue is the one of *manageability*. Using technology in the classroom or across a computer network involves specific technical and classroom management skills as well as sound pedagogy. The third challenge is *teachability*.

Areas of media education such as film and television have a richness of resources and teaching practices; moving image study also has a high degree of consensus about what key concepts and theories are relevant and teachable. However, in areas such as video games there is abundant material and debate, but not as yet a dominant theoretical perspective. Given the relative newness of video games, the lack of a single theoretical perspective is to be expected. This chapter will cover the key issues related to the first two areas outlined above but, given the nature of this book, its main focus is on *teachability*.

The elephant in the room

A further challenge to teaching new media is what might be called the *specificity* of the subject: the specific characteristics of the 'new media' themselves. Arguably, the supposed universally applicable key concepts of 'text' and 'narrative' are problematic when applied to computer-based media. Even the concepts of 'audience' and 'producer' may be put into question by the prevalence of social networking and user-generated content. What is certain, however, is that these difficulties need to be grasped in order to understand the rest of what might now be referred to as 'old' media, which are in the process of being heavily 're-mediated' by the computer-driven technologies, e.g. TV and video on demand, BBC iPlayer.

Computer technology is the 'elephant in the room' of this study. Developments in the speed, capability, capacity and affordability of personal computing power have driven media changes, especially in the last 20 years. The computer's role has itself been a representational issue in popular culture and the Media. Utopian and dystopian visions of the new technology have indeed been partly instrumental in the development of new media applications: for example, the term 'cyberspace', used to describe the domain of new media, was adopted from author William Gibson's (1984) cyberpunk classic novel, *Neuromancer*.

One of the most interesting common features of the areas of study referred to as 'games' and 'Web 2.0' is that they are the most stubbornly 'computerish' of the new media, because they remain resistant to the assumed drift towards the convergence of audio-video technologies into a 'home media centre', or universal portable devices controlled by media-conglomerate content providers. While new devices, such as the iPhone, may eventually bring about this convergence, new media have fostered a culture of resistance among many of its audience. Personal computer users have the reputation of being *actively* engaged with the new technology, having developed the ability to 'hack', 'rip', 'burn' and 'mod' their texts of choice. An active minority of computer users has indeed more than resisted the blandishments of the media giants: they have collaboratively developed *open source* software alternatives, and a succession of new entrepreneurs and products challenge conventional business models and structures. The recently dubbed 'Web 2.0' is one of the most important waves of innovation.

Web 2.0: the law of unintended consequences

All technologies tend to be used in ways that were unintended by their inventors. The internet was originally developed as a tool for scientific, academic and government communications: the World Wide Web was envisaged as a giant hyper-textual library. The combination of commercial exploitation and audience usage has created what has now become known as 'Web 2.0'. Web 2.0 is not a new technology as such, rather it is a naturalisation of the Web into the texture of everyday life – the label '2.0' stresses the Web's continual incremental development.

Technologically, one of the chief outcomes of the Web has been the end of *milestone* software releases and the ushering in of an era of *perpetual beta* versions of software. New media are an important part of the global economy and are at the heart of modern media corporations. As with previous developments in media technology, new media have accelerated the process of remediation, bringing about changes in the function and practices of all existing media platforms.

The new media have also challenged the business models of traditional media producers. In common with others, Tapscott (1997) in *Growing up Digital*, views the new media as a potentially radical challenge to globalisation and corporatism. Other, more critical commentators, have described the ethos of Web 2.0 as a way in which billionaires can make money through making people feel good about working for nothing. The apparently counter-cultural values of open source applications, such as Linux, depend on an abundance of free labour from a willing pool of enthusiasts. Similarly, social networking sites such as MySpace and Facebook work only by harnessing the time and personal data freely given by its users.

What is now retrospectively called 'Web 1.0' or 'eMedia', are the many forms of media distribution and computer applications that were made possible by the Netscape internet Web browser. The development of the Web browser gave users the ability to capitalise on the hypertext media language (html) invented by the so-called 'father of the Web', Tim Berners-Lee.

Another Tim, Tim O'Reilly (2005) gave a name to what has now become known as Web 2.0. This new set of applications is powered by the same technologies from which the Google search engine emerged, but more importantly it is motivated by new ways of thinking about the Web. Applications cited as typically 'Web 2.0' include: social networking sites such as MySpace, User Generated Content (UGC) sites such as YouTube, and new participative media forms such as blogs, podcasts and wikis. They have all existed since the 1990s, but by the 2000s they were being used by a 'critical mass' of consumers. This usage was partly due to the increase in high-speed internet broadband access, and to the Google search engine's power; but principally because of the many small, useful and entertaining applications that made the Web a part of everyday life.

By bringing the Web into the domestic sphere, media usage began to be transformed in ways that were largely unanticipated by the big players of the media industry. In using technologies that detect what has been called 'The Wisdom of the Crowd', Google began to level the playing field of media production and distribution. Exceptionally successful applications – what are often referred to as 'killer applications' – such as YouTube, emerged rapidly and without the need for the prolonged and heavy marketing that earlier 'dotcoms' (an appellation taken from a company's final section of its website address: '.com') such as Amazon had required. These new applications arguably continue to challenge the media industry at every level of the supply chain.

Worried about their continued existence, large media corporations felt they had to ask a number of difficult questions in key areas:

* *Regulation and control*: 'How do I stop people downloading stuff?'
* *Finance*: 'How do I get people to pay for stuff?'
* *Production*: 'How can I make a living when everyone's doing it for free?'
* *Distribution*: 'Where has my audience gone?'

Media Studies 2.0

For media educators and theorists, the interactive and game-like nature of Web 2.0 content challenges the validity of textual analysis concepts born in the era of mass media. With reference to O'Reilly's (2005) list of distinctions between 'Web 1.0' and 'Web 2.0', authors such as Gauntlett (2007), and Dovey and Kennedy (2007) have enumerated the differences between what might be termed 'Media Studies 1.0' and 'Media Studies 2.0'. Gauntlett's article 'threw down the gauntlet' for New Media Studies in a way that had a huge impact on British Media Studies, not least by providing a compelling rationale for re-designing the GCE (2008) and GCSE (2009) specifications (see Chapters 6–8), which belatedly placed new media at the core of the subject, rather than treating them as a peripheral, bolt-on study. Gauntlett's (2007) original article is essential reading for any media educator; the following two extracts map out some of the major challenges it offers. According to Gauntlett, 'Media studies 2.0' differs from 'Media Studies 1.0' in that:

> The fetishisation of 'expert' readings of media texts is replaced with a focus on the everyday meanings produced by the diverse array of audience members, accompanied by an interest in new qualitative research techniques.

This call for a shift from an 'expert' to an audience focused approach is perhaps the most contentious challenge as it is tempting to apply the established conceptual toolkits when studying New Media. It is by no means certain, however, that a 'semiotic deconstruction' of a website or a 'Proppian analysis' of a Role Playing Game (RPG) is useful or appropriate. The study of 'Everyday Life' is an academic discipline that abandons structuralist textual analysis for a more ethnographic approach.

Gauntlett's second challenge is in relation the nature of the texts that we choose to study. In Media Studies 2.0:

> The tendency to celebrate certain 'classic' conventional and/or *avant garde* texts, and the focus on traditional media in general, is replaced with – or at least joined by – an interest in the massive 'long tail' of independent media projects such as those found on *YouTube* and many other websites, mobile devices, and other forms of DIY media.

In the pre-YouTube world it was self-evident that an expensively produced MTV music video was more important than a self-produced low-budget music promo. In the Web 2.0 world (despite attempts by the major recording companies to reassert control) this may not always be so. The following case study looks at this area in more detail.

The wisdom of the crowd in popular music

The wide use of file-sharing sites such as Napster quickly undermined the music industry's financial structure. The demise of high street stores such Woolworths and Zavvi has been blamed in part on the consequences of 'free' digital distribution of music. Alongside the economic change – from bought to free or subscription music – there is a parallel change in popular music culture. The 'directories' or 'canons' of pop music (what O'Reilly [2005] refers to as the 'taxonomy') and the musical genres that have been hitherto constructed by 'experts' such as music critics, Artistes and Repertoire (A&R) men and disc jockeys (DJs), are gradually being supplanted by the Web 2.0 practice of 'tagging'. Tagging is part of what O'Reilly (2005) calls 'folksonomy' or 'the wisdom of the crowd'.

Tags work by collecting data about the decisions and preferences of individual computer users and turning them into a powerful predictive tool. The Web 2.0 audience is made of a collection of individual 'tag clouds' that describe personal and collective patterns of media consumption. Using tags, sites such as LastFM produce personalised 'music radio', which both caters for the user's tastes and offers suggestions for new choices. Commercially, this practice opens up a long tail of products that can be recommended to listeners, a practice exploited by Amazon for instance. Some social music sites, such as Audiofarm, offer an eclectic alternative to the mainstream (although many more do not). Economically, such sites provide many independent artists with small incomes, rather than the traditional model of providing large incomes to very few artists.

The experience of iTunes, however, seems to indicate that this long tail of artists can diminish once a site becomes popular. The mainstream, commercially marketable artists reassert their dominance. Arguably, the lack of expert tastemakers can make online music sites random and unsatisfying. Sites such as HypeMachine address this by using the recommendations provided by music bloggers. Music blogs, written by self-proclaimed experts and enthusiasts, are also the source of an astounding quantity of 'free' music, which may be the main appeal to the average user. A&R men in record companies certainly comb the blogs for the 'next big thing'. The *blogosphere* seems to be the new form of journalism in the field of music, just as it is in other cultural fields. Web 2.0 applications such as *Technorati* even automate the process of finding where the buzz is on the Web.

At present music blogs offer a huge diversity of opinion, although we may soon see the must-read musical equivalent of *The Drudge Report*, which according to Wikipedia (en.wikipedia.org) is 'a conservative news aggregation website. Run by Matt Drudge with the help of Andrew Breitbart, the site consists mainly of links to stories from the United States and international mainstream media about politics, entertainment, and current events as well as links to many columnists'. *Ain't It Cool News* (AICN) is 'a website founded and run by Harry Knowles, dedicated to rumours and reviews of upcoming and currently playing films and television projects, with an emphasis on science fiction, fantasy, horror, comic-book and action genres. It combines gossip from anonymous and unverified sources as well as news and reviews' (ibid.). *Popbitch* is 'a weekly UK-based celebrity and pop music newsletter and associated website dating from the early 2000s. Much of the material for the newsletter comes from the *Popbitch* message boards, frequented by music industry insiders, gossips and the casually interested. The board has at various times been credited for celebrity rumours (both false and true) appearing in the press, and the coining and subsequent usage of many phrases'.

Looking at the Web's impact on popular music does not mean having to discount mainstream marketing initiatives such as *The X Factor* on television. Arguably, the rise of TV talent shows is part of an industry response to the perceived death of the single record brought about by new technology and the internet. As such, it is an example of an important concept in new media: *remediation*.

Remediation

One of the big controversies in looking at 'new media' is how the 'new' has an effect on the 'old'. This idea of 'remediation' had two articulate champions with two very different points of view: Marshall McLuhan and Raymond Williams.

McLuhan (2001), a 'techno optimist', believes that remediation increased human capacity in an almost organic way:

> after more than a century of electric technology, we have extended our central nervous system itself in a global embrace, abolishing both space and time as far as our planet is concerned. Rapidly, we approach the final phase of the extensions of man – the technological simulation of consciousness, when the creative process of knowing will be collectively and corporately extended to the whole of human society.
>
> (McLuhan 2001: 3)

Williams (1974) takes a more pragmatic, perhaps pessimistic, and Marxist view:

> The physical fact of instant transmission has been uncritically raised to a social fact, without any pause to notice that virtually all such transmission is at once selected and controlled by existing social authorities.
>
> (Williams 1974: 127)

Although their debates took place long before the internet era, their arguments are still applicable and have recently been much used in the debate between different schools of thought in relation to new media *cybertexts*.

Cybertexts: the difference between the Web and games

Although there is a large and increasing crossover between the Web and games, these two applications of computer technology tend to be viewed in strong binary terms and with a contrasting amount of cultural capital. Despite being born from the same technology as the Web, games tend to be seen as the Caliban rather than the Ariel of the enchanted isle of new media world. Lister *et al.* (2003) draw the following helpful distinctions:

The Web	Games
Creative communication	Mindless entertainment
Public space	Private/Commodified space
Adult	Child/Youth
Fluid identity	Hyper-masculinity
Immersive	Addictive
Interactive	Reflex 'twitch'
New reality	New delusion
Art and Literature	Trash culture toys
Objects to think with	

Figure 3.1 Comparative values attached to the Web and games

Adapted from Lister, M., Kelly, K., Dovey, J., Giddings, S. and Grant, I. (2003: 263).

Media theorists initially conceptualised the Web in terms of hypertextuality and cyberspace. Both concepts tend to privilege the 'text' and the technology rather than the audience. Parallel to this approach however, the emerging discipline of 'games studies' (or ludology) has developed a different emphasis with a much stronger appreciation of the audience and its involvement with new media within everyday life and the domestic sphere. According to Aarseth (1997), both the Web and games are cybertexts and can be read using similar techniques of analysis. One of the other characteristics that they share is 'multi-modality'; they can be read in a number of very different ways according to how they are used.

Modalities

One of the principal applications of social semiotic theory is the idea of modalities. Modalities map the different ways in which texts and behaviour can be meaningful to those who participate in and/or use particular media. Gordon Calleja's (2007a) model of 'game involvement' uses six modalites to interpret the experience of game playing – which can also usefully analyse many Web 2.0 applications. It is an active model of player *involvement* that assumes a multimodal complexity at the heart of the game playing experience, rather than players being passive consumers of the game experience. Calleja's modes of involvement are:

- tactical;
- performative;

- affective;
- shared;
- narrative;
- spatial.

Tactical involvement

> . . . tactical involvement represents engagement with all forms of decision making made within the context of the game. This includes interaction both with the rules . . . with the broader game environment and other players.
>
> (Calleja 2007a: 236)

This form of involvement can also be called 'game-play'. It is argued by ludologists that this is the core of the game experience, with its distinct set of rules within a magic circle of significance. According to this theory, games are not essentially narratives. Unlike narratives, games do not have to 'mean' anything, they do not have to refer to or represent anything outside the internal coherence of their game-play. The ludological approach is rooted in the work of Johan Huizinga, such as the 'magic circle' metaphor often cited by those who follow his approach:

> The arena, the card-table, the magic circle, the temple, the stage, the screen . . . are all in form and function play-grounds, i.e. forbidden spots, isolated, hedged round, hallowed, within which special rules obtain. All are temporary worlds within the ordinary world, dedicated to the performance of an act apart.
>
> (Huizinga 1970: 28–29)

While games are the 'purest' forum for tactical involvement, any media text with a degree of interactivity or problem solving demands the exercise of some tactical skill. The skilled use of a search engine, website or database requires the participant to understand and 'play by the rules' in order to achieve an outcome – the outcome may be mainly functional but satisfaction can be gained by 'winning' the answer. The archetypal 'geek' is a description of someone whose greatest satisfaction is in understanding and using the underlying rules of a system. One of the most puzzling aspects of video gaming for the non-player is the willingness of players to use maps, so-called 'walk-throughs' (literally step-by-step guides) readily available, pre-programmed codes that give the player advantage in some way – 'cheats' and shortcuts pre-engineered into the software. The idea of tactical involvement explains this approach to gaming nicely: the greatest tactical satisfaction is to beat the system *but without stepping outside the rules.*

Performative involvement

> Performative involvement relates to all modes of avatar or game-piece control in digital environments, ranging from learning controls to the fluency of internalised movement.
>
> (Calleja 2007b: 208)

One of the areas of computer gaming that has received much academic and media attention is the issue of personal identity raised by games' avatars. Cyber-theorists such as Donna

Haraway (1991) have argued that avatars are self-constructed, post-modern, identities that incorporate human and machine in a new *cyborg* (CYBernetic ORGanism – part human and part machine). Controversy about role-playing in persistent game-worlds such as *Second Life* generally centres on the tiny minority of players who identify themselves obsessively with an unrealistic idealised persona. Research into players in MMOGs (Massively Multiplayer Online Games) such as *World of Warcraft* shows that experienced players tend to choose avatars according to their game-play attributes (what they can do) rather than their attractiveness as personalities (who they would like to be). Players in open-ended games ('Paidia' games in ludological terms) like *Second Life* may well use avatars differently from those in 'Ludus' (strictly rule-based) games.

It is also possible to apply the concept of performative involvement to Web applications, particularly to Social Network Sites (SNS), which often involve the elaborate construction and maintenance of an online identity. Media coverage has largely focused on the capacity for misrepresentation and deceit in SNS, whereas research into SNS users shows most people use them to keep in contact with people with whom they already have face-to-face dealings, indicating that SNS deception is limited by 'self-policing'.

Affective involvement

> The practiced effort required to engage with games places particular emphasis on the need for them to be compelling enough to sustain this effort . . . The cognitive, emotional, and kinaesthetic feedback loop that is formed between the game process and the player makes games particularly powerful means of affecting players' moods and emotional states.
>
> (Calleja 2007a: ibid.)

Involvement in a game involves an emotional investment that is facilitated by the game's design. The aesthetic beauty, or 'realism' of a game-world, or the kinaesthetic pleasure of well-configured movement controls all add to the tactical pleasure of game-play to produce a rich gaming experience. As with many pleasurable experiences, to the outside observer game experiences seem to have elements of compulsive behaviour, or even addiction. Much research has been directed at the cognitive and affective effects of gaming on young people, and true to such 'effects' research, findings are often sharply divided between those that find harm – Anderson and Bushman (2001), and those that find benefits – Buckingham (2000, 2007a). The two research camps are irreconcilable since they come from different theoretical perspectives, use different research methodologies and have different standards of 'proof'. Internet usage has generally escaped demonisation because of its information and education uses; SNS, however, have begun to suffer similar negative stereotypes to those attached to video gaming and MMOGs.

Shared involvement

> Human controlled agents allow an infinitely wider range of communication as well as responding in more unpredictable ways, making the shared involvement more intense when other humans are present in the environment, whether they are being interacted with directly or act as an audience to the player's actions.
>
> (Calleja 2007a: 237)

Many online games such as MMOGs offer players the capability to communicate, interact and cooperate with other players (or at least, their avatars). Games such as *World of Warcraft* have developed integral elaborate social networks through 'forums', 'guilds' and shared missions. The appeal of 'persistent virtual worlds' such as *Second Life* is almost entirely due to their capacity for social interaction as are popular SNS, which are entirely constructed around various forms of shared involvement. Any SNS member is continually asked to participate in social activities such as quizzes, games, discussions and forums as well as making their profile and diary available to other site members. The willingness of SNS members to publicly share personal information has been the cause of some 'stranger danger' fears in the Media; but perhaps just as much of an issue is the willingness of participants to share their personal information with the organisations that provide 'free' SNS services in return for this valuable personal data.

Today, marketers can even learn about the stories that we tell ourselves about ourselves; they are represented in the profiles of our social networking sites . . . young people don't mind so much that they share their 'friends lists', conversations and navigational habits not only with their acquaintances but also the companies who interpret much of this data. With these firms (and possibly government bodies) as daily confidantes, latent possibilities for total control have opened up (Scholz 2008).

Narrative involvement

There have been numerous discussions within game studies about the role of narrative in digital games. The more vigorous, and at times heated, of these took place during the so-called narratology–ludology debate (Calleja 2007b: 149).

Game studies theorists such as Aarseth (1997) and Juul (2003) have fiercely resisted application of literary, or cinema-derived narrative theory to games and hypertexts. According to these ludologists, the underlying structure of a game is a set of rules that has very little to do with story structure: what, for example, is the narrative of the shape-placing game *Tetris*? Games, according to Juul, are defined by six common features, which can be used to frame investigative questions for any game, see Figure 3.2.

Despite the ludological objections to applying structural narrative theories, such as those of Propp or Todorov, some game genres do have strong elements of classical narrative.

Game features	Investigative questions
Rules	What are the rules of this game?
Variable, quantifiable outcomes	What are the possible outcomes?
Value assigned to possible outcomes	What are the most valued outcomes?
Player effort	What makes a player 'care' about the
Player attachment to outcome	outcome?
Negotiable consequences	What (if anything) does the player get out of the game that relates to his/her own life?

Figure 3.2 Investigating game features

Role-playing games such as *World of Warcraft* self-consciously refer to existing mythic or fantasy story worlds, such as 'Middle Earth' in Tolkien's work. Other popular games relate to movies, or even to 'real-life' scenarios. It does not seem difficult to come to the conclusion that there can be games with *no* narrative, games that *also* have narrative, but never games that are *only* narrative. Calleja (2007b) suggests that we can usefully look at two kinds of narrative:

> For the scope of the current analysis, two perspectives on narrative will be helpful. On one hand, we can look at narrative elements like a game world's history and background, or the back-story of a current mission or quest. I will refer to this as the 'designed narrative'. On the other hand, we can take narrative to refer to the player's interpretation of the game-play experience. I will refer to this as 'personal narrative'.
>
> (Calleja 2007b: 87)

Some theorists suggest that if there is a dominant narrative form in games then it is a *spatial narrative* (rather than a temporal narrative, as in literature and film). The designed narrative of a game can be compared to a detailed map of the whole story-world. The 'personal narrative' is the individual journey through this world.

Spatial involvement

Typically, video games create 'worlds', 'lands' or 'environments' for players to explore, traverse, conquer and even dynamically manipulate and transform (Newman 2004: 108).

Games and the Web produce computer-generated virtual spaces for human minds to inhabit. The possibilities and perils of such interaction and territories have excited the imaginations of science fiction writers such as William Gibson noted above. A spatial narrative may take time to traverse but not as a time-based narrative; rather it is a progressively revealed *map*. Jenkins (2004) uses film theory to suggest there are four ways in which this map can be used to create a satisfying narrative:

- evocative spaces;
- enacting stories;
- embedded narratives;
- emergent narratives.

Evocative space is created by 'using pre-existing narrative competencies', referring to story-worlds with which the audience is already familiar, either from other media texts, media platforms or genres. Thus *Grand Theft Auto* (GTA) can evoke American cityscapes by reference to classic crime thrillers. Evocative space is somewhat akin to movie mise-en-scène.

Enacted space is the spatial narrative created by the pursuit of a goal, the overcoming of obstacles and the resolution of conflicts. In a traditional 'platform game', an enacted spatial narrative would be resolved on completing a 'level'. The analogous film studies concept is mythic story structure: Joseph Campbell's (1949) work, for example, *The Hero with a Thousand Faces* (3rd edn, 2003) inspired Disney scriptwriter Christopher Vogler (2007) to create a map of the 'Hero's Journey'. In classic heroic narrative the hero's quest involves the navigation of this territory.

Embedded narrative: in film theory there is a distinction made between the time-limited 'plot' of a film and the virtually unlimited productivity of the 'story-world' from which the plot draws its elements. Like film, games can create enigmas that refer to and reveal glimpses of the larger story-world.

Emergent space: in one important respect computer games (and some Web applications) are more game than text. Players are often allowed to interact relatively freely with virtual environments and the objects in them in order to produce 'creative' outcomes unanticipated by the author of the cybertext. *Second Life* and other *Sim* (simulation) games are 'virtual toy-boxes' in which participants can individually or collaboratively have a cumulative impact.

Cybertexts and ergodic literature

Aarseth (1997), however, has pointed out that this apparent interactivity is limited. In the cybertext, navigation is *ergodic* (translatable as 'path-work'), meaning that instead of being 'read', it requires the participant to make a sustained effort to follow a particular path through a labyrinth of alternatives. Like someone in a maze, the player must work out a path through the text. According to Deleuze and Guattari (2004), a labyrinth can have a simple linear structure, an apparently open 'net' structure, or an unpredictably organically branching rhizome structure (in horticulture a rhizome is a rootstock, a creeping underground stem by means of which certain plants, mint or bamboo for example, propagate themselves). How the apparently open cyberspaces are navigated therefore is largely determined by the initial design of the space. The different ways in which players navigate their ways though the cybertext are determined partly by the different game genres.

Studying games in the classroom

Possibly the most engaging way to work with games is students making their own. How realistic this is in terms of class time and relevance for Media Studies will depend on the Awarding Body specification; Burn and Durran (2007) demonstrate how games production can be effectively managed at Key Stage 3. For those who want a quick dip into game design, Michigan Institute of Technology produce a web-based application called *Scratch*. Its website (http://scratch.mit.edu/) has freely downloadable software and an extensive online support community, which includes ScratchEd for educators. *Scratch* works on any computer with a recent version of Java (a general purpose programming language) installed – the vast majority of Web browsers are compatible. More advanced 3D game design and commercial game design applications, such as MissionMaker and Game Builder may be bought with educational discount prices.

The economic and industrial aspects of games can be approached by researching careers in the games industry. The UK media training body Skillset has a comprehensive set of resources, as do a number of other 'gamer' sites. (See 'Useful websites' for all of these suggestions.)

The idea of 'teaching' games in the classroom can seem daunting, but using a data projector linked to a console or PC enables a whole class to watch a player's individual experiences. One interesting way of demonstrating 'game-play' (the 'ludic' aspect of a game) is to ask an 'expert' player to guide a complete novice through a game level or mission. Another way is to ask the 'expert' to 'walk through' the narrative 'story-world' of a game and explain the character and attributes of his/her chosen 'Avatar'.

MMORPG games such as *World of Warcraft* (*WoW*) and *Runescape* are rich resources for the classroom. *Runescape* has the added advantage of being free, whereas *WoW* is a subscription-based game. However, immersive console games and MMORPGs are not the only games that can be studied in a classroom setting. Game based social networking sites such as *Club Penguin, Gaia Online* or *Neopets* can also be used. These SNS sites allow a whole class with computer access to have a shared online gaming experience.

As a precaution and part of the preparation for teaching games and SNS, most teachers will find it necessary to convince their ICT services department to 'unblock' what somebody has deemed to be 'time-wasting' sites. It is vitally important that any discussion and negotiation with ICT colleagues takes place well before embarking on a sequence of lessons focusing on games and Web 2.0.

Away from the classroom, students can research games through media concepts such as Industry and Audience, and apply specific theoretical perspectives. Industrial practices such as spin-off games from films such as *Quantum of Solace* provide excellent examples of multiplatform products in a multinational matrix of media corporations. Conversely, *indie* game companies, such as Jagex (www.jagex.com) and 'in-house' and 'third-party' game producers can be compared. Student research into the history of the ongoing 'console wars' is also an engaging and relevant institutional study. The so-called 'razor blade' financial model used by game console producers (sell consoles at a loss, but make a big profit on licensing games) will surprise many students. For those students who want to engage with specific games at a more theoretical level one of the best approaches is through an exploration of how game players relate to games. The 'modalities of involvement' model above is one approach to such study. The social impact of games can also be researched by students through an examination of media coverage of various 'moral panics' and applying the competing perspectives of *effects* theorists and their critics, e.g. Barker and Petley (2001), and Gauntlett (2007a).

Studying Web 2.0

Use of the internet in education has been heavily promoted for over a decade and ably supported by academics such as Professor Stephen Heppell (www.heppell.net), and the government agency charged with promoting and supporting innovative and effective use of ICT in schools, British Educational Communications and Technology Agency (Becta) – until it fell victim to the coalition government cutbacks in 2010. However, its website is still extant (www.becta.org.uk).

Many Web 2.0 applications are difficult to use in class precisely because their social networking capabilities are regarded as a waste of time within the educational setting. However, Web 2.0 applications such as blogs, journals, wikis, forums and chat are highly productive whether using intranet applications, such as Moodle, or one of the many freely available commercial and educational applications. Indeed, they are already part of the formal options in some GCSE and A level courses. Although teachers need to learn how to manage and moderate online student interaction, with a little perseverance these interactive forms allow students to collaborate on shared projects and to evaluate their own work alongside others in a group setting.

While it is, perhaps, understandable that teachers may be concerned that students will abuse their ability to 'post' comments, generally young people observe online protocol scrupulously, if only because their contributions are made in public. Even more than with games, the Web is a medium to which young people can genuinely contribute. Most curricula can support the making of Web pages, posting videos and production of audio and video podcasts. The barrier to entry is far lower in relation to Web applications than any other media. It is only a small step from posting 'random' clips on YouTube to entering online material for commissions on such sites as the short documentary website 4Docs (www.4docs. org.uk) and creative productions on the BBC's Blast website (www.bbc.co.uk/blast). This is an area where with a modest investment in staff training, teachers can genuinely facilitate meaningful entry into the Media.

Summary

Media Education is topical and opportunistic. It seeks to illuminate the life-situations of learners. In doing so it may place the 'here-and-now' in the context of wider historic and ideological issues.

(Masterman 1995)

One of the defining characteristics of media education is study of the ephemeral world of media usage and evolving technology. When Masterman wrote his Media Studies manifesto in the 1980s, the principal 'new media' of the time were the VCR and camcorder. Importantly, the camcorder encouraged students to engage practically and creatively with visual narrative. The VCR enabled teachers to pause the flow of exciting, ephemeral television and film and, supported by excellent moving image education resources, followed the lead of Film Studies to focus on detailed examination of specific authored texts.

Arguably, in the following 20 years, this version of media education blurred the wider media education mission in the interests of *teachability*. Although Media Studies specifications changed little, the media certainly did. Digital technology (the *technicity* of new media) created new and converging media forms, and Web 1.0 rapidly developed into Web 2.0 and the domestic sphere. The novel characteristics of digital forms and various modalities of active audience involvement in the now not so new media are urgently prompting media teachers to re-engage with the here and now. This chapter offers accessible resources, pedagogy and pre-emptive organisation strategies to address (largely unfounded) concerns about the educational appropriateness and *manageability* of forms such as social networking sites and whole class games teaching.

In responding to the evolution of media technology and its new generations of users, media education should correspondingly evolve its own analytic discourse from 'Media 1.0' towards 'Media 2.0'. While there are areas of conceptual continuity there are also substantial shifts away from textual dominance to meanings created by processes (of active audiences), the effects on corporate media, fresh perspectives on narrative, and the rich new investigative territory of ludology. The outline of Media 2.0 theoretical perspectives offers rigorous and stimulating support for teachers to engage with the *teachability* of internet forms and computer games, and to meet the requirements of the 2008 and 2009 Awarding Body specifications that put eMedia at the heart of Media Studies. The new media require media teachers to plunge again into the situated culture of media audiences and production: it is after all where the students live.

Further reading

Buckingham, D. (2007) *Beyond Technology: Children's Learning in the Age of Digital Culture*, Cambridge: Polity.

Essential reading for students and teachers; rigorous, academic and accessible, the book is a thorough and well-reasoned analysis of the growing divide between schooling and the Media, and the technologically rich cultural lives young people live outside school. Chapters include: 'New Media and Children's Culture', 'Rethinking the Educational Potential of Computer Games', and 'Digital Media and Learning in the Home'.

Gee, J.P. (2008) *What Video Games Have to Teach Us About Learning and Literacy*, 2nd edition, Basingtoke: Palgrave.

Rightly called a 'transformative work', this second edition is an updated and revised version of Gee's classic work on video games. It is not a media education text *per se* but is essential reading to develop thorough knowledge and understanding of games. Chapters include: '36 Ways to Learn a Video Game', 'What does it mean to be a Half Elf?', 'Why doesn't Lara Croft obey Professor Von Croy?' and 'What should you do after you have Destroyed the Global conspiracy?'

Recommended resources

Practical guides to teaching video games in the classroom

Burn, A. and Durran, J. (2007) *Media Literacy in Schools: Practice, Production and Progression*, London: Paul Chapman Publishing.

McDougall, J. and O'Brien, W. (2008) *Studying Videogames*, London: Auteur.

Newman, J. and Oram, B. (2006) *Teaching Videogames*, London: BFI/Palgrave Macmillan.

Websites

BBC Blast: Commissions work from young people – www.bbc.co.uk/blast/

Becta: Government agency supporting ICT in Education – www.becta.org.uk/

Digra: The Digital Games Research Association – www.digra.org/

Edge: The gamer's journal – www.edge-online.com/

Four Docs: Resources and commissions for documentary makers – www.channel4.com/culture/microsites/F/fourdocs/

Gameology: Games Studies resources and commentary – www.gameology.org

Game Studies: The International Journal of Computer Game Research – http://gamestudies.org

Game Builder: Fully specified game design software – www.garagegames.com

Half-Real: Jesper Juul's site (The Dictionary is particularly useful) – www.half-real.net/ and www.half-real.net/dictionary/

Heppell.net: Stephen Heppell (new media and e-learning expert) – www.heppell.net/

MissionMaker: Easy to use PC game making software for education www.immersiveeducation.com/missionmaker/

JISC: IT Research for HE and FE – www.jisc.ac.uk/publications/publications/twWeb2.aspx

O'Reilly: Tim O'Reilly's Web 2.0 resources – www.oreillynet.com

Skillset: How to train for a career in new media – www.skillset.org/games/

Scratch: Cross platform game making application from MIT – http://scratch.mit.edu/

Theory.org: David Gauntlett's indispensable site – www.theory.org.uk

Chapter 4

Global and local in media education

Roy Stafford

Introduction

The National Curriculum (NC) at KS3 and 4 requires schools to consider a range of cross-curricular 'dimensions' as potentially unifying areas of learning that 'span the curriculum' and 'help young people make sense of the world' (QCA 2007a). There are several dimensions and they are meant to be seen as integrative with each other as well as with NC subjects. 'Global dimension and sustainable development' and 'identity and cultural diversity' are two of the dimensions that concern media teachers. 'Sustainable development' should interest media teachers also, but in a chapter of this length space is limited.

There is a long history of debate within media education about developing this multi-disciplinary discourse within a 'whole school' policy. The political and institutional history of English education has meant that a narrower view of 'media studies' as a subject has been more successful so far both as a discrete subject post-14 and as a model for housing media work within English. The possibility of engaging with 'dimensions' is exciting – even if they are not mandatory requirements, there is clearly a will to support the work.

Any media teacher appraising the QCA documents on the two dimensions listed above will immediately notice the possibilities for media work. This is hardly surprising, but what is more important is to recognise two factors:

- the dimension documents promoted by QCA are in themselves media texts that represent ideas about global issues, identity and diversity from a particular perspective and from within a specific institutional and cultural context;
- the history of media education and the development of media theory reveal distinct struggles over concepts such as 'globalisation' and 'representation'.

What this means is that support documents need to be approached with critical awareness and media teachers need to be prepared to argue against some of the assumptions that may underpin the approaches suggested for cross-curricular work.

The focus in this chapter will be on underlying principles and some of the most important and contentious issues that might fruitfully be explored in media work at KS3/4 and in a more developed way at KS5 within film and media studies teaching.

Global/local and diversity

There are many ways to theorise what 'globalisation' might mean. In the second edition of the *Media Student's Book* (Branston and Stafford 1999) globalisation was said to occur when:

- activities take place in a global (not national or regional) arena;
- they are deliberately organised on a global scale;
- they involve some interdependency, so local activities in different parts of the world are shaped by each other;
- communication between and about activities was instantaneous.

Although the four points above were retained in the 'Whose globalisation?' chapter of the fourth edition (Branston and Stafford 2006), the introduction suggested two further considerations:

- globalisation processes have meant that for some people, life seems to be lived in a 'borderless' world of instantaneous access to images of events and to goods and services via the ever-expanding world of internet communication;
- one particular economic system – the 'free market system' or 'global capitalism' – now permeates most of the globe.

The recession that has hit 'global capitalism' since 2008 has both proved the impact of instantaneous changes within the global economy and cast doubts on how the economy will function in the future. However, given the 'crisis in capitalism' that hit world markets in 2008 and 2009, the last bullet point above may need to be revised in a future edition of the book.

The concept of the global is *dynamic*. Two other related issues are:

- the inequalities of access to the global economy (and global media);
- the perception that one economic and cultural power dominates global cultural and economic exchange – the United States of America.

Again, how academic scholarship and political campaigners have theorised these relationships has changed over time. For instance, the term 'third world' is now rarely used in academic discourse and there are still struggles over concepts of 'North' and 'South' (as distinct from 'Western') and the more politically charged use of 'over-developed' and 'under-developed' (which emphasise the power relationship underpinning global exchanges). Within Media Studies, these kinds of debates have crystallised around two related concepts – 'cultural imperialism' and 'hegemony'. Whatever media teachers would like to explore in classrooms will usually be underpinned in some way by consideration of these concepts.

Cultural imperialism and hegemonic Hollywood

This concept derives from the idea that after the process of independence struggle and the effective de-colonisation of the former territories of European imperial powers, the newly independent states were then 're-colonised' by US (and European) cultural power – film, television, popular music, global branding, etc. This form of domination, it is argued, is more insidious since it is seen as invited rather than imposed. The debate has thus been developed using the concept of hegemony.

Hegemony means the control by one group over others exerted through persuasion and consensus. Originally confined to issues concerned with political control, hegemony has long been used to describe the control over media communications by groups within societies and in global terms the control exerted by specific national media industries over those in other countries. The hegemonic position of the major Hollywood studios in global film and television is the best example of how this issue arises within media education.

A good example of US hegemony in television is the long-established sale of US TV shows at differentiated prices to television stations across the world. If a UK school has an international partner overseas, an interesting exercise might be to undertake a content analysis of what kinds of TV programming are available locally. The likelihood is that in many countries local programming will be augmented by filmed drama, especially 'universal' formats such as crime thrillers and family melodramas produced by Hollywood studios and their affiliates. The US television industry has been built on the basis of 'syndication' – the process by which high production costs for US broadcast are offset by income from re-runs and sales to overseas buyers. Shows such as *Friends* or *24* are sold at differentiated rates ranging from the highest in the UK and Germany to much lower rates in Africa or Latin America. In smaller markets, the deal is seen as beneficial to both sides. The US producer gains revenue for very little cost and the local broadcaster has access to material with production values that cannot be matched locally. Consider, for example, the portfolio of US shows listed by the Kenyan private TV station KTN on its website, www.ktnkenya.tv, which included *House, Heroes, CSI: NY* and *The Sopranos* in May 2009.

Media theorists have seen this kind of development as having a range of possible negative outcomes. The most obvious is that local producers are unable to compete with imported programming and that this will in turn stifle the development of local talent, preventing the possibility of an indigenous filmed entertainment industry able to create local fictions with their exploration of local identities and cultural traditions. The implication is that US hegemonic cultural power leads eventually to an homogenisation of local culture around the world – what has sometimes been termed the 'MacWorld' effect – the efficient production of a bland product with some nods to local taste, but essentially the same product everywhere.

There are several objections to this view of a simple equation of:

global media power = US hegemony

and they prompt important considerations in teaching about Hollywood. The hegemony argument:

- risks seeing the local audience as passive – they may actually 'read' or 'use' American programming in different ways than in the US;
- risks suggesting that there is locally a traditional culture that is itself stable and somehow free from all the problems inherent in an American lifestyle;
- ignores the powerful impact of other cultural production 'flows' that may compete effectively with American programming in some markets (for example films and television from other global producers such as Latin American *telenovelas*, Hindi Cinema etc.).

To return to the example of African television broadcasts, one of the main developments in the last five years has been the broadcast in many African states of English Premier League Football (and the promotion of replica shirts and other forms of branding). One of the reasons for these developments is the large number of African footballers now playing in the Premiership and the very high celebrity profile that some players have achieved. In Nigeria, and increasingly in other African states, the most popular form of filmed entertainment is 'Nollywood' – the unique video film industry that claims for itself a production output surpassed only by India and the US. Nollywood is now having an influence outside Africa, not least on the diasporic populations of West Africans living in the UK and the US. ('Diaspora' here refers to the existence of communities with a clear sense of identity related to that of the country of their family origin. In the UK this means a wide range of communities from all parts of the world.) The whole question of diaspora audiences for all kinds of media production from countries outside Europe and North America (i.e. a 'contra-flow' of cultural power) throws doubt upon the cultural imperialism thesis.

Corporate media power

Whatever the challenges to US cultural hegemony, it is still a powerful agent in disseminating American cultural ideas. Hollywood films dominate every theatrical film market in the world (i.e. more than 50 per cent of box office or the largest single market share) bar the four Asian markets of India, China, Japan and South Korea. Even in Pakistan in the midst of Taliban attacks in 2009, a BBC reporter was offered Michael Jackson CDs and Angelina Jolie DVDs in a Punjabi video and music store (BBC 2009).

The important argument may well be about the model offered by American media business practices and the ways in which these have been adopted and adapted by entre-preneurial producers across the world. At the time of writing, what is apparent is that US media corporations, especially Hollywood studios, are engaging with producers with quite different cultural bases in India and China. Even when, as in India, American business methods may be seen as adaptable, the likelihood is that the media business models that emerge will be new. A further question will be – what will happen to the currently marginalised media producers in languages other than Hindi or Mandarin? Will they have more or less chance to develop independently?

The problem of hegemonic Hollywood in UK media education

If the preceding discussion seems esoteric in terms of teaching in English classrooms, it is nevertheless important for any understanding of the central problem associated with studying 'global media texts' in a UK context.

It is possible to study media texts produced in all parts of the world and to access them via English-language productions. Since English is the language of business, international politics and cultural exchange, there are English language newspapers printed in most countries as well as websites offered in English. There are also many English language radio stations worldwide and since the development of internet radio, more radio stations have become accessible from the UK. Several of the world's major television broadcasters also produce 'world television services' (e.g. Al Jazeera and Die Welle as well as CNN and BBC World), which may be available via satellite connections in the UK. Some of the suggested materials in QCA's National Curriculum support documents on the Global Dimension are produced in English by European and North American aid agencies. There is a tradition in Anglophone Africa of 'development media' produced in this way.

But although these 'English medium' services can provide factual information about different countries, they are limited in the range of representations they offer and the extent to which they can provide access to local cultural activity. Therefore, if English school students are to get any sense of what popular culture might be like in other countries, the most accessible form is likely to be filmed entertainment produced in a local language. Popular music also offers opportunities, but arguably not as many as film (with which it shares some of the problems outlined below).

Ideally, all students should be studying at least one modern foreign language. In the UK, this could well be Mandarin, Arabic, Urdu or Hindi as much as Spanish, French or German. The confusion in the English schools system, with the weakening in language provision at Key Stage 4 while it is encouraged at Key Stage 2, does not help. Where modern foreign language provision is well established, there will be clear opportunities to link media education work directly to explorations of other languages in their cultural context. For the majority of students, however, access to films from other cultures is likely to mean subtitles. In some countries, dubbing is the common mode of access to foreign language filmed material (e.g. in larger European countries and parts of Asia). In the UK it has largely died out – something that some European film producers regret and that has undoubtedly narrowed the film market for films from non-English language producers.

There is a prejudice against subtitling within the UK generally and unfortunately within education as well. Partly, this is simply a matter of unfamiliarity – subtitled films are rarely, if ever, shown on the two main terrestrial TV channels (BBC1, ITV1). Many school students have never seen a subtitled film in the cinema and teachers, conscious of this fact, may lower their expectations of what is appropriate for their classes. Experience of organising cinema screenings for a variety of school groups suggests that subtitling is not really a problem for students at KS3 or above (or even at KS2) – unless they have specific reading difficulties. If the film is appropriate in terms of narrative, genre and style, the subtitles will usually reflect this.

Hollywood and the problem of the popular

The central issue for media teachers in selecting material for study of global issues focuses on the general UK familiarity with American popular culture. This is particularly the case for the forms of filmed entertainment enjoyed by most school-age students. So much so in fact that official film culture in the UK posits Hollywood as the norm and all other forms of cinema, including those British films that do not adopt the Hollywood model, as 'specialised' (the term used by the UK Film Council). Within Film and Media Studies a similar approach to the perception of Hollywood hegemony leads to a situation where films are classified according to the ways in which they are 'not Hollywood'. In other words, students will often approach a film to discover how it differs from the Hollywood norm, rather than starting from how the film works in the context of its own production and reception by a local audience.

While it is sound pedagogical practice to begin with what the student knows, in the case of films outside Hollywood, this approach runs the risk of approaching such films in a negative way. It is compounded by the use of the term 'World Cinema', which can be found in some Film and Media examination board specifications and which is routinely used in marketing non-Hollywood films. As with 'World Music', the term is both offensive and misleading. It works to confirm that American films have a unique identity, but all others can be lumped together as 'non-American'.

In the film industry, the term 'international' performs the same function as the world market is routinely split into two – 'North America (US and Canada)' and 'International'.

A further complication is that films are distributed internationally largely on the basis that the only 'popular genre films' that can be sold overseas will be American. In reality, most of the non-English language films sold internationally are what used to be called 'art films' or 'arthouse films' and although such films may offer an insight into the culture of their country of production, they may be both less accessible to a general audience because of their cinema aesthetics and in any case aimed at an international rather than a local audience.

There are several major film industries outside Hollywood that make a broad range of popular films – comedies, action films, melodramas, thrillers, etc. Such films do enter the UK, primarily for diaspora audiences. They are also brought into the UK on DVD or purchased on the internet. Mainstream UK cinema or DVD distributors do not distribute most of these films. Hong Kong/Chinese and Turkish films follow this pattern, as do video films from Nigeria and Ghana. The main non-English language films in the UK are the Hindi (and occasionally Tamil) films, which although distributed through mainstream cinemas and video stores are still not properly integrated into the UK film market. All of these films would be interesting to use in classrooms. Many are now subtitled (although perhaps not very well in some cases), but so far there is little evidence of this happening. Instead, careful choices must be made from what is easily available via mainstream sources.

Popular films from India, Hong Kong, etc. are likely to appeal to an audience of 13-year-olds, partly because cultural differences are to some extent compensated for by familiar action and music sequences. Unfortunately many of the action films that might actually raise interesting social questions, such as *City of God* (Brazil/France 2002) set in the *favelas* of Rio de Janeiro in the 1980s, are classified with an 18 or 15 certificate. There is nothing to prevent a teacher screening an 18 or 15 certificate film for younger students, but parental consent should be sought and judgments of suitability made. Other considerations are that the excitement created by violent action may both engage some students but also get in the way of a possible discussion of wider issues. Some films, like *City of God*, may also be simply too long to easily screen in school situations (although an after school film club showing may be possible).

Case Study I: Exploring 'global' questions through *Not One Less*

In the case study that follows, a film that could be used with any school group from KS3 upwards is offered for classroom work on 'the global dimension':

> Education for the global dimension encourages learners to evaluate information and events from a range of perspectives, to think critically about challenges facing the global community such as migration, identity and diversity, equality of opportunity and sustainability, and to explore some of the solutions to these issues. Learning about the global dimension offers opportunities for schools to address their duty to promote community cohesion. The global dimension addresses social, political, environmental and economic issues that are of direct concern to young people.
>
> (QCA 2007b: 2)

Not One Less, China 1999 (106 minutes) is a film directed by the most famous filmmaker in China, Zhang Yimou. Zhang is a unique figure straddling the international art film market and the popular film market in China. In 2004 his epic 'martial chivalry' film *Hero*, with Hong Kong action star Jet Li in the lead, topped the North American box-office charts. *Not One Less* is the direct opposite – a low budget film about a young girl in rural China.

Plot outline

The schoolteacher in a small village has to leave for several weeks to visit his dying mother. The village chief appoints Wei Minzhi, a 13-year-old village girl, to act as a stand-in teacher. He promises that she will be paid if, when the teacher returns, all the children – 'not one less' – are still attending the school. When a boy runs away to the local city, the girl determines to go to the city herself to find him and bring him back.

Not One Less is filmed in the style known as 'neo-realist' and traceable back to attempts to make films about ordinary lives first seen in France in the 1930s and Italy in the 1940s. Since then, the idea of filming on location with non-actors from the local community has been adopted by filmmakers around the world, often because they don't have budgets for studios, stars and special effects. Zhang Yimou would know this film history, although similar films made in Iran during the 1990s possibly inspired him. This is a global style of filmmaking, but it depends on literally finding its story in the everyday lives of local people. The stories often hinge on universally understood incidents in people's lives, even if the cultural context may be unfamiliar – a good example of the 'universal' depending on the 'specific'.

The film offers several illustrations/explorations of global issues:

• it deals with a universal story of a 'country' person going to the city and encountering 'urbanisation'.

Whether UK students are in an urban or rural school, they may be unaware of the major shift in the UK population from the country to the town in the early nineteenth century. Here is a chance to link to economic history or economic geography to other texts such as nineteenth-century novels that students may be studying in English (especially the novels of Elizabeth Gaskell or Thomas Hardy).

In much of Asia and Africa, the population shift is very much a contemporary social issue (e.g. the Mumbai slums of *Slumdog Millionaire*) and the film explores some of the challenges that the move creates for Minzhi. *Not One Less* also:

• highlights the lack of resources for rural education;
• emphasises both income difference and access to 'modernity' issues for rural and urban populations.

One of the issues about representations of rural communities around the world, especially in Asia and Africa, is that they appear on television screens in the UK only when the villagers are victims of famine, flood or man-made disasters (what might be described as 'victim reporting'). The representations in *Not One Less* are of an ordered society (although see the arguments about propaganda below) in which people are poor, but not starving. They have a clear idea about the value of the little they have, but they are also conscious of what a consumer society might bring and how systems of privilege work (one student is removed from the school to receive special training as an athlete).

Additionally, the film:

*   shows the power of global brands, even in rural China.

In one scene, the children who have all worked hard to earn a little money are tempted to spend it on a single can of Coke. Coca-Cola is one of the most well-known logos in the world. How is it used here? Is it an example of Hollywood-style 'product placement' or a subtle critique of globalisation? There are several TV sets in the film – all Sony models. The film was co-produced by Sony.

Finally, *Not One Less*:

*   highlights the role of television in societal change.

In the final part of the narrative Minzhi goes onto the local TV News in order to make a tearful plea for the boy to return and as the film ends a TV crew descend on the village. The film was popular in China and Wei Minzhi became something of a celebrity. An article on an English-language Chinese website (www.china.org.cn/english/features/cw/ 214270.htm) outlines how appearing in the film inspired the village girl to determine to become a filmmaker herself.

Classroom work

Not One Less is an accessible film that should generate discussion on the points above and provide a stimulus for further work. One possibility is to consider the character function of Minzhi in the story (and her subsequent 'real life' career). On this occasion it would be useful to compare Minzhi as the 'hero' of the narrative with the familiar heroes of Hollywood narratives. The answers to the following questions should give us insights into the fictional world that she inhabits and how it is different from that of a Hollywood film.

*   What kind of quest does Minzhi undertake?
*   What is her goal?
*   What does she 'win' at the end of the film?

On a more practical basis, students could try to write an outline for a UK film in which a school student faced a task comparable to Minzhi's.

*   What would be the equivalent story?
*   How and why would a UK story turn out differently?

One of the differences might arise from the 'institutional context' of a UK production. *Not One Less* was a co-production between private film companies and the Beijing Studio, which is controlled by the Chinese state. The film was heavily criticised by some in the West as being too supportive of the Chinese Communist Party and the various state agencies: for example, in the 'happy ending' to the film and because the real horrors facing a young person alone in a strange city are not shown. Director Zhang has experienced both sides of this reaction in his long career. Some of his films have been banned in China for being too critical and others, besides *Not One Less*, have been seen as apologias for the Chinese leadership and the communist system. China is a difficult place to make films in terms of censorship, but is everything plain sailing in the UK? Students can consider:

- What kinds of constraints filmmakers face here?
- Is their story likely to be filmed?
- Is their type of film ever likely to get shown to a wider audience?

The style of the film

Media education asks students to consider 'films as films' – to approach the film as a careful construction of viewpoints rather than simply as a 'window on the (real) world'. It is useful, therefore, to look closely at a particular scene and note how skilfully the director and his crew create the appearance of reality through use of camerawork, sound and editing. *Not One Less* is just as 'constructed' as any Hollywood or Bollywood film. The difference lies in the nature of the story. Again, students will probably not appreciate this until they have actually tried to create a narrative sequence themselves. Since *Not One Less* includes several classroom scenes students could shoot a few minutes of footage in their own classroom and compare the differences made by:

- the camera (where it is placed, choice of shot, angle, movement);
- how the images are composed and framed.

Other suitable films dealing with global/local issues

An interesting contrast to *Not One Less* is a Chinese film made a couple of years later. *Beijing Bicycle* (France/Taiwan/China 2001) borrows its title from a famous Italian neo-realist film, *Bicycle Thieves* (Italy 1948). Its story covers the attempt by a young man from the countryside to earn money in Beijing as a bicycle courier. He aims to eventually own the relatively expensive bicycle supplied by the courier company through payment on an instalment basis and is devastated when the bicycle is stolen. The narrative then shifts to the thief, a boy from a lower middle-class family who has little money and needs to impress his girlfriend at a quite prestigious city school. In this sense the film draws on the universal 'youth picture' genre and could also be used in conjunction with the 'identity' dimension covered below. *Beijing Bicycle* is a certificate 15 film, but could be used with care at KS3.

If there is not time to use a full-length feature film in class, the Iranian feature *The Day I Became a Woman* (Iran/France 2000) offers the possibility of using a three-part film with each of the three stories running about 20–25 minutes. Although there are some links between the stories they also stand alone. The three stories deal with three stages in the lives of women on the island of Kish, off the Iranian coast. The stories have elements of surrealism and 'magic realism' and offer images of a distinctive Muslim community. The context of production is also interesting. The director Marziyeh Meshkini is the second wife of Mohsen Makhmalbaf. The Makhmalbafs are a radical family of Iranian filmmakers that includes Mohsen's daughters Samira and Hannah who are also directors (see www.makhmalbaf.com). The film is a U certificate.

Identity and diversity

The identity and cultural diversity curriculum dimension helps learners to gain a broad understanding of the country they are growing up in: its past, its present and its future. They learn about its range of cultures and traditions, its political system, values and human rights, how it has evolved to be as it is, and in particular, how they are able to contribute through democratic participation to its future development.

Pupils will engage critically with the following questions:

- Who do we think we are?
- What connects us with and distinguishes us from others in the UK and the rest of the world?
- What are our roles in shaping a cohesive society?

(QCA 2007c)

This curricular dimension requires a focus on the media studies key concept of representation. Discussion of representations and particularly issues concerned with what might be termed 'identity politics' has been key to the development of media education. Indeed, many teachers have been attracted into media education because of a desire to teach about identity issues. In the 1970s and 1980s much media work was concerned with anti-sexist and anti-racist education. Such work has never been straightforward and what has distinguished the media education approach has been awareness of the complexity of representation issues (see Chapter 2).

Media texts are careful constructions, 're-presentations' of aspects of reality that are consciously or unconsciously selected by producers. The meanings of these texts are not fixed and depend on who is reading them and in what context. 'Identity' is both derived from and asserted through an engagement with both 'lived reality' and a wide range of media texts. We are not 'free' to read texts in any way we please. Some texts are prescribed, some are proscribed and we need to be assertive in selecting and circulating texts that somehow speak to us or for us. In this sense, 'identification' with certain kinds of media texts becomes a political act.

In order to communicate effectively and economically, media producers and audiences rely upon the conventions of media language and in particular the process of 'typing' – creating shorthand character types that are easily recognisable. In any society where power is not shared equally (that is, in every form of human organisation) it is probable that typing will become part of a process of circulating images, which reinforces that inequality of power.

One recent example of this has been the demonising of large numbers of young people in the UK as 'hoodies'. Through reference to a popular form of clothing that makes it more difficult to see the wearer's face, a potent visual symbol of aggressive and 'feral' youth has been created. This negative typing has had several 'real' social effects, not least increasing distrust of young people by older groups in the population.

However, the recognition that many forms of *typing* can have negative effects, does not mean that the primary work of media education should necessarily be to identify 'bad' representations and to promote 'positive' ones. But this is what tended to happen for many years – as part of both anti-racist and anti-sexist education. It is worth recognising that typing is most effective when it is based on some form of 'lived experience'. Hoodies became a powerful symbol because many young people wore them – the 'negative effect' came from the way the symbol was used by producers and read and circulated by audiences.

Failure to recognise this leads to what has been described as the 'burden of representation'. This has been particularly a problem for Black and Asian media authors in the UK. Faced with uniformly negative images of black youth in the UK during the 1970s and 1980s, writers and directors felt constrained by pressure to create positive images. When Hanif Kureishi broke out of the conventional typing of British Asians to create Omar, the hero of *My Beautiful Laundrette* (UK 1985), he created a complex and controversial character who both confirmed and transcended the *type* within an overall text that included more familiar types. The success of the film not only introduced an international audience to interesting British Asian characters, but also it also helped to liberate Black and Asian authors in the UK.

More important than creating positive images, is to create a diversity of texts and images coming from a more diverse group of producers. Media education in the classroom is about access to that diversity and through it exposure to the ways in which identities can be represented. The case study below explores one of the key ways in which identity issues are represented in the category of films that might be described as 'youth pictures' (i.e. films whose primary audience lies somewhere between 13 and 23 years-old – but rarely the whole age group).

Case Study 2: *Pressure* (UK 1975)

Horace Ové's feature was the first African-Caribbean British film, made on a low budget and with considerable ingenuity. The opening sequence offers a perfect example of how identity issues can be represented in film. After some evocative sounds of birdsong and waves on a Caribbean beach, the song *Pressure*, a 'story-song' in the style of a soft reggae/soca hybrid plays over drawn title cards that depict scenes from the early years of a Trinidadian family making the move to Britain. The first photographic sequence begins with a close-up of egg and bacon frying in a well-used pan and the sounds of Capital Radio discernible through the spitting of fat. Next to the stove is a dish of salad. The egg and bacon is the breakfast of the younger of two sons, 'Anthony', who emerges dressed in what appears to be school uniform. Mother is humming along to a gentle reggae tune on the radio and Tony turns down the volume. As his mother serves breakfast, his older brother (who appears not to live in the flat over a grocer's shop) comes up the stairs after picking up a ripe avocado from the shop below and sits down at the table. Unlike Tony who was born in Britain, Colin was born in Trinidad. He's wearing a long parka jacket and a woollen hat as he peels the avocado and adds hot pepper sauce. Colin speaks in a mixture of Trinidadian patois and Black American slang, whereas Tony speaks with a London accent. They squabble about eating habits and what to call the fruit (which is 'zabuca' in Trinidad). The two are seated opposite each other and as the camera cuts between them we see Tony in a head-on MCU (medium close-up shot) as in response to Colin's taunt about his tastes, he utters the immortal line: 'So what's wrong with fish and chips, bacon and eggs and Gary Glitter.' The framing allows us to see a tea cosy and an open packet of *Mother's Pride* sliced bread in the foreground, Tony in his school shirt and jumper with tie in the middle-ground and behind him a Gary Glitter poster. Colin calls him 'English boy' and refers to the 'Black food' that their mother used to make.

This lengthy description is justified in order to demonstrate how Ové introduces the issue of growing up in the then racist society of West London in 1975. The older brother has been politicised by his experience and is consciously asserting his Caribbean identity. The younger brother has grown up believing himself to be identified with the culture he has been born into. What a close reading of the 'signifying systems' of the film (the music, camerawork, sound, dialogue, decor etc.) shows us is that identity in film, especially in films dealing with struggles over identity in adolescence, is often signified by:

- use of language;
- choice of food and drink;
- clothing and hairstyles;
- popular cultural referents such as music, football teams, pin-ups, etc.

Similar scenes exist in a whole range of films. Here are just a few examples:

Save the Last Dance (US 2001): A white girl from a small town in the north-east US finds herself moving to Chicago to an inner-city and mostly African-American school. A would-be ballet student, she accepts an invitation from a black girl at the school to visit a club. In the next scene she learns something about life in the inner city and is quickly 'transformed' into someone not totally out of place. Her hair and clothes are altered and she is taught some of the slang terms to use – and not to use.

Anita and Me (UK 2002): This adaptation of Meera Syal's autobiographical novel is an excellent resource for exploring identity issues. The central character of the film, Meena, is the child of an Asian couple in a small mining village in the area of the midlands known as the Black Country in the 1970s (again, music plays an important part in evoking time and place). She has a vivid imagination and the film details the summer when the 12-year-old Meena 'grows up' as a result of her meeting with Anita, an older white girl. It is important that all the events in the film are seen from Meena's perspective. Meena wants to eat fish fingers instead of her mother's home cooking and this is taken up later in the film when Anita is invited to tea and is bewildered by what she is offered to eat.

A useful contrast to any of the preceding three films – all created by filmmakers from outside the dominant community – is to look at some of the films of director Shane Meadows. Meadows is another filmmaker using his own biography as a source of ideas and characters in films such as *A Room for Romeo Brass* (UK 1999), *This Is England* (UK 2006) and *Somers Town* (UK 2008). *This Is England* is an 18-certificate film, but this should not prevent judicious use of clips from a film that offers plenty of examples about how a sense of self-identity is formed. The little seen but recommended *Love + Hate* (UK 2005) tells a simple 'Romeo and Juliet' story about a relationship between a white boy and Asian girl in Blackburn.

Further examples of British films that explore social class as well as gay and lesbian issues in adolescent relationships include *Get Real* (UK 1998), *Beautiful Thing* (UK 1996) and *My Summer of Love* (2004). Outside the UK, one of the most successful films to use with school groups is *La haine* (France 1995), featuring a trio of friends, Jewish, North African and West African, resisting what they see as an oppressive French state. A much gentler film, but highly recommended, is *Le Grand Voyage* (France/Morocco 2004) in which a young French Moroccan man is required to drive his father to Mecca. On the way, the son learns about his father and about himself and what it means to be a second-generation migrant. (See Note at the end of this chapter.)

A practical exercise

Finally, one way of following up analysis of scenes such as those outlined above – or in preparing for an analysis – is to ask students to script and storyboard and then, depending on time and resources, shoot a short video sequence based on the following scenario:

When two cultures clash

Two characters with different cultural backgrounds meet for a meal.

One is 'host' and therefore responsible for the food and drink and the 'ambience' of the meal. Students should decide:

Who are the two characters? What is their sense of 'self-identity'? How are they dressed?

Where do they meet? How is the set 'dressed'?

What food and drink is served?

What music is playing?

How does the host try to make the guest welcome?

How does the guest display evidence that s/he is experiencing a different culture?

The scene will need a few lines of dialogue, but the whole scene should not exceed five minutes if it is filmed. The aim of the exercise is to encourage the students to explore what 'cultural difference' feels like for the participant, but also to focus on the way in which the experience is represented to audiences.

Summary

The first part of this chapter addresses the cross-curricular dimensions of 'global dimension and sustainable development' with a focus on the global, and 'identity and cultural diversity' in the second part. It shows how media texts, concepts and active pedagogy can shape and enhance cross-curricular enquiry into the dimensions' themes.

Students are guided beyond well-intentioned acquaintance with a 'range of [global] cultures and traditions' (QCA 2007c), diverse identities in the UK, and issues that are of interest to them. Political implications and contentious issues are tackled through questioning media discourse, representations and industrial practices. Identity politics operates in the dominant social representations circulated by mass media, which often prefer selectively constructed types to reflections of cultural diversity. The global distribution of American TV series illustrates how economic power fosters cultural hegemony.

Several media with perspectives, issues and cultures from different parts of the world are accessible in the UK through English language media such as newspapers, radio via the internet and television stations such as Al Jazeera via satellite connections. However, film provides the main case studies and illustrates how to avoid simplistic analysis, even at a cultural theory level. The cultural imperialism thesis is challenged by active audience theory and the 'contra-flow' of films in response to Indian and Nigerian diaspora demands in the 'West'. Engagement with diverse texts from less familiar producers is a fruitful means to critique dominant corporate stereotypes.

Films, even non-mainstream products with subtitles, are the most inviting media for students to engage with different cultures. Personal stories about everyday lives, such as the Chinese film *Not One Less*, enable them to explore the 'universal' from the 'specific'.

Familiar issues such as the power of global brands and the role of the Media in social change stimulate broader awareness, such as population shifts from rural to urban life. Social class, sexuality, generational relationships in American, French, Moroccan and British films offer further ways to consider what 'connects us with and distinguishes us from others' (QCA 2007c).

The overall genre of youth films invites discussion of diversity and social cohesion through global and UK comparisons. Personal biographical films such as Syall's and Meadow's root particular British cultures in the Midlands and recent history, and the second-generation immigrant themed films provide a common issue in global and British identities.

Further reading

Branston, G. and Stafford, R. (2010) *The Media Student's Book* (5th edition), London: Routledge.
  Please refer to the 'Further reading' recommendation at the end of Chapter 2.

Recommended resources

Films

All the films in this chapter have been released on DVD in the UK. Some may have gone out of print, but are likely to be available via Amazon, Amazon Marketplace, Play.com, e-Bay and other DVD retail websites.

Supporting background material

Supporting background material for all the films in this chapter may be found at http://itpworld.wordpress.com.

Section Two

Curriculum

Chapter 5

Media education and English in Key Stage 3 and Key Stage 4

Jenny Grahame

Introduction

Since its inception in the late 1980s, few aspects of the National Curriculum for England and Wales have been as contentiously debated or as politically sensitive as the English curriculum for Key Stage 3 and 4 students. This strategically important transitional phase between primary education and the formalised assessment of the GCSE courses has suffered collateral damage from the consistent intervention of successive governments, from the 'Back to Basics' campaigns of the early '90s and subsequent brutal curriculum revisions, through the introduction, critiques and ultimate acceptance of SATs, the New Labour Literacy Strategy and Framework years, to the recent opening up of the Revised 'Big Picture' National Curriculum in 2007.

Throughout this same period, the media landscape has changed beyond recognition in terms of its products, the technologies and platforms through which they are accessed, and the opportunities for audiences to interact with and generate them. Equally importantly, there has been a major shift in the perceived significance of the Media and cultural industries to the British economy. How are these changes experienced by young people in schools at Key Stages 3 and 4? At the time of writing, English teaching is redefining itself with a revised curriculum and the introduction of a new and radically different suite of English GCSE specifications, which is likely to impact dramatically on classroom practice, and may transform the ways in which media is integrated into Programmes of Study (PoS). How far is an increasingly mediated English curriculum enabling them to understand and fully participate in the changing digital world of the twenty-first century?

This chapter will attempt to offer a broad overview of the state of play for media education for students aged 11–16 in the English curriculum. Its starting point is the relationship between the two subjects, the ways in which they have accommodated each other, and the compromises required in incorporating media teaching into English. It will explore the new opportunities opening up for media study, and practical strategies for exploiting them to develop media skills both within and despite the constraints of the English PoS. A selection of classroom practices will suggest a variety of approaches, consider the longer-term impact of new technologies and new forms of assessment on teaching and learning in English, and briefly explore some classroom activities that demonstrate the ways Media Studies practice might inform, inspire and re-engage students in an English curriculum for the twenty-first century.

Media Education in English – the back-story

In 1991, in the early pre-SATs years of the then 'new' National Curriculum, the English and Media Centre published a teacher's handbook (*The English Curriculum: Media Years 7–9*) on ways of integrating media education into KS3 English teaching. Revisiting the book in the course of researching this chapter, I was struck by how little the field appears to have changed. While the case no longer needs to be made for the importance of media literacy and its inclusion as part of Subject English, much of the classroom practice described in the book has developed remarkably little. It explored generous conceptual interpretations of the seemingly reluctant inclusion of media in the then Programmes of Study (PoS) for English; considered the different ways in which media texts could enhance and extend conventional approaches to literary study, generate engaged and purposeful talk, and scaffold different types of writing; attempted to map where and how differently the Media might be studied in other subject disciplines, in the primary curriculum and in specialist Media Studies; and puzzled over the problems of developing a workable framework of progression for media learning in a then largely undocumented field.

Nearly 20 years on, its examples of hands-on classroom activities, schemes of work and models of delivery are still recognisable in much current departmental practice; the obstacles to cross-curricular and whole-school approaches are still largely unbroached despite the innovative inroads of specialist schools; we still know relatively little about how children learn about the media – with the exception of the 2011 report of the ESRC project led by the Centre for the Study of Children, Youth and Media.

This stasis is perhaps unsurprising given the recent dominance of the National Literacy Strategy, which many would argue has exercised a particularly instrumental and deadening influence over much teaching and learning in English, restricting the range of permitted text types, opportunities for creativity, and dialogic debates about the purposes and philosophies of the curriculum, and imposing uncomfortable compromises for teachers committed to Media education. Similarly, the pressures of accountability exemplified by the limited repertoire assessed in KS3 SATs has, for over a decade, militated against risk-taking and curriculum innovation in all but the most visionary or well-resourced of institutions. However, this period has also seen some significant changes, both despite and in resistance to, the incursions of the Literacy Framework. Most obviously, the range of media, platforms, modalities and learning technologies with which young people now engage has grown exponentially with digitisation, both in and out of school. The digitised delivery of the curriculum in classrooms increasingly needs to be addressed and has been formally acknowledged in the re-thinking strategy that has informed the 2007 revised English curriculum.

Multimodal English – a new phase?

While previous versions of the National Curriculum for English focused on a detailed and prescriptive framework of learning experiences, increasingly circumscribed by the National Literacy Strategy, the revised 2007 curriculum has become more 'friendly' to media education in a number of ways:

- It is underpinned formally for the first time by a series of four key concepts: Competence, Creativity, Cultural Understanding and Critical Understanding. Interestingly these concepts have for some time circulated, although in a different combination, within media education; indeed, Film Education's annual conference is entitled 'CP3: Critical Practice, Creative Process, Cultural Perspectives'. While they are framed rhetorically rather than practically, there is no doubt that their openness and flexibility invite a broader definition of appropriate study texts, and a more inclusive approach to the development of literacy skills.

- There has been a loosening of the structural prescriptions and at times mechanistic micro-objectives of the Literacy Framework, which if followed to the letter exercised a disproportionate impact on teaching and learning, and were considered by many to be inimical to media education.

- This strongly skills-based curriculum has formally acknowledged the range of literacy skills required for citizens of the twenty-first century in its many references to 'multimodal' texts. A somewhat uninspiring term – why not simply 'media'? – multimodality can however become the semantic loophole through which, for example, to develop Speaking and Listening. A popular TV show can be legitimately discussed as a multi-platform vehicle, on screen, online, through press coverage, SMS and on social network sites; under the Reading strand a Shakespeare play can be analysed in a variety of formats and media, from page to stage to heritage movie to classic TV serial to graphic novel to remake to TV ad and beyond. These are not new examples, neither are they assessment-proof; inevitably multimodal study will be assessed in terms of the three conventional English strands, and the media learning will be evaluated only in terms of students' communication skills. But they are a start.

- The Revised PoS and their interpretation by the Awarding Bodies for the English GCSE 2010 specifications suggest a new commitment to offering students a wider range of creative and analytic opportunities for learning with and through media. There is active encouragement for the use of multimodal adaptations, the use of moving image media as stimulus for talk and creative writing, and for the study of spoken language. The challenge for media education is, as it always has been, to find ways of exploiting these activities so that media texts are not merely transparent vehicles for skills development, but are in themselves objects of investigation and analysis, and situated in a broader cultural context.

- The revised curriculum reinforces individual subject disciplines with a number of over-arching cross-curricular 'dimensions', of which, significantly, technology and the Media is one. The aim is to provide opportunities across the curriculum for students to 'consider media as both consumers and authors of content', to engage with critical questions about the reliability of online content, and to acquire digital communication skills. Despite a skills-based agenda more closely identified with ICT than with media education, and a focus on access and competence rather than critical and political enquiry, this dimension offers further opportunities to find ways of integrating the study of media into a wider range of subject areas, and in theory at least opens the door to new forms of inter-disciplinary collaboration.

So, with cautious optimism, the time might be right for a resurgence of interest in the study of media in English. What follows is a brief overview of the development of ideas about the Media within the curriculum, and a snapshot of the current state of play.

Media and English: a (very) short summary of a long history

The relationship of media study to the English curriculum has a long history, which has been well documented and much debated over the last 70 years. Chapter 1 outlines the rich and entertaining history to be mined from exploring differing cultural perspectives over the decades, ranging from the need to inoculate students against the moral dangers of advertising and popular cinema in the 1930s, to Cold War moral panics about the subversive influence of American horror comics and the arrival of rock and roll in the 1950s. The early 1990s Tory government exhorted teachers to reject the cultural relativism of a Chaucer and Chips/Milton and McDonald's English curriculum that might span both literary heritage and popular culture. Within ten years, however, and the dawn of the new millennium, the rhetoric had changed to accommodate the massive impact of new technologies and digitisation, and the range of different stakeholders in the school curriculum. As a result, the terms of debate have shifted to take on board not only the cultural and moral implications of the vast spectrum of multi-platform media forms and practices now on offer, but also on the increasingly complex technologies used to 'deliver' knowledge in schools.

Thus, the relationship between English and media has been shaped by a series of contradictory rationales that have underpinned subject development and that share a defensive attitude to the Media. Late twentieth-century English aimed (often reluctantly) to develop critical media reading skills as a way of protecting young learners from manipulation, bias and misinformation. It implied a range of ideas about discrimination, notions of value and quality, and a focus on media effects and influences exemplified in 'dumbing down' discourses. While early twenty-first-century English teachers would now challenge these views, they still inform some practice in English, and are perhaps residual in the unimaginative and restrictive pairing of non-fiction and media texts in GCSE examinations.

Aligning the concepts

Much thought has been given to finding ways of refining and simplifying media concepts to sit more comfortably alongside those of other 'host' subject sites, in particular the English curriculum. In the early 1990s, the British Film Institute (BFI) Education Department, at that time a strongly influential voice and lobbyist in curriculum development nationally, published two innovative Secondary Curriculum statements identifying six core 'aspects' of the Media that could both provide a framework for specialist Media Studies teaching at a variety of levels, and be inflected across a range of other subject curricula. Over the next ten years, in the light of increasing government intervention militating against cross-curricular innovation, the BFI refocused its training and lobbying attentions on a contro-versial strategy to integrate formal media education into the English Curriculum as an entitlement for all students. Strategically, it made sense to anchor teaching around concepts and approaches in English that most overlapped with Media Studies rather than previous frameworks, including the BFI's six 'aspects'. A simpler formulation of language, audience, institutions and representation, the four key concepts adopted by Media Studies examination specifications, might fit more effectively within the highly politicised arena of English, and might be easier for hard-pressed teachers in the frontline of endless curriculum intervention and governmental opprobrium to tackle. The result was an investigative model of three over-arching concepts, which underpin all forms of textual study, whether those texts are individually authored poems, plays, novels or industrial collaborative products such as news media, ads, film or TV, on and offline:

- *Language*: How does the text/s make meaning through camera, sound, editing, design, performance, mise-en-scène? What is the role of narrative, and how is it structured – and how does it relate to other examples from the same and other genres?
- *Producers and audiences*: Who made the text/s, how and why – and how might this affect their meaning? Who is the text for, how will they access it and make sense of it?
- *Messages and values*: How does the text represent individuals, groups, events, places, ideas? From which viewpoint/s do we see them?

These key questions have informed and extended the work of many English departments, however, their relatively successful incorporation into English has not been universally welcomed by the Media Studies community. In some schools there is a culture of distrust and rivalry between English and media departments, and a sense that, having fought fiercely for recognition, resources and status, hard-earned specialist media expertise risks dilution and institutionalisation. Indeed, despite the fact that a large majority of media teachers come from an English background and may even teach in both areas, in many schools the two subjects areas are quite separate and, on occasions, hostile to each other – perhaps a consequence of long-term inequalities in support, budget and training opportunities.

This is short sighted; at the root of best English practice lies a set of textual assumptions shared with, and arguably strongly influenced by, Media Studies. For both subjects:

- Texts are polysemic: they can be read in a variety of different ways according to what readers/audiences bring to them. There is no one fixed 'right answer'.
- All texts, in whatever form, are constructs that represent particular points of view; there is no such thing as a value-free or 'transparent' text.
- To be literate in a range of modes and text types, students need to become both readers and writers; the production of texts is as important, and as essential to understanding, as analysis.

Teaching media in English: where?

English departments incorporate aspects of media study, with varying acknowledgements of key concepts and principles, into their teaching in very different ways. These variations are often closely related to local authority policy, institutional status, structural position within the school and student intake, and of course to the socio-economic and cultural context of the school. A QCDA report (*Media Matters: A Review of Media Studies in Schools and Colleges, QCA 2005*) reviewed the ways media education is organised within English departments' practice. It found a wide range of approaches, including:

- Departmentally resourced self-contained schemes of work about the Media, usually where Media Studies exists separately or is co-taught at KS4 or 5, and media expertise is available. Schemes of work frequently incorporate both analysis and low-tech production; have a strong focus on concepts of representation and audience, and some reference to industrial practices, albeit simplified.

- Occasional schemes of media work, frequently film-based, according to the expertise of individuals within the department. Students' access to media will vary depending on the enthusiasm and interests of their class teacher.
- Short media-led activities integrated across the PoS. Here media processes such as storyboarding, poster-making or adaptation from print into a visual or aural medium are used to help students 'get inside' a text, extend their reading skills, and stimulate writing and talk – strategies actively encouraged in the National Curriculum Subject Orders.
- An end-of-KS3 media project to replace the SATs-shaped hole left at the end of Year 9, offered as an enrichment activity, and occasionally undertaken in collaboration with other departments – for example, Art or ICT. In some schools this might take the form of a fully realised media production, e.g. a documentary about the school, a school-based advertising campaign, or an immersive or 'deep learning' activity such as a newspaper production simulation or a website design.
- Dedicated Media Studies lessons throughout the Key Stage. A few schools (often but not always specialist Media Arts) have demonstrated their commitment to media work with a single lesson a week for all students throughout KS3, allowing for the structured development of both analytical and practical media skills beyond the remit of the English curriculum, and preparing students for entry to GCSE Media Studies. Anecdotal evidence suggests that many departments would favour a similar model but they are unable to meet the resourcing or organisational demands of such a large-scale curriculum development.
- Starting specialised Media Studies work in Year 9. Since the demise of SATs a growing minority of schools systematically prepare KS3 students for Media Studies as an option at KS4.
- A single extended media study unit undertaken during each key stage. At KS3, these are frequently related to the study of a full-length feature film, a genre study or a structured simulation, often focusing on advertising. At assessment-dominated KS4, only the extremely popular AQA GCSE English specification has offered the opportunity for media coursework. Despite the motivation generated by the unit, it was framed instrumentally to assess writing for analysis, review and comment, and could not fully reward critical or creative engagement with the texts.
- Co-teaching GCSE English with GCSE Media Studies at KS4, as an alternative to the traditional dual certification model of English with English Literature. A range of anecdotal and statistical evidence suggests that such co-teaching can result in substantially improved achievement and results, particularly for boys, who seem to show greater motivation when studying a course that has a more even balance between fiction, non-fiction and media texts. In some cases results in both subjects have increased by up to 15 per cent.

The lack of sustained research into media teaching and learning makes these structural approaches difficult to evaluate, particularly given the huge variations between curriculum organisation, resourcing and philosophy in schools, Similarly, the lack of understanding of progression in media learning has made it difficult for English departments to plan a coherent developmental media curriculum across the two key stages. Thus, in many schools students may receive a fairly random series of media experiences that do not necessarily 'join up' as a coherent body of knowledge or understanding. English teachers and consultants frequently comment on their wish to encourage more media teaching, to access more media training and to incorporate media work more systematically into their departmental curriculum. However, current funding priorities 'rarely cover' policies, and the advent of new GCSE English specifications, which have effectively monopolised INSET opportunities for English teachers, have recently dramatically reduced such opportunities. The next section of this chapter offers an anecdotal snapshot of existing practice and potential developments at Key Stages 3 and 4.

Teaching at Key Stage 3

Media Matters confirmed the common-sense wisdom that activities based on making or analysing print media were those most commonly undertaken within English; by far the most frequent media task involved production of a leaflet, advert or poster – activities that students might experience several times a year. Sadly, despite clear enthusiasm for the requirement to study a wider range of digital media, particularly the moving image, change has been slow. The report indicated that:

> Work on newspapers, magazines, and print advertising remains at the heart of classroom practice; particularly in Year 7 and 8, with a particular focus on non-fiction and information texts, in preparation for the somewhat minimalist assessment requirements of the GCSE examinations pairing non-fiction with Media. Teaching focuses mainly on features of non-fiction writing, on differentiating 'fact and opinion', and on Audience and Purpose. While attention is paid to layout and presentation, these visual aspects of meaning are often dominated by concepts of bias, information retrieval, language and persuasion; the study of 'news', its values, ownership and production context are rarely studied in their own right.

Advertising, including charity and campaign advertising, is taught across the age range by the vast majority of English departments, often repeatedly and not surprisingly given the rich speaking and listening repertoire involved. The prevalence of advertising is possibly due, in part, to the availability of well-established teaching resources and easier access to online and broadcast material. Commercial and campaign adverts are ideal micro-texts for the close study of the moving image; they also allow for comparison with print-based advertising, internet or viral campaigns, and other forms of persuasive rhetoric. The advertising industry itself is addressed implicitly through simulation and practical work, but institutional perspectives are often seen as falling within the province of Media Studies.

Film is overwhelmingly the medium of choice, reflecting the popularity of cinema with both students and teachers of Media Studies, and its construction as an art form with a 'higher status' than TV or other moving image forms, and thus 'safer' than more populist or contentious media forms. The most popular approach by far is the literary adaptation; indeed, for many departments this remains the only sustained moving image work undertaken at KS3, generally as a support – and on occasions as a substitute – for the literary original, usually a pre-twentieth-century novel or Shakespeare play. The demands of the literary text are privileged, at the expense of the film as film. Increasingly, however, teachers appear to be recognising the limitations of this approach, and considering the adaptation process as a cultural phenomenon in its own right as a key feature of the new GCSE English specifications; we will explore this issue later in the chapter. Other film-based schemes of work in English often focus on specific genres (horror, science fiction and the US teen movie feature most prominently), with an emphasis on the affective aspects of film language, generic conventions, characterisation and narrative structure. At KS3 less attention is paid to the social and institutional context of the film, its production processes or promotional machinery. The study of short film is rapidly becoming a staple feature of many KS3 English classrooms. This area of study demands further research, particularly in view of the powerful, but as yet unsubstantiated claims made for the use of film in developing literacy skills advocated by the BFI's Reframing Literacy initiative. We will return to this later in this chapter.

Interestingly (and perhaps politically, in view of 'dumbing down' debates), work on popular television texts has been less popular with teachers at KS3, although the advent of YouTube has opened up new opportunities for focused and language-rich extracts – where the filtering systems of schools and local authorities allow them to be accessed. Narrative genres such as soap opera and sitcom are often taught with a focus on issues and themes, or to model narrative structure and characterisation. While work on these genres sometimes results in creative projects that are closer to literary study than media analysis, teachers with expertise in Media have been able to introduce concepts of institution and production, and to increase students' understanding of the industrial and editorial constraints that have characterised these texts. Other forms of TV drama such as the one-off play or drama serial are rarely taught, perhaps demonstrating English teachers' preference for the study of identifiable generic conventions, and their consonance with the 'text-types' required for English. Similarly, the study of factual TV and documentary is used as stimulus for speaking and listening assessment, group debate, or as support for argument writing, but rarely as an object of study in its own right.

The study of online media and the virtual world, an increasingly dominant feature of the specialist Media Studies specifications, remains in its infancy, in response to the moral panics about internet safety circulated in the popular press, and the consequent protectionist filtering policies of local authorities and school ICT managers. Despite the expectations that students will encounter the full range of screen-based multimodal texts, in practice at KS3 these are often restricted to printouts of web pages and analysis of the technical features of web design. Discussion of the impact of social networking, text messaging and other forms of digital communication is often conducted through print coverage rather than the technology itself. However, an increasing number of schools have been able to develop partnerships with new approaches to the analysis and marketing of computer games – and in some cases to the actual production of games.

Writing in media: ongoing problems with production

In many schools, providing opportunities for pupils to 'write' in media in KS4 English is still fraught with difficulty, despite increasing acknowledgement of the value of practical media work and its huge popularity with pupils. The logistics of organising, resourcing and undertaking this type of work are still awesome. There are huge differentials in resourcing, ranging from no facilities whatsoever to access to the full range of digital production technologies, and enormous variations in teacher expertise and confidence. Equally importantly, a perceived lack of time in an already overcrowded and assessment-led curriculum is compounded by timetabling, which militates against extended group work.

The case for kicking against these logistical obstacles is complicated by the absence of assessment requirements: media production skills are not formally situated in either the PoS, or within the GCSE specifications; there is therefore no requirement to evaluate or assess them. As a result it may be easier to simply ignore them – or to leave them to the Media Studies department, which has the kit, the technical expertise and the remit to deliver them.

Media and Key Stage 4 English: new specifications, new opportunities?

While the ideal KS4 curriculum would be a continuum developing the newly SATs-free media opportunities of KS3, the reality is that most English departments, however innovative, will be led by the longer-term requirements of the GCSE specifications. In their latest 2010 revisions, these are organised in terms of three separate but overlapping qualifications. Students are entered for one of two routes: either a single stand-alone English specification, incorporating aspects of language and literature, or for a double qualification comprising both English Language and English Literature: the expected preferred route for those considered likely to continue to A level Studies. Many schools will teach these two routes in combination, to allow maximum flexibility and delay entry decisions as late as possible: a complex scenario that will require some difficult choices of content and approaches.

Thus all students, whatever their ability, follow programmes of study requiring them to:

- Analyse and write 'non-fiction and media texts' under controlled examination conditions. In practice, this will usually mean working on print information texts – leaflets, newspaper reports or feature articles – to demonstrate their skills of information retrieval, comprehension, understanding of the features of text types, including layout and presentation, identifying points of view, and writing in appropriate forms for specific audiences.
- Read and write about texts from Shakespeare and the English Literary Heritage in lesser or greater degree depending on their chosen route. These may be assessed either in examination, or as controlled assessments, which allow teacher-set assignments within prescribed parameters and thus more personalised and innovative task setting. All specifications encourage the use of multimodal approaches and moving image media to engage and stimulate students, although they will not be assessed for media skills.
- Demonstrate speaking and listening skills of presentation, discussion and role-play; all specs recommend the use of multimodal and popular media approaches to generate informed and engaged talk.
- Write creatively, generally as controlled assessment as above. Again, the use of multimodal stimulus is encouraged; the AQA specification in particular requires that at least one task is prompted by study of the moving image.
- In addition, the study of spoken language is a feature of all the new English Language specs, and exemplified by the language of popular media.

There are notable exceptions to this broad overview. The Edexcel Awarding Body has broadened the scope of the non-fiction and media examination requirement with a pre-released compilation of themed non-fiction material that will include at least 50 per cent moving image or screen-based texts. It also offers a stand-alone spec entitled 'English Studies:

Digital Literacy', which requires students to both analyse and to produce digital texts. This has both external assessment through both unseen examples and a pre-released digital compilation; and controlled assessment through the planning, construction and post-production evaluation of a digital text in an appropriate medium. This new and innovative model is perhaps the closest so far to what might be recognised as Media Studies practice.

At the point of writing, before the specifications have been finally approved and while they are still subject to QCDA amendment, it is difficult to predict the impact of the new English GCSEs. The Awarding Bodies have explicitly invited the study of media and multimodal texts to demonstrate a commitment to a broad and inclusive set of literacies for students in the twenty-first century. From a media education perspective, these opportunities represent a major advance, and a sea change in the frequently contentious relationship between English and Media. However, the complex assessment structure of the specs may pose problems for departments committed to co-teaching media alongside English; it is also clear that these changes will have a backwash into the KS3 curriculum as teachers re-think their practice in terms of the demands of their GCSE choices.

So what actually happens in the classroom? Some examples of practice

The following brief accounts of teaching activities represent a range of tried and tested approaches that reflect the shared premises and conceptual overlaps between English and Media Studies outlined earlier in this chapter. In most cases, they could be developed, amplified or revisited at any point over the 11–16 curriculum, depending on the nature of the texts and skills around which they are anchored. However, bearing in mind the complex organisational demands of the GCSE curriculum, they are organised here in strands around the PoS that are likely to inform the ways departments will organise their schemes of work.

Media and reading: approaches to literature

I Exploring a key moment in a text: using adaptations

The use of film and TV adaptations of texts from the English Literary Heritage is probably the single most common form of media work undertaken in the English curriculum. Showing the film of the Great Big Book or a Shakespeare play makes a text accessible, engaging for students, speeds up the reading process, and is a well-earned 'carrot' at the end of a difficult reading process. But film adaptations are frequently under-used, and under-problematised, resulting in the 'Luhrmann syndrome' – as evidenced by the thousands of GCSE coursework essays claiming that *Romeo and Juliet* opens with a TV screen, urban riots and a helicopter.

In order to understand that a literary text can be interpreted in an infinite variety of ways, from different perspectives in different cultural and historical contexts, and interpreted differently by different producers and directors, students need to experience a range of adaptations from different time periods. And as with any close textual analysis, meeting the entire text head-on does not necessarily help to develop the sorts of critical and analytic observations students will be required to demonstrate in writing; short clips are frequently far more productive, in tandem with some of the following strategies:

Scheme of work

Asking for more: multimodal approaches to Dickens

Aims: to develop close reading skills around an iconic literary text and to explore the ways different eras and producers have interpreted it, the impact of moving image technologies on the original text, and the reasons for its relevance and cultural significance over time.

- In small groups, students take on the role of researchers for a new TV production company commissioning new drama adaptations from the English Literary Heritage. They conduct simple online research into recent adaptations in film and on terrestrial TV channels, and some very limited audience research into the appeals of such drama. These might be homework tasks, or resourced by a few examples of recent press coverage for class study. Groups report back on their findings in a shared written report or group presentation, and discuss as a class, in relation to the Dickens text they are studying.
- Groups are now invited to pitch for the commission to produce a new updated adaptation of *Oliver Twist*, and to produce a sample storyboard or camera script for the iconic 'Asking for More' sequence of the novel. They are directed through a close reading of the original text, with prompts for the consideration of camerawork, soundtrack, mise-en-scène, editing, appropriate casting and performance. They produce treatments for the sequence, and present them to the class, with a rationale for their choices and interpretations of theme and characterisation. They are compared and evaluated. Where students are also studying Media Studies at GCSE level, and if time and resources permit, they could go on to produce their extract digitally.
- Students now watch and critique several clips of the scene from a range of moving image adaptations covering as wide a time frame as possible. There are scores of these dating back to 1909 silent cinema; particularly useful are the 1922 version starring Jackie Coogan, David Lean's expressionist post-war classic, *Oliver* the musical, the Polanski film, and the 2008 TV serialisation. Different groups in the class can compare these with their own treatments, and evaluate them in various ways, tracking such aspects as the media language of camera, sound and lighting; variations in mise-en-scène; casting and performance and its impact on the representation of Oliver and the workhouse authorities; the differing perspectives on childhood or poverty, etc.

This sequence of work fulfils a wide range of reading objectives, and presents opportunities for group or individual Speaking and Listening assessment, and for the development of practical media skills. Media Studies teachers might also inflect it to address wider issues such as the function of the literary heritage for the film, broadcasting and other cultural industries, and the impact of developments in media technologies.

This scheme of work, with full supporting classroom resources including DVD extracts and teaching notes can be found in *Doing TV Drama* (English and Media Centre, 2009).

Figure 5.1 Asking for more: multimodal approaches to Dickens

- A chosen adaptation is integrated throughout the learning process, interspersed with reading and performance, prediction exercises and brief creative writing activities.
- Key scenes most important for close analysis are screened from two or three contrasting versions, time periods and formats, including looser contemporary retellings based on the original. Use storyboarding activities to consolidate understanding of the significance of a key moment.
- Students record a director's commentary for a key scene, to think through the filmic and editorial decisions behind the ways the text has been adapted.
- Students draft an alternative voice-over soundtrack for a key scene that reflects the characters' true feelings or thoughts.

Such activities help students to understand that all adaptations are reconstructions/ interpretations; there is no correct or completely faithful version. They also raise questions about the cultural significance of the original text, generate debate about its meanings and value over time, and speculation about its longevity. The outline scheme of work below incorporates these ideas with a range of practical approaches from Media Studies, can be taught at a variety of different levels, and adapted to a variety of heritage texts.

2 Exploring the language of a text: media transformations

While the fully fledged production of media texts may be a step too far for the majority of English departments, the literacy practice of reading/analysing through writing/production is a well-tried creative strategy that can be undertaken with minimal resources, and used to focus close study of the language of a wide range of both literary and non-fiction text-types. For example, a key Shakespeare scene can be unpicked variously as a magazine feature, news item, photographic montage or film poster, a still-image trailer of digital photographs presented in Photo Story, iPhoto or PowerPoint, the narrative of an advert, or retold in the contemporary language of a crime drama or soap opera. Here, students' own cultural expertise as consumers of media genres or form is drawn on as a framework to unpick imagery and metaphor, rhythm and structure, or theme, as required for a full understanding of the original text. Similarly a dense information text such as a factual newspaper article or feature can be made more accessible by re-versioning it as the basis for questions for a TV game or quiz show, a story strand for an existing soap opera, a treatment for a *Newsround* or *Blue Peter* item, or even the format for a new TV reality show. Such activities are both memorable and highly entertaining; they also allow students a degree of subversion and acceptable parody, which can be usefully unpicked for revision purposes.

While English teachers are often wonderfully creative in constructing appropriate textual transformation activities as ways into difficult texts, they sometimes miss the opportunity to incorporate aspects of media concepts and knowledge that might be highlighted simply by a small tweak of the task, as Figure 5.2 suggests.

3 Making media texts: Creative production activities around personal interpretation

The approaches outlined above all stop short of full production work; but the technologies now available in most schools mean that it is increasingly possible for students to construct their own interpretations of short texts using ICT software to capture, sequence and edit

---

Transforming *Romeo and Juliet*

- To support the close study of a difficult Shakespeare scene such as *Romeo and Juliet* Act I scene 5, students analyse the well-known TV advert for Levi's jeans based on the scene from *A Midsummers Night's Dream* in which Titania meets Bottom in ass-head mode; the advert opens with theatrical curtains and uses an edited version of the text transposed to an American street-gang stand-off on an urban street corner.
- Students compare the advert to the original text, and explore the way it uses the language and imagery of asses and bottoms to highlight the unique selling points of the jeans, and its impact as a marketing strategy.
- This can now be used in reverse as the model for an advertising task based on the scene students are working on, with a structured brief to promote products tied to the language and imagery specific to the scene; in the *Romeo and Juliet* example this includes hands, lips, pilgrims and other religious iconography. Students now become creative teams in an advertising agency briefed to 'sell' hand-cream, lip gloss or nail varnish, to storyboard an appropriately edited version of the text, to construct a pack-shot that exemplifies the symbolic nature of the original imagery, and to present their pitch persuasively to their account manager.

This very flexible sequence of work can be amended for a wide range of language-rich or difficult extracts including prose, poetry and non-fiction; it can be undertaken as a 'light-touch' starter-type activity, or extended across one or more lessons. The Levi's Midsummer advert is easily available at www.tellyads.co.uk, www.visit4info.co.uk or alongside 20+ other Levi's adverts in *Doing Ads* (English and Media Centre, 2008).

Figure 5.2 Transforming *Romeo and Juliet*

digital images; there is evidence that as teachers become more confident with whiteboard technology this is becoming an increasingly popular approach to support the reading of short stories and poems. Poetry in particular has always been associated with the visual image, both as a source of inspiration and an analytic tool, but the availability of applications such as Photo Story, iPhoto and PowerPoint, or software such as PicturePower3, now makes it possible to create visual readings of image-rich texts with little additional hardware, as Figure 5.3 on page 84 suggests.

Media for speaking, listening and spoken language

The most powerful site for media education in the English curriculum is without doubt the programme of study for Speaking and Listening, and it is in this area that many of the most innovative classroom approaches can be found. The following examples of typical classroom activity provide a brief snapshot of ways in which media texts and processes generate purposeful and engaged group debate (one of the GCSE assessment criteria), provide the context for 'real world' talk for specific audiences and purposes, and opportunities for creative interaction and collaboration:

Creative production activities

Creating a graphic poster-poem
In an ICT room or using a suite of laptops, students can re-present the text of a poem in Word, using their choice of size and style of font, colour, layout and use of white space to construct a visual representation of the significant elements of structure, rhythm, metre and imagery. These can then be printed out as A4 or A3 posters, and wall-mounted for comparison and as study texts for other classes.

Creating a digital poem from a sequence of found images
Provide students with a range of figurative, metaphorical and literal images – as hard copies, or in digital form, sourced through Google – which represent themes and ideas expressed in the poem. In small groups, students discuss and create their own reading of the poem, and select a sequence of images to illustrate their interpretation. They can then rehearse and record an audio reading of the text, and synchronise it with a slideshow of images (or a paper cut-and-paste storyboard if working with hard copies), to present to the class. In comparing the images selected for each group reading, students can actively engage in quite sophisticated analyses of their differing interpretations, and the relative impact of anchoring the meaning of the verbal language with different types of image.

Comparing poems digitally
The process can be extended to compare two contrasting poems on a similar theme – for example from clusters of poems in the relevant GCSE poetry anthology; here, a single bank of images might be used quite differently to illustrate two thematically linked poems from different historical periods, or from different cultures. The images provide useful visual scaffolding, which can later be used as a framework for comparative writing.

Further variations include students sourcing or capturing their own digital image-bank, or indeed, if resources are available, constructing and editing a moving image video poem from scratch – a useful exercise for students also taking Media Studies at GCSE level.

Figure 5.3 Creative production activities

Whole-class debate

Extracts from popular television genres and their cross-media platforms – particularly documentary and reality TV formats, celebrity interviews, talent shows such as *X Factor*, issue-based story lines in teen drama series or soaps and music videos – offer legitimate and pupil-friendly opportunities for the discussion of the representation of groups and individuals, the values of celebrity and consumer culture, and the 'dumbing down' discourses in the tabloid press.

A radio debate

- Students analyse clips from *Brat Camp*, a reality show in which unmanageable teens are forcibly detained in harsh conditions in the American desert to modify their behaviour.
- They read and discuss a range of perspectives from the show's production team and psychologists, blogs and chat room responses from experts, former participants and viewers of various ages.
- In role as various interested parties (participants, parents, counsellors, critics, producers), they prepare and take part in a 'live' radio phone-in debate representing a range of different points of view on the issue.
- Hosted by the teacher, to ensure full participation, the debate is recorded, allowing students then to evaluate their own and others' performance and responses. The activity can be recycled for a wide range of different popular formats.

A version of this activity, based on *Big Brother*, appears in *The Key Stage 3 Media Book* (English and Media Centre, 2002).

Figure 5.4 A radio debate

Role-play and simulation

Media production activities, real or simulated, whether in the form of a newspaper editorial meeting, development of a new TV show, or judging a short film competition, offer the ideal context for speaking and listening in unfamiliar situations, for audiences beyond the classroom and for purposeful presentations with cross-curricular links. The group development and presentation of an advertising campaign for a new product, a charity, public health issue or cause is one of the most productive and popular of classroom activities, and allows for the painless introduction of information about the organisation, market research and practices of the advertising industry.

The study of spoken language

This newest feature of the new GCSE English 2010 specifications explicitly invites the investigation of media texts as examples of spoken language in the real world. Exemplar tasks suggest comparisons between scripted and spontaneous talk on television – for example, the authenticity of soap opera dialogue as compared to the unscripted speech of a current affairs discussion, workplace-based documentary or reality show such as *The Apprentice* or *Secret Millionaire*. Further real-world examples might include the study of transcripts of talk around game playing, telephone communication or a comparison of transcriptions of social interaction and communications on social network sites.

A branding simulation

- Students study and evaluate the functions and significance of branding through the study of logos, slogans imagery and constructions of brand identity – developing useful skills of reading and image analysis.
- They analyse TV, print and online examples from a single campaign that focuses on brand identity rather than a specific product, and discuss the use of visual symbols, design, layout, colour coding, etc. in constructing a brand personality.
- Small groups then work on the development of a Fairtrade clothing brand, which draws on input from both the Citizenship and Art departments. Their brief is to develop a presentation and visual identity that emphasises the environmental and humanitarian principles of the brand rather than its individual products. Each group targets a particular audience demographic, ensuring a range of different outcomes.
- Following their presentations, which must be accompanied by visual aids, students then compare their research, planning and branding strategies with a case study from the company whose campaign they have previously analysed, thus relating their own experiences to those of the real world.

Variations of this simulation have been used with students from Year 7 up to AS level; the processes remain the same, but differentiation is provided through decreasing degrees of support and the increasing complexity of secondary texts. A fully resourced version of the simulation is provided in *Doing Ads* (English and Media Centre, 2008).

Figure 5.5 A branding simulation

How real is reality TV talk?

- Students are provided with a transcript of the introductory voice-over of a new reality show, and invited to comment on its language features, tone and register.
- They listen to the extract from which it was transcribed, and evaluate the impact of voice, register, dialect and timing. They then watch the full extract, to see how the meaning of the spoken words is affected by the inclusion of graphics, images, insert and cutaway extracts, and visual edits.
- They compare this scripted voice-over with further extracts of unscripted (but of course highly edited) talk from the participants in the show. They use their findings as the basis for a study of the ways in which spoken language varies according to the range, demographic and functions of the speakers, and how it is mediated by the format of the show and its editing processes.

Figure 5.6 How real is reality TV talk?

Media and writing

While print media examples are predominantly used to model writing and production around non-fiction forms and genres, such as editorial and argument writing, moving image media are frequently used in English as stimulus for creative writing. This is perhaps the most media-friendly aspect of English, as acknowledged in the new GCSE specs; the AQA controlled assessment Writing tasks, for example, are categorised under 're-creative' writing (taking a text and turning it into another), and 'write-ons' (taking a prompt such as a picture, and developing writing from it), as well as a compulsory creative task requiring writing stimulated by a moving image text; other Awarding Bodies adopt similar approaches. The range of opportunities here is limitless, and requires little explanation.

Stimulus for extended writing derived from popular literary and moving image genres such as crime, chick lit or romcom, science fiction and fantasy is particularly useful in engaging recalcitrant writers; there is a substantial body of research suggesting that boys in particular are strongly motivated by the use of moving image clips that provide visual prompts for detailed writing about place, character and atmosphere, and that move them beyond simple narrative retellings towards more complex and sophisticated language and viewpoints. The use of trailers, opening sequences, music video or short film can teach important lessons about pace, point of view, showing rather than telling and subtext in narrative development.

An alternative, if under-researched, approach to this conventional model of stimulus/ creative response has emerged recently with the increased availability of production technologies that enable students to create their own digital texts in still or moving images and use them as the basis for non-fiction or creative narrative writing. A single lesson constructing a short video sequence in the suspense or horror genre can provide concrete visual stimulus to support students who find it difficult to think outside a story outline.

Making a still-image documentary

- Students analyse the impact and meanings created by a range of still digital images that represent different aspects of environmental concern. They select a limited number as the basis of an argument about one specific aspect – e.g. climate change or pollution.
- Using a software program such as PicturePower3 or Photo Story, they sequence, crop and edit their images and draft a voice-over commentary that develops their argument; this is recorded and evaluated by the class.
- The still-image movies they have produced become the scaffolding for a piece of creative or argument writing,
- Using different banks of images, the same process can be used as the stimulus for poetry writing, or for narrative.

An account of a similar activity successfully developed with underachieving boy writers is available from www.englishandmedia.co.uk.

Figure 5.7 Making a still-image documentary

The example in Figure 5.7 uses simple editing software incorporating still images and sound-recording facilities to engage and structure student argument writing by supporting reluctant writers.

Studying short film

While most of the examples of practice described here situate media work pragmatically in the context of the English PoS, it is important to remember the huge pleasures generated for both students and teachers by schemes of work that are led by media study, rather than simply served by it. One notable example – the only one there is space for in this chapter – is the recent emergence of short film as an increasingly valued media form that brings together the textual practices and skills of both English and Media Studies, and that lends itself particularly well to cross-curricular study.

Short film has always been studied in English as a particularly rich source of work on narrative, language and representation. The British Film Institute has been highly proactive in highlighting its value in developing literacy from Key Stage 1 onwards, through publication of a series of influential and inspirational compilations, from *Story Shorts* in the primary curriculum to *Real Shorts* and *Moving Shorts* at Key Stages 3 and 4. It has used these rich resource collections as the basis for national training and research in its Reframing Literacy initiative. The English and Media Centre included four shorts in its best-selling *Key Stage 3 Media Book*, and published its own compilation, *DoubleTake*, which also includes short films produced by Film and Media A level students; there are a vast number of other resources available, both from Film Festivals, university film production departments and the major broadcasters.

Short films are ideal media texts for the English classroom. They can be viewed repeatedly over a single lesson, and lend themselves to very close textual analysis; they are complete texts in themselves, with clearly defined narrative structures, and often high production values; they are often interestingly quirky and generically hard to classify, so they offer students unfamiliar perspectives, styles and voices. Their stories are often based around a moment in time, a crisis or a turning point, rather than extended plot development, requiring ellipses of time, and unconventional characterisation. And if well researched, they can provide a mine of illuminating information about their production processes, and the aesthetic and editorial decisions made by the director. They thus offer multiple opportunities both for self-contained 'film study', but also for highlighting transferable concepts, approaches and skills that can be linked to other types of texts.

The ubiquitous review-writing task – traditionally one of the most overused and poorly accomplished in the curriculum – need not be the only outcome; the activities in Figure 5.8 require a close textual analysis of the film but also yield a variety of writing outcomes appropriate for English.

Conclusion

At the point of writing the conclusion to this chapter, the relationship between media education and English is teetering on the brink of the unknown. The draft English GCSE specifications are moving towards approval, and first glimpses of final controlled assessment tasks suggest that the interpretations of 'multimodal' approaches, and the moving image

---

Writing from a short film

Students watch and deconstruct a short film narrative with an unexpected twist (for example from *Double Take*, described above), told visually with no dialogue. Using the visual images, themes and structure of the film as a starting point, they can:

- create and refine their own narrative re-telling, told from the viewpoint of the protagonist, developing their own take on atmosphere, mood, tension and sense of place;
- script an alternative soundtrack for the film that amplifies or changes its meanings;
- construct a director's commentary;
- recreate the narrative in a contrasting format – e.g. as a factual news report, a poem, another media genre;
- move on to create their own narrative with a twist, either in prose, as a treatment or in script format;
- compare the film with another short on a similar theme, focusing on the film techniques of camera language, sound and editing, and on their different representations of character and voice;
- with access to editing software, re-edit the film to create an alternative narrative, and produce an evaluative commentary explaining their rationale and the impact of their decisions.

Figure 5.8 Writing from a short film

prompts and stimuli proposed for creative writing and for the study of spoken language are rather less generous and open than the specification guidelines have suggested. In addition, the sheer volume of content to be covered, and the narrowness of the assessment focuses of the set tasks will undoubtedly challenge the opportunities for genuinely speculative and creative media study, if only because of the time and resource constraints in which teachers and students will be operating. And on a bigger-picture level, the recent acquisition of a coalition government, and the inevitable reductionism of a Tory-run education department is likely to impact unfavourably on the development of media literacy within the English curriculum – as ever, the first target for policy intervention.

However, here too we have been before – and survived. The new generation of teachers who have grown up with a more inclusive and multimodal experience and understanding of literacy, and for whom communication and creativity through social media is as natural as for their students will not be willing to reject this newer heritage to prioritise print, chalk 'n talk and canonical study. Conservative rhetoric and a protectionist discourse may superficially dominate in the short term; but the pedagogic demands and long-term impact of the digital wired-up world on the ways in which meanings are made are not going anywhere. Media and English will remain entwined for the foreseeable future.

Further reading

Barratt, A.J.B. (1998) *Audit of Media in English: A BFI Education Research Report*, London: BFI Publishing. This research report shows how schools were interpreting the National Curriculum requirements for teaching about media as part of the English curriculum. It provides media teachers with a very clear account of the possibilities and problems (still) likely to be encountered in schools: from teachers' positive attitudes towards, and desire to be involved in, teaching the media to a lack of confidence and a need for further training in the area.

Buckingham, D. (2003) *Media Education: Literacy, Learning and Contemporary Culture*, Cambridge: Polity. David Buckingham's book provides beginning and experienced media teachers with a comprehensive overview of the debates, theories and principles underpinning the teaching of media. He also provides a detailed and compelling rationale for a form of media education that is theoretically rigorous and manageable in practice. It includes a section on 'Media Education in Language and Literature Teaching'.

Hart, A. and Hicks, A. (2002) *Teaching Media in the English Curriculum*, London: Trentham Books. Based upon thorough school-based research, the book illustrates how teachers of English and Media have developed curricula that draw on the fact that students watch, hear, understand and avidly discuss television, radio and film. The book offers strategies for teaching and evaluating the results of their work on the Media in the classroom.

Hobbs, R. (2003) 'Approaches to instruction and teacher education in media literacy', in *Higher Education Research & Evaluation*, 1, January 2003, 58–64 http://academic.mediachina.net/article.php?id=5530. The concept of literacy has expanded to include digital, visual and electronic media and popular culture. The paper identifies three rationales that are emerging from various stakeholders in education and government in both developed and developing nations that support media literacy. The paper considers the educational and social implications of expanding the concept of literacy to include critical analysis of media texts and media practices.

Quy, S. (2007) *Teaching Short Films*, London: BFI/Palgrave Macmillan. This book is a comprehensive and insightful theoretical examination of the forms and functions of short films from a variety of production contexts. It develops a conceptual approach to the analysis of short films and builds on this foundation to provide helpful advice for teachers and students who are producing their own short films by including a framework for the production process and demonstrating how practical work can be used to engage with key aspects of the Media Film Studies curriculum.

Recommended resources

Teaching materials

British Film Institute educational resources at Palgrave Macmillan www.palgrave.com/bfieducation: *Moving Shorts* and *Real Shorts*.

English and Media Centre publications – www.englishandmedia.co.uk/publications/index.php: *Doing Ads* (2008), *Doing Reality TV* (2010), *Doing TV Drama* (2009), *DoubleTake* (2007), *English Allsorts* (2008), *The Key Stage 3 Media Book* (2002), *Movie Power: Scripting* (2007), *Picture Power 3* (2006).

Chapter 6

Media Studies GCSE (1)

Possibilities and practice

Elaine Homer and Elaine Scarratt

Introduction

The challenges for the teacher new to GCSE Media Studies – finding the means and time to acquire subject knowledge, theory, skills, managing practical activity – can seem overwhelming. Enabling students to engage with contemporary issues and the role of the Media in society additionally requires teachers to keep up to date with changes in media ownership, regulation, technologies, audience consumption and innovations in media forms. Documentation can be demanding – the 2009 specifications, partly due to regulation impositions, are more prescribed and detailed than their legacy counterparts. All these elements require a disproportionate amount of preparation time for a few periods a week on a busy timetable. To ease the new media teachers' GCSE workload the main aims of this chapter are to provide:

- the Awarding Bodies' key specification requirements;
- issues to consider for planning schemes of work;
- an exemplar course plan;
- advice on managing practical work;
- technical resources;
- advice on preparing students for external assessment.

The specificity and detail of the 2009 specifications can mask the underlying routes through their courses, which are overall more structured than previously. The outlines here indicate how apparently multi-faceted learning and formal specification requirements can be integrated and shaped into informed choices and manageable courses. This background context informs an exemplar AQA Single Award course plan, the controlled assessment unit of which is amplified in Chapter 7 into an extensive scheme of work.

The overview here can be followed up on the Awarding Bodies' websites, which have extensive regularly updated online teacher support materials, including teacher guides to the specifications; and the Awarding Body endorsed books (some with attendant if pricey online packages), which have teaching and learning advice, and assignment and assessment criteria tailored activities with classroom friendly high production values.

The Awarding Bodies

The three main GCSE Media Studies Awarding Bodies are AQA (Assessment and Qualifications Alliance), OCR (Oxford and Cambridge and RSA Examinations) and WJEC

(Welsh Joint Education Committee). They share similar broad structures and ethos but are highly distinctive and offer genuine choice of well-crafted courses – also designed for continuity onto their respective Media Studies A levels. The 2009 specifications maintain their predecessor's breadth of learning, but the reduced outcome load means that course durations can be imaginatively exploited for other activities – extended introductory units, extra assignments from which final submissions can be selected, cross-curricular projects, community and local media industry partnerships.

However, time can be very relative depending on student intake. It can take much longer than expected for students to complete work, especially practical productions – and the control restrictions mean that less learning can be undertaken for homework. Whole school events also need to be factored into planning such as time out for work experience, modular exams in other subjects, mock exams (although as Chapter 7 shows these can be integrated into a scheme of work), sports days, festivals and so on. Similarly adequate time has to be given for thorough exam topic and exam technique preparation, especially for OCR and WJEC note-making on 'unseen' texts.

Only AQA offers a Double Award course leading to two GCSEs; it may seem unrealistically demanding on the school timetable, but there are increasingly flexible modes of delivery for GCSE Media Studies. Each Awarding Body has online course plan variations, which may be delivered in different timeframes such as a one-year course, starting in Year 9, in conjunction with GCSE English, and so on. OCR has the most flexible course as it is unitised and, like WJEC, offers additional exam entry in January. OCR's Individual Portfolio (Unit B321) is separate from the Production Portfolio (Unit B324), its other controlled assessment assignment, thus creating the opportunity for a modular course. Controlled assessment units can be submitted when appropriate for students and OCR examiners visit centres to moderate the marking, though it is a regulatory requirement that at least 40 per cent of the assessment for all specifications must be at the end of the course. OCR has also incorporated the Disability Discrimination Act (2005) into the external assessment by offering a choice of audio or audio-visual texts for the compulsory Section B topic in the external assessment.

Commonalities and differences

This section considers the specification's rubric and key informing principles. Page references are from the latest online editions of the specifications at the time of writing (AQA 1.4 2010; OCR July 2009; WJEC 12 April 2010), and are referred to by their Awarding Body initials.

Levels of control: this regulatory element emanated from political impetus to ensure consistency and parity for candidates, to promote independent learning, and curtail plagiarism. How each specification has innovatively interpreted and applied these constraints provides instructive comparisons of their teaching and learning strategies. Levels of control focus on task setting (high), task taking (medium) and student supervision (medium–low), so task setting is a prime consideration. Past concerns about appropriateness and quality of production work have led to highly directed (and supportive) task setting in all specifications – AQA's are prescribed. It is also the most directed overall, which may be helpful to less experienced teachers; those with more experience will find room for interpretation as Chapter 7 demonstrates. OCR and WJEC have more freedom within broad frameworks for 'written' tasks. All offer stimulating assignment choices, which have been developed from successful legacy work.

Assessment weightings: 60 per cent controlled, 40 per cent external. The initial classification of Media Studies as an academic subject, prior to final 2009 specification approval, allocated 25 per cent controlled assessment. Challenged by media education stakeholders it was changed to the 'applied' weighting of 60 per cent to acknowledge characteristic media education pedagogy of developing students' critical faculties through both analysis and production. However, the key consideration is the amount of content and nature of the external assessments. OCR and WJEC require significantly more topic knowledge and analysis than AQA.

Assessment Objectives (AOs): see specifications AQA p. 24, OCR p. 25, WJEC p. 11 for full versions. The four AOs distil the expected breadth and rigour of learning: knowledge and understanding (AO1); analysis and response (AO2); research, planning and presentational skills (AO3); product construction and evaluation (AO4). They are given similar assessment weightings, however classroom planning will need to note how they are applied to each assignment. Additionally WJEC and OCR reduce AO3 to allocate 10 per cent and 9 per cent respectively more to analysis and response (AO2); a balance that is reversed for AQA and indicative of their more demanding external assessments noted above.

Aims and learning outcomes: see AQA p. 7 repeated p. 24, OCR p. 5, WJEC p. 3 for full versions.

These are four generic statements that flesh out the AOs and promote multi-faceted learning. OCR, however, has a modification in the first one. 'Develop enquiry, critical thinking and decision-making skills through . . .' is continued by AQA and WJEC as '. . . issues that are important, real and relevant to them [learners] and to the world in which they live', whereas OCR continues '. . . the study of media texts, audiences and institutions.' OCR appears more traditionally academic than the student centred discourse of AQA and WJEC, but all Awarding Bodies aim to stretch and challenge candidates through subject accessibility.

Engagement with digital technology: the specifications accommodate less technologically confident teachers but firmly embed digital media with varying degrees of compulsion and the option to use and study digital media and related issues, and centres are expected to have adequate hardware and software. AQA and WJEC include digital media texts in their external assessment papers and strongly promote study of convergence throughout. OCR and WJEC welcome digital evaluations for the main production assignment.

Presentation: responses may be submitted in a wide variety of ways (WJEC), possible formats include 'annotations, charts, bullet points, continuous prose or a combination of any of these' (AQA p. 10). As well as engagement with decisions about conveying content in effective formats, the aim is also to avoid reliance on essays and so clearly differentiate Media Studies from English. Choices of format should reflect the subject's full range of visual, audio and written potential as appropriate to the task whether it is creative or critical, and for controlled or external assessment. The permitted lengths of assignments are quantified in 'words' as an approximate collective noun for the various formats.

The four media concepts: the conceptual framework of Media Languages, Audiences, Representations and Institutions is integral to all aspects of GCSE Media Studies teaching and learning, and generic to all specifications. However WJEC significantly varies its conceptual organisation into a three-part 'framework' of 'study areas' (WJEC pp. 7–9), but with minor variations in taxonomy. 'Media texts' (genre, narrative and representation) integrates media languages within these three areas to highlight its role as creating meanings. 'Media organisations' selects marketing and promotion, regulation and control, and personal, social and ethical dimensions to explore the implications of industry practices such as conflicts between the individual and organisations, and issues about online environments. 'Media audiences/users' is an early formal foregrounding of audiences as active participants.

Areas of study

The specifications and teacher guidelines should be referred to for detailed lists and some differing terminology and organisation, but the areas of study are broadly categorised as media forms, platforms and topics. Media forms are the 'type of communication used to create content' (AQA and WJEC), a sitcom may be in the form of a radio or TV programme. Platforms are the technology used to deliver the media forms. Terminology varies significantly across the boards but it covers three processes: print, audio-visual (or Moving image) and electronic (or Web-based technologies/New media). AQA's aim for detailed guidance (p. 6) makes rather complicated reading with selective combinations of forms/ platforms (Print and electronic publishing) and cross-forms/platforms media (Advertising and marketing, Popular music and news). The structure and terminology are also at odds with AQA's more streamlined A level version of forms and platforms (print, broadcast and e-media). WJEC and OCR prefer an uncluttered focus on media forms and topics rather than itemising platforms as well, but expect they will be studied in relation to the convergent nature of the Media. Media topics overlap the other two; topics may be based on media forms, issues, genres, technologies, etc. such as advertising, celebrity, television drama, animation. All the external assessments are based on media topics, as are AQA's Assignments and OCR's comparative analysis.

Controlled assessment

All the controlled assessments have two parts. One combines analytical and pre-production tasks as explicit requirements in AQA and OCR and implied standard practice for WJEC; the other is a major production including research, planning and evaluation. These latter three elements attract less assessment weighting than their counterparts, but have intrinsic status as skills that require teaching, affect production quality and enhance critical understanding through reflection on creative decision-making. The specifications differ numerically in their assignments, but require students to have a broad experience through a range of media that must include print and audio-visual forms. The minimal requirements are: AQA three discrete media forms/platforms in controlled assessment, OCR minimum of two media in controlled assessment and three media across the whole course; WJEC three media across the whole course including audio-visual and print in the controlled assessment.

Key learning

Introductory units can be structured in several ways. Chapter 7 gives a broad introduction to audio-visual language and is also focused on preparation for, say, Action adventure movies, the AQA (2011) and OCR (2010–2013) examination topics. WJEC recommend developing students' critical autonomy through exploring how meaning is created in a wide range of media forms before embarking on the first formal textual investigation in the second half of spring term.

AQA

Unit 2: Understanding the Media

Three assignments chosen from assignment banks of prescribed tasks.

Assignment 1: Introduction to the Media (Language and audience)

One option from a choice of eight combined analytical tasks and research and planning tasks.
500 'words'.

Assignment 2: Cross-media study

(Representation and institution)
One option from a choice of six combined analytical tasks and research and planning tasks using two media forms.
1,000 'words'.

Assignment 3: Practical Production and Evaluation

(All concepts)
One from a choice of six prescribed topics with production tasks.
Planning and research 12 pages maximum.
Evaluation 700–800 'words'.

Note: the exam topic must not be used for controlled assessment.

OCR

Unit B321: Individual Media Studies portfolio

One assignment with two parts: (Language and representation).
Comparative analysis of two texts minimum from the same or different media/contemporary or non-contemporary/from any national context.
An accompanying production exercise (planning and evaluation) 800–1,500 words, or 10–15 slides, or 3–5 mins podcast.

B324: Production portfolio in Media Studies. (All concepts)

One from a choice of 12 set briefs.
The portfolio comprises:
-The production
-Appendix with all planning materials, including discarded ideas.
-Production log: evidence of individual contribution to research and planning, with an evaluation in a choice from four formats: written commentary 500–800 words, or PowerPoint 5–10 slides, or Podcast/audio presentation 3–5 mins, or DVD with extras 3–5 mins.

Note: the three external assessment topics cannot be used for controlled assessment.

WJEC

Unit 2: Creating for the Media: investigating and producing

Two textual investigations; at least two media, one must be print.

Textual Investigation 1

(Genre)

One option from a choice of three prescribed titles to investigate one main text with references to several others.
400–850 'words'.

Textual Investigation 2

(Narrative or representation)
Centres select one from a choice of four (narrative) or three (representation) prescribed titles and use one main text with references to others, all chosen by the centre. 400–850 'words'.

Production tasks

(All concepts)
One choice from 21 set options; centres may create their own briefs subject to WJEC approval.
Research: 2–4 types of evidence.
Planning: evidence of 2–4 planning stages.
Evaluation: 300–500 'words' in a freely chosen form.

Note: one textual investigation may be based on the exam topic. Neither textual investigation may be based on the production topic. The production topic cannot be based on the exam topic.

Figure 6.1 Comparison of specification controlled assessments

Assignment 1 of AQA analyses the language of media texts and how they are constructed to appeal to target audiences. Cross-media study considers the interdependence of media texts, how producers seek synergy where possible and how choice of form influences the nature of a product, for instance print and online versions of magazines. OCR encourages in-depth analysis of at least two texts and their 'representations of individuals, groups events or places are created and what socially significant messages and values are constructed', understanding should be enhanced through contrasting texts (OCR p. 8). WJEC advocates wider textual reading through using a main text and subsidiary texts. This also invites higher comparative skills and allows for some historical (five years or more) comparison. Textual Investigation 2 on representation (of gender) could take *Ugly Betty* as its main text plus extracts from a couple of lifestyle magazines and a trailer for *The Devil Wears Prada* (2006). A variation could be to contrast male and female appeal texts, such as an episode of *The Inbetweeners*. AQA and WJEC make engagement with the changes that digital media have brought explicit by foregrounding a focus on 'cross-media' products and 'convergence' respectively.

Assessment criteria are helpfully specific and itemise learning; they can be used to focus formative feedback, indicative marking for formal assessment and indeed classroom planning.

The overall aim is student critical autonomy, and personal insight and engagement is rewarded. As well as developing skills of 'enquiry, critical thinking and decision making' through analysing media texts, students learn how to research products and audiences, solve problems, use practical skills to creatively construct products, and how to evaluate them. Working through these stages enables students to develop, apply and reflect on their understanding of all four key concepts. The purposes of the pre-production tasks are to learn technical skills for the major production and to 'demonstrate' (AQA), 'highlight' (OCR) and 'reinforce' (OCR and WJEC) understanding. Product construction entails application of technical and representational codes, format and generic conventions learned through textual analysis and product research. The specifications formalise this process by integrating analytical and planning tasks in all controlled assessment 'written' assignments and, in the case of AQA and WJEC, their external assessment as well.

The control element is intended to ensure that students' undertake appropriate tasks; their work is 'authentic' without any plagiarism; has 'integrity' without over-reliance on help; and is assessed consistently and fairly. It requires students to work under informal supervision except for research tasks, which are permitted limited supervision. Students must produce a bibliography of clearly recorded sources used in research and analysis, with indications of how each resource was useful. Group work is encouraged for audio-visual production units (maximum four students for AQA and WJEC, five for OCR); students must produce clear evidence of their individual responsibilities and contributions. Logs of key creative decisions and selecting planning evidence directly apparent in the finished product are just a few such pre/production strategies. Evaluations can also evidence individual contribution by students indicating their responsibility for specific work and ideas.

Course planning

Issues for planning schemes of work

Choose case studies that appeal. One of the advantages of media study is that it taps into students' enjoyment of the Media, which can be capitalised on to engage their interest and extend their thinking. The case studies in Chapter 7, such as teenage magazines and popular music genres, have contemporary relevance and tackle themes that students can relate to such as representation of childhood, race and family.

Set briefs with scope for originality. Set briefs that provide students with the scope to be original and creative, e.g. a concept, logo and original images for a campaign advert. Opportunities for students to choose their own case studies, for example in music promotion, sustain their interest and encourage them to develop independent research skills. Integrate homework activities that draw on their knowledge of the latest trends, how they consume and what is popular. In this context exploit media teachers' knowledge of music and trends from different eras to contrast with the students' experience and provide historical perspective. The music promotion unit in Chapter 7 also fulfils the requirement to study texts from other cultures as students opt to research varied music genres and their historical and cultural context. Open-ended practical assignments provide opportunities for students to create culturally diverse outcomes and briefs can be set to encourage students to challenge negative racial stereotypes.

Incorporate differentiation strategies. Differentiation is by outcome for both types of assessment, however ability levels are formally enabled, not least by option choices. Students undertake progressively more complex AQA assignments and extended outcomes so understanding and skills develop and are consolidated during the course. OCR exemplar production tasks have wide variations in complexity; and WJEC allows a wide margin of 'words' for assignments. The textual investigation title options move from the mainly descriptive, e.g. 'Investigate how genre conventions are used . . .' to the critical 'Investigate how far [chosen text] conforms to genre conventions' where issues such as hybridity and intertextuality are expected to be tackled.

The requirements for combinations of analysis, evaluation and production skills create opportunities for students to achieve in different ways and can be enhanced by differentiation strategies. The various media forms (print, audio, moving image and web-based technologies) are easily linked to specific learning styles (visual, auditory and kinesthetic), which are also catered for by the expected diversity of outcomes formats. The different evaluation formats offer similar opportunities, though students should have skills training and prepare for each to ensure that their points are focused, e.g. scripts for audio formats, a themes for each PowerPoint slide. Less confident writers can present annotated print productions and screen grabs for AQA evaluations.

Promote active learning. Speaking and listening activities in varied groupings encourage debate – planning meetings, interviews, presentations, role play, e.g. a press conference interviewing a band about their career, or an advertising pitch in response to a brief. All the specifications advocate enquiry, and 'investigation' is a recurring term. Gifted and talented students relish the opportunities for independent research and flexible open-ended briefs, including the production for which they can be stretched by encouragement to be group leaders. Others develop through more structured approaches that break down the learning – scaffold analysis through modeling on the smart board, share interpretations through discussion, text annotation, structured questioning and writing frames; extended writing such as a press release or evaluation can be tackled in successive stages. For productions they can be steered towards tasks and roles they will find manageable and able to identify in their evaluations.

All specifications aid focused course planning. The directed and exemplar tasks point to breadth of form and platform coverage; identification of associated media concepts and

AOs in the assignment outlines and assessment criteria highlight ensure they are addressed and appropriately distributed. Different types of learning and skills development are prompted by the combinations of analytical, and research and planning tasks. It is the teacher's role to accommodate the restrictions on unit content combinations (including with the exam topic), make initial choices of rich texts and issues that appeal to and stretch students, to set clear and stimulating briefs, provide a range of outcomes, and to plot the cultivation of specific skills for independent work in the productions and external assessments. To this end it is advisable to work backwards from the exam topic(s) and main production media form(s).

A two year course plan for AQA Single Award Two Year

This AQA scheme of work, amplified in Chapter 7 where adaptations for OCR and WJEC are noted, covers all controlled assignments for 'Unit 2: Understanding the Media', and integrates exam preparation for 'Unit 1: Investigating the Media'. Each assignment is set as an industry brief or simulation and students respond in role – an approach that also prepares them for the in role response in the external assessment and 'Unit 4: Responding to a Media Brief in the Double Award'. As the Unit 1 exam topic changes annually reality television is used as an example only.

Skills development in the course plan

Research skills

Occasionally subject information research is needed for production content, such as campaign adverts. The main research areas are product research – products of a similar nature to learn conventions and to avoid repetition, audience research and industry sources. Research into products can be annotated print images such as film posters or CD covers, or screen grabs.

Quantitative and qualitative research into potential audiences is a fundamental aspect of media industry practice and should be integrated into all tasks, practical productions and exam preparation. Typical tasks might include primary research into an audience's preferences and habits based on surveys or questionnaires, structured interviews or written feedback from focus group discussions. Secondary research might include accessing industry data, e.g. BARB for television audience viewing figures, magazine media packs for reader profiles, etc., that can be presented as reports including charts and graphs.

Research tasks have low levels of supervision and so can be completed for homework. It is a regulatory requirement that students acknowledge all sources and explain what they learned. To enable independence, research skills should be modeled and evaluated in lessons – e.g. devise a questionnaire, pilot it in class, review its strengths and limitations, model how to search on the internet, evaluate sources and how to create an appropriately referenced bibliography.

Planning

Planning can be evidenced by notes, minutes of meeting, drafts/sketches with their ideas represented as mood boards, pitches and synopsis, thumbnail sketches, flat plans or mock-ups

YEAR ONE
Term 1

INTRODUCTORY UNIT: Media language and practical skills taster.
AO2, AO3
Topic: Film language and promotion
Concepts: Language (inc narrative, genre), and industry.
Case studies: *Kick-Ass* (2009), *Raiders of the Lost Ark* (1981).
Analysis: Film posters, sequences, websites.
Skills: Storyboarding, filming steady shots in a narrative sequence, in camera editing.

UNIT 2: UNDERSTANDING THE MEDIA
Assignment 1: Investigating the Media
AO2, AO3
Concepts: Audience, media language
Topic: Print
Form/Platform: Magazines/Print and electronic publishing.
Case studies: Teenage magazines front covers: *Sugar*, *Match!*
Analysis: Comparisons of the language chosen to target magazine audiences.
Research: Media packs, industry reader profiling and circulation, primary audience research (questionnaire).
Planning: Front cover mock-up, treatment, evaluation.
Skills: Print design, layout, image manipulation (Photoshop), thumbnails, pitch.

YEAR TWO
Term 4

Assignment 3: Practical Production and Evaluation
AO3, AO4
Topic: Advertising and Marketing.
Form/Platform: Advertising/Print or TV.
Concepts: All.
Case study: Children in campaign advertising: *Ventriloquist* (NSPCC), Barnardo's, *Think!*.
Production: 30-sec TV advert, or three magazine adverts.
Research: Campaign subject information; products, CAP Code, students' productions; target audience research, feedback from mock-up/rough edit screenings.
Planning: Pitch, production schedule and (as appropriate) thumbnails, mock-ups, photo-shoots, storyboards.
Analysis: Evaluation (written); and production log or blog as preparation.
Skills: Filming, editing/photography, DTP and image manipulation.

Figure 6.2 AQA single award course plan

Term 2

Assignment 2: Cross-media study
AO2, AO3
Concepts: Representation and institution.
Topic: Promotion of music.
Form/Platform: Music video/TV, websites.
Case studies: Arctic Monkeys, Beyonce, Dizzee Rascal.
Analysis: How an artist is promoted and represented in music videos and internet sites.
(written or PowerPoint).
Research: Publicity photos, CD covers, audience media use re. music artists.
Planning: MySpace page mock-up and music video storyboard with annotated evaluations.
Skills: Storyboarding, photo-shoot with digital camera, PowerPoint presentation, campaign planning, web-page flat plan.

Term 3

Exam topic taster and mock exam
Case study: **TV talent shows**
The X Factor
Britain's Got Talent
Cross-media music promotion, synergy, celebrity, industry manufactured careers.

Term 5

UNIT1: INVESTIGATING THE MEDIA
AO1, AO3, AO4
Concepts: All.
Exemplar Topic: Reality television.
Case studies: *Big Brother* (Jade Goody race row), *I'm A Celebrity . . . Get Me out of Here*, Japanese game shows.
Research and planning – concepts and skills:
Codes and conventions.
Style, presentation, values.
New technologies.
Representation, issues of bias, values, current debates.
Celebrity culture.
Audiences, popularity and appeals.
Scheduling.
Practice hand-drawn skills for practical tasks.

Term 6

Preliminary material
Students research and plan their responses to the brief sent four weeks prior to the exam.

Figure 6.2 continued

for print and electronic media and scripts, contact sheets, storyboards (hand drawn or photographic) for audio and moving image. Storyboards should clearly convey the narrative, genre/style, mood shot timings and sequence pace, so should be annotated for camera – types of shots, camera movement, transitions, shot duration; sound – dialogue, music and sound; and key action. Remember, students are required to demonstrate their creative ideas and understanding of media language rather than their ability to draw.

Practical skills

Small-scale low-tech skills are taught and integrated in the assignment briefs from the start, as are the high-tech Unit 3 Practical Production skills for filming and DTP.

In the introductory unit students learn how to construct detailed storyboards with full filming instructions, and use digital video cameras to frame and compose shots. In Assignment 1 they photograph original still images and manipulate them using Adobe *Photoshop*. The low-tech planning skills are also developmental activities for WJEC and AQA external examination practical tasks. AQA pp. 15–16 has useful guidance notes for evaluating students' technical skills; and OCR pp. 50–57 has an excellent thoroughly detailed list of assessment criteria for such skills in all media forms.

Equipment

As controlled assessment is 60 per cent of the course and entails a high proportion of practical work, centres are expected to be adequately equipped and there is plenty of advice about appropriate technology in Awarding Bodies' online resources such as teachers' handbooks. Equipment preferences and access are influenced by many local factors so the following list, used for the AQA course above, is offered as an indication of the type of equipment and facilities needed for a class of about 24 students.

Recording

- Six digital cameras to create original images.
- Four mini DV video cameras: can be used with Macs or PCs with firewire cards installed.
- *Edirol* recorders and microphones.
- Accessories: firewire cable, tripods.
- USB cameras immediate upload – check compatibility.

ICT facilities

- Screening: preferably a ceiling projector and Smart board screen, good sound and blackout.
- MP3 file storage: liaise with network technicians to ensure settings are adequate.
- Access to the internet and library for research.
- Use dedicated computer access or book into whole school facilities such as ICT suites or recording studios.
- PCs preferably with DVD drives and burning software.
- Stand alone computers (or mini networks) with DVD drives and burning software.
- Colour printer/scanner.

Editing software

- Video editing: iMovie is popular, easy to use, and usually part of the 'bundled' software with Mac computers; for PCs Windows Moviemaker can be downloaded free.
- DTP package, e.g. Quark or In-design.
- Print image manipulation: Adobe Photoshop.

- Audio editing: Audacity available free to download.
- Podcast packages: Garageband for Mac, Podium for PC.
- Sound effects can be downloaded free from Word online.

Consumables

- Mini DV tapes, writable DVDs, batteries.

Storage

- USB drives, portable hard-drives.

Managing the production

Often teachers are either over anxious about managing productions or assume that students can just 'get on with' practical work. It is crucial to plan and structure activities throughout from research to final evaluation. Devise basic templates for planning processes (AQA has several in the online Teacher Resource Bank) and keep copies in the shared area or in the classroom for easy access. Including skills development from the course start gives time for students to practise and experiment with different technologies and production techniques. The following list of essential points to support effective practice can be supplemented by other observations about practical work in Chapter 11 and organising courses in Chapter 13.

1   Show high quality examples of previous students' work as stimulus models – graded examples on display motivate students to want to produce their own; they can also be used for discussion about the technical requirements and workload implications. Introduce assessment criteria (and itemised technical skills in unit outlines) at an early stage so students develop informed self and peer assessment.

2   Demonstrate and induct students on how to operate equipment such as a still or video camera, how to set up a tripod, or use editing software. Model how to create a product; design principles and how to use the equipment to make meaning with appropriate forms and conventions. Other possibilities are to book in another member of staff: a technician demonstrator, or a student expert to offer demonstrations or support for students.

3   Provide formative feedback and offer ongoing support throughout to help students to critically assess and develop their production work; feedback notes could form part of their production logs/blogs.

4   Enable students to use original material as much as possible, or if found material is justified it must be manipulated to show creativity.

5   Ensure that roles and responsibilities for group work are clearly defined so individuals have evidence to meet specification requirements. All the specifications have 'collaboration' guidance for maximum group numbers, which are linked to production media forms. Video production work more efficiently with large groups (four-AQA/ WJEC, five-OCR) and is easily divided into roles that can be rotated such as camera person, director, lighting, sound and editor. This is more akin to industry practice and so beneficial preparation for Double Award students who will be tested on such knowledge.

6   The increased formal presence of planning in the 2009 specifications indicates how essential this stage is to a successful production outcome. Allow adequate time for research and planning – and prevent students from surging ahead with productions until you are satisfied with the thoroughness of their preparations. Be aware that editing is time intensive even for a two-minute sequence, and factor in time for uploading videos.

7   Set interim deadlines for progress report 'tutorials' to maintain pace and to keep students on schedule.

8   Establish strict rules, systems and clear guidelines for off-site, and onsite production work outside the media 'classroom' area and scheduled lessons. Any such activities should have management agreement; use the school's permission system for out of lesson students. A school-headed letter covers student filming in public areas – though some schools have been asked to notify local police! However, if students want to use buildings, even if it is a shop front, transport, tube stations, etc., they should seek permission from appropriate personnel in advance. Offer enrichment sessions for access to equipment out of lessons. Students must not use violent props such as fake guns and knives, especially off-site – serious crime squads react very quickly.

9   Security and logging of material. Ensure that students take responsibility for labeling tapes and disks, and safely storing them. Video files must be organised into folders and back-up established; e.g. school networks should run back-up tapes. Editing work on stand-alone machines can be backed up on a portable hard drive. Encourage students to use USB storage devices, especially for digital print and web design work.

10 Evaluation. The practice for previous specifications to write lengthy evaluations was prohibitively challenging for many students so all Awarding Bodies provide prompts to support succinct reflections (AQA p. 16, OCR p. 13, WJEC p. 19). Choosing a preferred 'written' format (AQA) or electronic format with visual images, and/or sound (OCR and WJEC) further enables more focused analysis. Whatever the presentation format, students should continue to combine practice with theory and critical awareness throughout the production process (research – final product). Build in opportunities for critical reflection, such as peer review and plenary sessions, to make critical connections between the decisions they make during the production and media concepts and issues – e.g. how the conditions of production, institutional constraints, attempts to appeal to a target audience and so on influence the nature of their product. Make time to log important decisions in a production diary or blog, and to store evidence of how their ideas have evolved such as mock-ups and screen dumps.

External assessment

All the external assessments are written examination papers. The exam topics are prescribed and change frequently – AQA annually, WJEC bi-annually (but the specific aspects of the topic change in the second year and OCR topics more flexibly and helpfully remain for 'at least three years' (OCR p. 15). To ensure breadth of study there are restrictions, noted in Figure 6.1 above, on exam topics being used for controlled assessment. Exam papers and the AQA simulation cannot be used verbatim as future controlled assignment briefs. OCR and WJEC both have 'unseen' extracts to which students respond. The AQA exam is closer to controlled assessment in that students prepare responses to a brief released six weeks prior to the exam, but the tasks are 'unseen' until the exam. AQA and WJEC cover one media topic. Both include creative tasks that entail students applying all of the analytical and practical skills cultivated during their courses. Overall, OCR has the most traditional written exam format and the most demanding content preparation as two topics are studied. Figure 6.3 outlines specification requirements; note that the topics here and in the exam preparation section below are recent examples used for the purposes of illustration.

AQA	OCR	WJEC
Unit 1: Investigating the Media	**Unit B322 Textual analysis and media studies topic (moving image)**	**Unit 1: Thinking about the Media**
Written paper 1hr 30 mins. AO1, AO3, AO4 E.g. TV sitcom Pre-release simulation brief six weeks before exam. Students prepare response.	Written paper 1 hr 45 mins. AO1, AO2 E.g. Action adventure films **or** **Unit B323 . . . (Print)** E.g. Lifestyle magazines.	Written paper 2 hrs 15 mins AO1, AO3, AO4 E.g. Music Five compulsory questions.
Topic knowledge and understanding.	**Section A** Unseen stimulus	**Section A: Investigating** Unseen audio visual or print stimulus.
Four compulsory unseen Tasks: Task 1(A) Genre Task 1(B) Representation	3–5 minute extract (B322) **or** 3–5 pages (B323) Three compulsory questions: 1. Genre 2. Media language 3. Representation.	e.g. Music video 1(a) & (b) Narrative: language 2 (a) & (b) Genre 3. Representations 4. Organisations, audience: e.g. marketing
Research, planning and presentation; production and evaluation. Task 2(A) Pitch (for a new British sitcom). Task 2(B) Design task (for proposed sitcom website).	**Section B** Same topic and questions for B322 and B323. E.g. TV and/or radio comedy. One compulsory question with two parts: (a) Institution (b) Audiences	**Section B: Planning** e.g. Fan website 5. A short unseen planning brief with 5 compulsory tasks: Task 1 Choice of name for site. Task 2 Three features of it. Task 3 Plan design. Task 4 Explain design plan. Task 5 Explain a typical (specified) website feature.
All marks are equally weighted. Available in June only.	Note the different mark weightings. Available in January and June.	Marks overall combine in the questions to equal weightings. Available in January and June.

Figure 6.3 Comparison of specification external assessments

ASSESSMENTS

Considerations for external assessment preparation

Endorsed publications and online resources have teaching and learning guidance including specimen papers, student responses and examiner comments on them. Chief Examiners' Reports are essential feedback for course review and planning. The teaching approach for AQA and WJEC should be a summative case study that draws on the knowledge and skills the students have cultivated during the course rather than as a standalone new unit. However, this may not be completely apt for OCR's two topic requirements and courses that are modular or have parallel controlled assessment and exam teaching.

The exam papers are very different but relevant information can be extrapolated from the following general points:

- Ensure familiarity with exam paper formats, answer books and pro formas for practical work. Even if topics change frequently the order of questions remain the same in relation to conceptual knowledge, and the types of practical activities.
- For 'unseen' extracts students should learn effective note-making strategies, i.e. not to relay the required information through telling the film extract story/describing a page, but to cluster it according to the questions. Also practise the screening/watching/note-making protocols and timings.
- Prepare model answers, draft answer plans, choose appropriate forms of response and practise design skills, paying attention to the weighting of marks and related time management. Learn and test case studies, facts and terminology.
- Design tasks are marked for ideas and evidenced knowledge not artistic ability. Blocks of colour can be represented with a sample of colour and its word; storyboards (usually 10 frames) are rewarded for interesting and original ideas, appropriate framing and annotations of key action, camerawork, sound, duration, sound and transitions.
- Impress upon students the importance of using examples – specific textual detail from unseen extracts, and their case studies. Read questions carefully to ensure how many texts need to be referred to, especially for OCR Section B.
- Use appropriate tone and language for different forms of response and to address different audiences, for example, for essays and simulations.
- Provide exemplar essays/responses. Encourage self-assessment and peer assessment using mark schemes.

AQA

Exam topics are notified two years in advance, and the online guidance for teachers sets out areas of knowledge and exemplar mainstream texts into the yearly topic's media concepts, so teachers can research, plan and gather appropriate resources in time for teaching before the pre-release brief arrives. The focus is on contemporary texts, and cross media study should be included, though teaching some historical background is advisable for understanding the topic's development. A key performance indicator is knowledge of a range of texts in preference to in-depth analysis of a few, however the exam tasks are narrow and tightly focused. Wide-reaching study benefits students by providing a bank of materials from which they can draw ideas for the tasks. Wording and emphasis of the tasks will vary but reference to specimen and past papers provides useful indications of how to target the teaching and learning.

The brief is in the form of an industry commission, inviting proposals from the students to respond in role as potential clients. Teachers can explain it and ensure that students are fully aware of the implications of its instructions, which imply conceptual issues in the guise of project requirements, such as target audience profiles. Teachers then operate only in an advisory capacity, e.g. to provide supplementary resources, access to internet and library resources, guide research and analysis processes, ensure students plan succinct responses closely targeted to the brief's instructions, and to use the short exam time productively. 'Non-essay style' formats such as charts, bullet points, mind maps, etc. warrant marks for the top levels as well as continuous writing.

The concept based knowledge tasks prompt students to be discursive so they can access higher marks, e.g. for situation comedy as a topic: Task 1(B) discusses with some examples, the fairness of how social groups are represented. The practical tasks are supportive. There are bullet point prompts to focus the pitch for a new British sitcom in Task 2(A), and Task 2(B) enables students to work to their strengths with either a 'page' or an audio-visual design choice for a homepage for their proposed new sitcom.

OCR

The OCR website has very detailed online support with stimulating sample schemes of work and lesson plans for all exam topics; it is also building up ExamQuest resources. For Section B – Baker (2003), and Lewis (2008) are useful published resources for TV comedy audience issues, and programme title sequences (along with scheduling) are good indicators of target audience. The focus is on mainstream contemporary texts for Section A, though brief contextualising historical background is informative – and indeed essential for Section B for understanding radio station and/or TV channel ethos. 'Historical' (five years plus) case studies are acceptable, as are American programmes, for Section B, but should be currently broadcast in Britain so scheduling issues can be addressed.

Students should study a wide range of text extracts for Section A, as they may be asked to compare the clip with their own case studies. For a film topic at least one complete text should be watched to get a sense of a typical narrative. All four bullet-pointed language features in Question 2 must be addressed, though not necessarily equally. The Chief Examiner's Report for January 2010 (Moving image – Action adventure) notes that editing was a weakness, so students must ensure they comment on juxtaposition of shots and sequences, transitions, pace and continuity. Question 3, representation, requires analysis beyond description, for instance how a character's narrative purpose is indicated, how stereotypes might be deployed. Students also need to be prepared to identify issues implied in the sequence.

Key learning for Section B is clearly outlined in OCR p. 14 and detailed further on p. 49. Comparative skills developed for the individual portfolio can be applied here, and it is advisable to study texts that have significant elements of contrast, especially in the same format, so students have plenty to research and discuss. Contrasting a radio and a TV format may be more manageable if the same programme is used, such as *Knowing Me Knowing You*. Centres are encouraged to consider the broadest genre possibilities, for instance TV comedy animation such as *The Simpsons* and *Family Guy*, programmes that additionally provide opportunities to explore 'intertextuality' and parody.

WJEC

Although the topics for WJEC change every two years, the current and successive topics are notified together. All future topics (though not the years) are listed in the Specification (p.6) and Teachers' guide (p. 17). The Guide also has detailed guidance on the 2011–12 Music topic, and support materials are produced for each new topic online and for Awarding Body support meetings. The Guide also has approaches to another topic – science fiction – using the Media framework. Teachers may prepare for future topics by using them for controlled assessment in non-examination years, and/or within the restrictions (see Figure 6.1) for exam years. Students are advised to study a wide range of genres and forms for the exam topic 'during the period of their course' (Teachers' guide, p. 17).

WJEC requires study of convergence, which informs the aspects of the topic chosen for the sections. For instance music fan websites (Section B, 2011), industry websites (Section A, 2012) and magazines (Section B, 2012) are forms that carry several media or refer to several media within them. Students should aim to indicate this awareness elsewhere in their answers, and study a range of case studies with a strong presence across the media and/or via the Web, e.g. music – Lily Allen, Basshunter, Dizzy Rascal; television drama – *Dr Who*. The marks are equally weighted for Section A and Section B, but the lengthier paper duration reflects the time needed to tackle an unseen brief, so students have to allocate their time judiciously – the tasks though are fairly predictable in relation to the known section topic.

The GCSE Double Award is an opportunity for students to gain two GCSE qualifications in Media. It replaces the short-lived Applied Media GCSE and has a strong pre-vocational emphasis as both units aim for greater depth of understanding about industry practice.

Unit 3: Exploring media industries

Students study two industries from a choice of seven and investigate a range of organisations within them to find out about how products are targeted at audiences, the influence of

Unit 3: Exploring media industries	Unit 4: Responding to a media brief
External assessment. Written examination paper 1 hr, 30 mins. A01, A02 Section A: short answer generic questions on the industry practices listed in the specification. Section B: longer responses to a media stimulus.	Controlled assessment based on an industry-related set brief. The brief changes annually. A03, AO4 Students produce a campaign across two media industries.
Available in June every year.	Available in June every year.

Figure 6.4 AQA double award

ownership, job roles and working practices, finance and regulation, and the effects of technology on production and consumption (AQA p. 19). A specimen paper with sample answers is available at the online Teacher Resource Bank. Students apply their case studies knowledge to the short generic questions in Section A. Section B has an industry stimulus – the exemplar's is research findings into young people's use of 'old' and 'new' media. Students use their comprehension of the stimulus material and application of their accumulated broad industrial knowledge to give more extended responses in answer to prompts about the cultural and media practices indicated by the information.

Exploring media industries develops the institutional context research covered in each Single Award unit; see the scheme of work in Chapter 7 with units on magazine publishing, advertising, and music promotion and television. The schemes of work also have extension activities designed for Unit 3 level industry research. Where possible centres are encouraged to make links with local media companies, for visits, work-related experience and visiting speakers/workshops.

Much of the Media tends to be London-centric – Channel 4 offers taster days, and *The Guardian* does a simulation of producing a front page from that day's news streamed into their education computer network. However, cities are increasingly developing vibrant, if small, media businesses thanks to digital technology, and local newspapers and independent cinemas or arts centres with cinemas are useful and often helpful starting points. Double Award students could run the BBC national *School Report* project for KS3 students.

Unit 4: Responding to a media brief

Unit 4 builds on the skills developed for the cross-media and production units, and exam simulation brief experience in the Single Award. Thorough sample briefs and exemplar student responses are available in the online Teacher Resource Bank, which so far have been campaign advertising. The topics are likely to engage students since, in line with the Learning Aims, the issues are contemporary and of direct interest to the student age group for such as the 'Social Networking Sites and Personal Security' exemplar.

Students are expected to undertake extensive topic, product and audience research as well as thorough planning for two media forms. So they should embark on it at quite an early stage in the course. Unit 3 and Unit 4 could be taught concurrently especially if one or more of the industries is relevant to what the students want to (or be encouraged to) use for their productions. The units are reciprocal in other ways as working to industry briefs in role, students explore the functioning of the media institutions from an insider perspective and go beyond their personal response to deeper understanding of the purposes of industry practices and the constraints on production.

Summary

Most students who opt for Media Studies are excited by the opportunities to study subject matter of interest to them, be creative and use media technologies. Establishing a relevant, accessible, skills-based and challenging course will ensure in the long term that a broad range of abilities is attracted, and students are able to develop as independent learners. Media Studies also provides different roles for the teacher and opportunities for teachers and students to learn from each other.

As noted in the introduction, this chapter also provides a context for Chapter 7, which elaborates the controlled assessment section in the AQA course plan above with detailed schemes of work and case studies. The external assessment is not included in the course plan because of the frequent topic changes, but broad approaches and suggested exam preparations for all specifications are offered above in this chapter.

Further reading

Clark, V. and Harvey, R. (eds) (2002) *GCSE Media Studies*, London: Longman. Nominally an OCR legacy specification book but it has highly informative chapters on media forms, how to study them through media concepts, and clearly itemised key learning.

Specialist Media Education publishers:
   Auteur Publishing www.auteur.co.uk/. Specialist media education publisher; books include GCSE targeted study areas and exam topics, e.g.:

McInnes, R. (2003) *Action/Adventure Films: A Teacher's Guide* and *Classroom Resources*.
   British Film Institute (BFI) *Teaching Media at GCSE* series published by Palgrave Macmillan:

Baker, J. (2003) *Teaching TV Sitcom*, London, BFI.

Baker, J. and Toland, P. (2007) *Teaching Film at GCSE*.

Lewis, E. (2008) *Teaching Television at GCSE*.

White, M.L. (2007) *Teaching Digital Video Production at GCSE*.

www.screenonline.org.uk Schools can register free for access to the video clips in this extensive BFI television and film archive.

Recommended resources

Awarding Bodies

All Awarding Bodies provide online teaching support; at the time of writing these are more substantial for AQA and OCR, but WJEC plans to add to its online support with a parallel website with an online forum and upload facility and showcase of students' work. All have endorsed 'text' books with partner publishers, some of which are linked to online learning resources.

AQA – www.aqa.org.uk

Morris, R., Varkey, D., Robinson, K. and McInerney, J. (2009) *GCSE AQA Media Studies*, London: Nelson Thornes, linked to the online Kerboodle! *Media Studies Student Book*.

AQA planning model for teaching GCSE English with GCSE Media Studies – http://store.aqa. org.uk/resourceZone/pdf/english/AQA-ENG-MEDIA-W-TRB-PLANNING-GRID.PDF.

OCR – www.ocr.org.uk/mediastudies/newgcse.

Lewis, E., Rodgers, M., Morris R. and Goddard, J. (2009) *OCR Media Studies for GCSE*, London: Hodder Education.

WJEC – www.wjec.co.uk

Esseen, M., Phillips, M. and Riley, A. (2009) *GCSE Media Studies for WJEC*, London: Heinemann.

Specialist Media Education publishers
Auteur Publishing – www.auteur.co.uk
   A well respected, up-to-date specialist media education publisher. Publications include GCSE targeted study areas and examination topics, such as:

Baker, J. and Toland, P. (2007) *Teaching Film at GCSE*, Leighton Buzzard: Auteur.

Lewis, E. (2008) *Teaching Television at GCSE*, Leighton Buzzard: Auteur.

McInnes, R. (2003) *Action/Adventure Films: A Teacher's Guide* and *Classroom Resources*, Leighton Buzzard: Auteur.

British Film Institute (BFI) – www.bfi.org

The BFI produces the *Teaching Media at GCSE* series published by Palgrave Macmillan including White, M.L. (2007) *Teaching Digital Video Production at GCSE*. Schools can register free for access to Screenonline – http://www.screenonline.org.uk. The video clips in this BFI television and film archive are extensive and essential.

Chapter 7

Media Studies GCSE (2)

Schemes of work

Elaine Homer

Introduction

This chapter offers a comprehensive guide to constructing Unit 2, the controlled assessment section of a GCSE Media Studies course. Externally assessed Unit 1, which forms the final part of most centres' course plans, is not included because of the frequent topic changes, however Chapter 6 has some preparation strategies. This scheme of work is for the AQA Awarding Body specification, but the suggested texts and approaches can be easily adapted for OCR and WJEC. AQA was chosen on a numerical basis as the most directly useful to classroom teachers since the legacy specification accounted for over 50,000 of the 69,823 GCSE Media Studies candidates in 2008 (JCQ) and is likely to dominate the market, for a while at least, despite the inevitable migration between Awarding Bodies that accompanies the arrival of new specifications.

AQA is the only Awarding Body offering a Double Award for GCSE Media Studies; such a course may seem unrealistically demanding on the school timetable but, as noted in Chapter 6, there are increasingly flexible modes of delivery for GCSE Media Studies. This plan for a two-year Single Award course has equivalence with the OCR and WJEC awards, and reflects the initially preferred mode of delivery informally indicated by teachers at AQA training days. This may be because the Single Award is the closest to delivering the familiar legacy specification, and very few centres undertook AQA's Applied Media Studies, the Double Award's predecessor. However, as partnerships with the workplace are increasingly part of school life, the extension activities are designed as preparation for Double Award units, particularly 'Unit 3: Exploring media industries', and indicate how the more challenging concept of institution, which is the focus for the Double Award, can be made accessible.

The scheme comprises successfully piloted activities for all ability levels in a mixed comprehensive school with a culturally diverse intake. One of the advantages of teaching GCSE Media Studies is that it taps into students' enjoyment and prior knowledge of the Media. The tasks and choice of case studies aim to stimulate students through their pleasures and familiarity with the contemporary texts and issues, then build on this engagement to formalise their knowledge and extend their understanding. It is an enabling approach endorsed in specifications' aims and learning outcomes, which promote 'consideration of issues that are important, real and relevant to [candidates] and to the world in which they live' AQA (2009: 24) and WJEC (2009: 3). Applying their cultural capital to familiar topics and issues in the classroom means that students are likely to be more informed and willing to engage with detail and complexities, and so gain the abilities and confidence to tackle critical investigation in less familiar territory.

The overall teaching and learning strategy is to draw out conceptual knowledge and understanding from students through active learning rather than didactic teaching. Textual analysis, and speaking and listening activities, scaffold their thinking in preparation for 'written', research and practical tasks. All assignments begin with discussion points that flag up the debates and issues in the ensuing classroom activities, and end with the resources and worksheets.

The worksheets are detailed to illustrate teaching and learning approaches, but should be modified as appropriate for individuals, classes and specification restrictions. The course is presented in its chronological delivery starting with a pre-GCSE course taster unit introducing the learning, understanding and skills required for the three formal controlled assessment assignments. References to the latest version of the *AQA GCSE Specification 1.4* at the time of writing are noted as AQA (2009).

Year one

Pre-GCSE Course Scheme of Work: Introduction to Media Language (four weeks)

This taster scheme of work introduces students to all four key media concepts through film language study. It also provides a foundation (to be re-visited in depth at the end of the second year) for Action adventure films – the external assessment topic for AQA (2011) – and the OCR B322 Moving Image option (2011–13). Selected elements of the unit can be adapted for WJEC Textual Investigation 1 (Genre) or Textual Investigation 2 (Representation or Narrative). Students learn how film language in a narrative sequence constructs meaning for an audience, and they apply this learning by devising a storyboard and an in-camera edited video sequence. The unit combines analysis with production research and planning, which are preparation for the first two Assignments, and production skills for Assignment 3. The institutional focus is film marketing, especially the impact of the internet on how films are promoted; related issues are explored by students analysing the poster and website for *Kick-Ass* (2010). This institutional approach can be applied to any film genre, including action adventure films, and other audio-visual forms such as TV crime drama, AQA's external assessment topic (2012). The *Kick-Ass* case study can be extended for the Double Award's Unit 3: Exploring media industries, by investigating film classification and independent film production outside of the main Hollywood system.

Further research and resources: film industry

Research film classification at www.sbbfc.co.uk/

Visit www.screenonline.org.uk to research production, distribution and exhibition, and film industry roles.

Figure 7.1 Further research film industry

Scheme of Work 7.1 Introduction to media language

Key questions
- What is meant by the term 'genre'?
- What are 'audience expectations'? Where do they come from?
- What are the conventions of the action movie?
- What is a 'hybrid'?
- How are films marketed?

Week	Learning objectives	Activities
1	Explore how film is promoted Evaluate marketing strategies	How do you find out about the latest film releases? Make a list of how films are promoted. Read article on film promotion: **Worksheet 7.1**. List audience expectations of a superhero movie: typical settings, stock characters, props, costumes and themes. Analyse the film poster and website for *Kick-Ass* (2010): **Worksheets 7.2 and 7.3**.
2	Evaluate representations of heroes and villains	In pairs interpret action movie film stills. Representation of characters and their relationships. Narrative events. What has just happened? What might happen next?
	Describe and interpret narrative and genre conventions	Starter: sequence a narrative in groups, e.g. *Jurassic Park* (1993) in which Ellie restores electric power to the safety fence (science fiction/action adventure). Justify choices and how order creates meaning.
	Analyse and respond to moving image conventions/how meaning is constructed for the viewer through film language/continuity editing	Analyse narrative and genre conventions for a classic action chase scene from *Raiders of the Lost Ark* (1981). Compare it with *Lara Croft: Tomb Raider* (2001): **Worksheet 7.4**. Identify mission or task. Representation of good and evil characters. How excitement and tension are created for the audience. Exotic setting and racial stereotypes.
3	Apply continuity editing skills through storyboarding	Show *Guide to basic camera movements* (OCR online resource www.virtualmediastudies.com/): framing, eye-line match, shot/reverse shot. Create a hand drawn or digitally photographed eight-shot storyboard for a story in a specific genre called 'The Package'. Include LS, CU, ECU shots; create suspense and set up a cliff-hanger. Show the package's importance. Allocate specific roles: director, cameraperson, actors, shot logger, continuity monitor.
	Evaluation/justify choices	Annotate camerawork (shot types, angles, positions, movement), editing (duration, transitions), and soundtrack (music, dialogue, sound effects).
4	Video production skills	Show online video *180 rule – filming*. 180-degree rule and match on action. Practical activity: demonstrate video camera. Record narrative sequence. In-camera editing.

Worksheet 7.1 The impact of the Web on film marketing (extension reading). (Adapted from Homer 2008)

When you pay to see a film in your local multiplex, purchase the DVD, download a game on its promotional website or email a friend the latest trailer you contribute to its commercial success.

Film fans contribute to blogs, chat-rooms or social-networking sites to share their views. The film industry takes advantage of this communication opened up by the internet sometimes for covert market research; or to create hype about a film before it's in production and to circulate possible endings to judge fan response. Famously *The Blair Witch Project* (1999) website, which was established before a distribution deal, was used to build interest among potential fans. This low budget flick proved extremely profitable owing to the hype generated by this fan speculation and recorded as the highest profit-to-cost ratio.

Tie-ins are authorised products based on the movie that provide additional income and synergy through cross-media promotion. Since *Star Wars* (1977) demonstrated the profitability of tie-ins and merchandise the industry invests heavily in films with potential for toy and game licensing and other film branded products.

Kick-Ass (2010), an independently produced comic book movie made outside the Hollywood system has received positive reviews. However, the film has courted controversy over the age certificate for its violent portrayal of the character 'Hit Girl', an eleven-year old vigilante, and the explicit use of language.

Visit *Kick-Ass* (2010) official site: www.kickass-themovie.com/main.html to look at how the film was promoted.

Worksheet 7.2 Film poster analysis guide

Describe and interpret:

The purpose of the poster.
What the film is about.
The *genre* of the poster and how you know.
The *title* of the film, *tagline* and connotations.
The *dominant image*, *foreground* and *background*.
The characters in the poster, their relationship, facial expressions, body language and clothes.
The certification and suggested audience.
The overall appeal of the poster.
The production company and director.

Worksheet 7.3 Web analysis guide

Who has produced the site and why?

Who is the target audience for the site? How do you know? How does the website appeal to the audience?

What experience does the website offer the user?

Describe the key features of the homepage and entry to the site.

In what ways is the site entertaining and informative?

Comment on the best features; the type of information and how it is presented including icons, images, videos and opportunities for interactivity, sharing and fan response.

How might users navigate the content interact with features games applications and adverts?

What opportunities are there for fans to influence the success of the movie such as blogging, reviews and file sharing?

Worksheet 7.4 Film sequence analysis

(adapted from Bordwell and Thompson 2008)

Make notes on the connotations of the following:

Setting and props (representation of the exotic)

Location or studio? How are props used (symbolic narrative function) to signify genre?

Special effects (animatronics, CGI, pyrotechnics) and their effect on the audience.

Lighting – hard/soft, diffused, low key, high contrast, illumination, attached/cast shadows.

Colour – warm or cool tones.

Character representations (heroes and villains) and racial stereotypes

Body language, costumes, actions, reactions and dialogue.

Narrative events, structure and character roles (the quest)

How the story is put together/ordered; point of view; key events; themes?

Whose point of view is the scene from?

What is the situation?

What is each character required to do?

What is their motivation or reason for completing the task?

How do they react in the situation?

Framing, angle and editing (creating meaning and generating audience response)

How is attention focused on particular elements? Through framing, use of zoom.

• use of long shots to establishing setting;

• close ups to show thoughts, emotions and reactions in facial expressions;

• different angles to connote power or vulnerability.

Effect of camera movements and pace of editing.

Pick out details that create suspense, surprise, generate excitement and create drama for the audience such as editing and camera movements.

Sound

Evaluate how sound effects enhance action and the use of dialogue to build up suspense.

Consider use of volume to startle the viewer.

Low-pitched sounds such as clanking, thuds or thumps.

High-pitched sounds such as screams or instruments like violins.

Unit 2: understanding the Media

AQA's Unit 2 aims to enable students to 'develop an understanding of how and why media texts are produced as they are' (AQA 2009: 8). It comprises three controlled assessment Assignments selected from prescribed choices in three Assignment Banks. The unit is developmental, beginning with a single media form in Assignment 1, which leads to the two cross-media forms/platforms in Assignment 2, and culminates in the major practical production and evaluation of Assignment 3. Assessment Objectives (AOs) and mark allocations are noted in the schemes of work to aid planning for time allocation and resources. The specification provides breadth of experience as the assignments must cover three discrete forms/platforms, and no assignment may cover the external assessment topic. Since Unit 3 is the most demanding, centres are advised to choose the production form they wish students to undertake first, then to differentiate accordingly for the other assignments.

Research and planning

Independent research and planning are integral to each assignment, and demand sophisticated skills that should be explicitly taught from the outset. Most students can locate relevant information unaided, but they struggle to select what to copy, acknowledge sources, synthesise findings in their own writing, and use their own words. Access to a wide range of web sources is motivating and promotes autonomy, engagement and individual findings, but students also need to be guided to specialist media sites such as magazine media packs or the CAP Code. Frustratingly 'entertainment sites' are a major target of school or LEA web filtering programmes. If requests to temporarily unblock them are unsuccessful then creative solutions to mediate access are necessary such as making multi-modal resources for the school intranet designed in PowerPoint with print, audio, video clips and web-links.

Controlled assessment

There should be a clear distinction between pre-work activities in which shared approaches such as modelling and group discussion are permissible, and task-taking when students begin writing pieces for final assessment and for which feedback should be generic and predominantly addressed to the whole class. Outcomes can be in a variety of formats 'such as annotations, charts, bullet points, continuous prose or combination of any of these' (AQA 2009: 10).

Unit 2 learning outcomes (AQA 2009: 8)

A02 Analyse and respond to media texts/topics using media key concepts and appropriate terminology. 10%.
A03 Demonstrate research, planning and presentation skills. 10%.
A04 Construct and evaluate their own products using creative and technical skills. 10%.

Figure 7.2 Unit 2 learning outcomes

Key media terminology

Accurate and consistent use of media terminology in analysis and evaluation are essential, especially for attaining high grades. Making them a routine aspect of classroom dialogue by explicitly defining key terms, consistently modelling their use and expecting students to employ them are effective strategies to develop student confidence in learning and applying media terminology. There is a full glossary of terminology in the AQA online Teacher Resource Bank (see *Recommended resources* on page 136).

Assignment 1 Introduction to the Media: print – popular magazines (8 weeks)

Assignment Bank 1 – Introduction to the Media

Key concepts: Media language and audience
Topic option: Print – popular magazines
Analytical task: Comparative analysis of two magazine covers
Research and planning task: Magazine cover mock-up and 500 word treatment.
Marks: **Total 15** (AO2–10), (A03–5).

Figure 7.3 Assignment Bank 1 – Introduction to the Media

This assignment can be adapted for OCR B323 Textual Analysis and Media Studies Topic (Print) Lifestyle Magazines, and WJEC Textual Investigations Unit 1 (Genre) or Unit 2 (Representation).

Convergence can be explored through online magazine versions that include promotion of other media, and magazine brands in other forms such as *Kerrang! Radio*, *Kerrang! TV*.

Students compare *Sugar*, a lifestyle magazine for teenage girls with *MATCH!*, a specialist interest magazine for boys. The main learning points are construction of products for audiences, and identifying primary and secondary audiences. Student analysis should be supported at this stage. For instance, the media press pack research helps them to focus on identifying target readerships by demographic and psychographic groupings; and comparison of the pleasures the magazines offer is guided by applying Uses and Gratifications Theory. The magazines invite exploration of how gender stereotypes are constructed through media language; although representation is not required for Assignment 1, including such consideration of this issue is useful concept preparation for Assignment 2.

Breaking down the elements of exemplar texts for individual analysis or through expert groups sharing feedback (Worksheet 7.6) develops students' critical autonomy and prepares them for what the Specifications describe as 'controlled assessment task-taking'. Discussion activities can then relate textual findings to wider issues and debates (Worksheet 7.7). Such modelling demonstrates gathering and applying detailed evidence to support arguments in written analysis and so avoids student tendency to vagueness. During controlled assessment it is likely that weaker students will rely on magazine editions discussed in class, whereas the majority of students will be able to demonstrate critical autonomy and varied responses through choosing different editions of the publications to analyse independently.

The purpose of the primary audience research and psychographic profile is to ensure that students have a strong sense of their target audience from the outset to effectively plan their magazine covers and to evaluate their decisions about content and presentation style for audience appeal in the treatment. The mock-up magazine cover can be low-tech, but it is also an opportunity for induction in Adobe Photoshop. Students learn basic ICT skills and experiment with photography and DTP for the Assignment 1 planning outcome, which will enable them to become confident users in preparation for the Assignment 3 production. Useful support resources include the stages of magazine production illustrated with Photoshop screen dumps in 'The Creativity Issue' of *MediaMagazine*, September 2010; and graded exemplar coursework magazine mock-ups in AQA's online Teacher Resource Bank.

Key Questions Assignment 1 – Magazines

- What types of magazines do boys and girls read?
- What is the appeal of the teenage magazines formula?
- How do magazine publishers attract their readers?
- What assumptions do magazines make about their readers?
- Is there a future for print magazines?

Figure 7.4 Key Questions Assignment 1 – Magazines

Scheme of Work 7.2 Assignment 1 – Popular magazines		
Week	**Learning objectives/ Lesson focus**	**Activities**
1	Analyse magazine codes and conventions to question the assumptions made about gender, lifestyles, interests and aspirations. Controlled assessment task.	Key words: Denotation, connotation, magazine terminology. Starter: which magazine title is the odd one out? Explain why. Connotations of each. List five features of a successful magazine cover. Group analysis: annotate and report back on three *Sugar* and three *Match!* covers comparing similarities and differences of subject matter, presentation and appeal: Group 1: images (framing, poses, facial expression, eye-line); active/passive, individual/team player? Group 2: use of feminine/masculine colour schemes. Group 3: layout and composition, rule of thirds, Z narrative. Group 4: content (fashion, dating, sport, celebrities, heroes). Group 5: titles, language, audience. Read **Worksheet 7.5** to identify readership. Write up comparative analysis either in Word or as a presentation in PowerPoint. Analyse the cover for each magazine and evaluate its effectiveness: **Worksheet 7.6**.

2	Evaluate audience pleasures. Question the assumptions magazines make about readers' interests, aspirations and lifestyle.	Starter: class survey to compare magazines they read and online alternatives. Explore the reasons for their choices. Introduce Uses and Gratifications Theory (adapted from O'Sullivan, Dutton and Rayner, 2003: 118). Students link pleasures they identify in the magazine covers to the theory: Relate their own pleasures to the criteria: 1. Diversion/escapism – release from everyday pressures. 2 Personal relationships/companionship through characters or discussion with others. 3. Personal identity – compare experiences/explore problems. 4. Surveillance – information about what happens in the world. Agree/disagree statements: **Worksheet 7.7**. Plenary: What have you noticed about gender stereotyping and the use of particular teenage and racial groups in relation to selling products in lifestyle and specialist magazines?
3	Explore how audiences are categorised. Primary research: target audience. Evaluate the effectiveness of each research method.	Introduce brief: **Worksheet 7.8**. Visit the National Readership Survey (NRS) website to define socio-economic grading categories and psychographic profiles. Devise a questionnaire. Create a psychographic reader profile. Cover content: list current events, stories, reviews, trends competitions, celebrities ... Model and discuss internet research techniques, website validity, source referencing in a bibliography. Re-draft assessment essay, make links with debates.
4	Plan magazine content and style.	Produce sketches/thumbnails and draft treatment. Pitch their ideas to a small focus group for feedback.
5/6/7	Magazine construction (n.b. layout and composition).	Digital photography and Photoshop induction: layering, import an image, re-size, crop, colour fill, add text, text effects, opacity. Compose a cover shot. Devise title and cover lines. Construct cover. Record notes on design decisions each lesson.
8	Justify design choices.	Re-draft treatment.

Worksheet 7.5 Magazine factsheets (*MATCH!* and *Sugar*)

MATCH! magazine (weekly) UK's best selling football magazine.

Publisher: www.bauermedia.co.uk

Reader age profile: "7–16 year old football mad children and teenagers – predominantly boys with a median age of 12"

Content: "Football news and scoops"

"It is the ultimate football fix, bringing its audience closer to their football heroes. *MATCH!* magazine features the biggest stars, the best interviews, and the latest football news every week."

Circulation: 100,007 (ABC Jan–Dec 2008).

Promotional strategies: Freebies (tattoos, posters, mouse mat); competitions; collectables (*MATCH!* attack card). Online subscription deal for the magazines. Celebrity endorsement.

Online publication: www.matchmag.co.uk

Sugar magazine monthly teen glossy "Leading the teen market for 14 years."

Reader age profile: 12–16.

"There are over three million 11–19 year old girls nationwide and 94% of them read magazines. *Sugar* can reach 45% of the UK's teenagers" (*Sugar* media pack).

Content: Social awareness campaigns, opportunities to influence content, model in the magazine. "*Sugar* engages the reader by allowing them to do what they want to do! Readers can shape the editorial through VIP Club, monthly fiction pages and by actively testing products featured in the pages of the magazine."

Circulation: 158,835 (ABC Jan–June 2008).

Promotional strategies: Range of sponsorship and marketing opportunities including free gifts, money off vouchers and competitions (*Sugar* media pack).

Online publication: www.sugarscape.com/

Worksheet 7.6 Magazine cover analysis – how does the magazine appeal to the reader?

Target audience: Who is the magazine targeting? How do you know? (Age, sex, gender, psychographic profile.) Describe possible secondary audiences for the magazine? Who is not represented (consider race, culture, types of teenagers)?

Title: What is the brand identity and connotations of the title?

Dominant image/model or celebrity: What is the impact of the dominant image(s) on the reader?

Cover-lines: Explain what the cover-lines suggest about the content of the magazine and how they entice the reader to buy.

Layout and composition of the cover: Explain how the different elements are organised on the page and the appeal to the reader. Is this conventional?

Colour: Describe the colour scheme and effect. What does this suggest about the magazine audience?

Mode of address: Explain how the magazine addresses the reader – directly, informally, ironically?

Worksheet 7.7 Agree or disagree?

Do you agree or disagree with these quotations from *Sugar* media pack? Give a reason for each of your opinions.

"Teenagers have more money and more influence than ever before, but they are also at a difficult time in their lives. To cope with body changes and life choices, they need a trusted source of advice. Magazines are invaluable as a source of that advice."

Teenage magazines aimed at girls can encourage them to dress sexily and consider becoming sexually active too young.

Teenage boys lack a lifestyle magazine to give them the advice they need.

MATCH! sets a bad example because it represents men as macho, aggressive and arrogant.

Teenage girls are stereotyped as only being interested in fashion and boys – this is not true.

"*Sugar* is extremely inclusive – our aspirational content will always make the reader feel good about themselves. It's all about being the very best version of who you can be."

Worksheet 7.8 Brief: magazine publishing controlled assessment

Devise either a specialist interest magazine for a teenage boy or a lifestyle magazine for a teenage girl that to some extent challenges stereotypes; meets the interests of your reader and will secure advertising revenue.

Task 1: Provide evidence of independent research and good quality sketches/thumbnails. Design a questionnaire or structured interview to find out about young people's interests and what they look for in a magazine. Questionnaire tips: easy questions first and multiple-choice to prompt responses; use closed questions/ratings to measure, and open questions for attitudes and values.

Task 2: Define your ideal reader: age, social class, race, and create a psychographic profile including: personality, hobbies/interests, brand loyalty, role models and aspirations.

Task 3: Produce a mock-up of the cover either hand drawn, collaged or using ICT.

Task 4: Write a treatment. Describe your target reader and how the magazine cover will appeal to their interests and aspirations through:

- Choice of title.
- Content.
- Magazine strap-line.
- Use of celebrity.
- Any promotions or free gifts.
- Lead story/cover-lines.
- Visual style and presentation.

Design tips:

- Ensure your background size is A4.
- Take the key image photo against a contrasting background for easy cropping.
- Use a limited range of complementary colours/shades (rule of three).
- Don't forget appropriate price, and barcode.

Further research and resources: magazine industry

Visit a newsagent to identify the range of titles on the market.

Research different roles within magazine publishing. Look online for up-to-date media packs for magazines that include costs to place advertisements, readership profiles and circulation figures at publishers such as www.bauermedia.co.uk and www.ipcmedia.com.

Visit the NRS for social grade definitions and their questionnaire:
www.nrs.co.uk/lifestyle.html
www.nrs.co.uk/downloads/interview/DS-CAPI_protocol.pdf

The Audit Bureau of Circulation (ABC) reports on the trading performance of newspapers and magazines www.abc.org.uk.

Figure 7.5 Further research and resources: magazine industry

Assignment 2: Cross-media study – promotion of music (9 weeks)

Assignment Bank 2: Cross-media study

Key concepts: Representation and institution

Topic option: Promotion of music

Analytical task: Explore the way in which one band or artist is represented and promoted across two different media (music video and internet sites): 1,000 'words'.

Research and planning tasks: Mock-up design for a MySpace page promoting an original band or artist. Storyboard for a music video promoting the same band or artist.

Marks: Total 30 (A02–20), (AO3–10).

Figure 7.6 Assignment Bank 2 – Cross-media study

Students explore cross-media representation of the same music artist in a website and a music video, then produce a web page for their own artist. Synergy (AQA online *Glossary* p. 7) and the impact of the Web on music promotion are key institutional issues, and some discussion of active audiences and participation in social networking sites should underpin their analysis.

Prior learning from the pre-GCSE course Introductory Unit can be developed in three ways. Music video narrative structure can be compared with classical linear film narrative. Storyboard skills should be extended to include detailed notes about camerawork, transitions and timings in relation to visual image, music and lyrics. These annotations are often neglected but are essential for students to pay attention to visual style, mood and pace.

Finally, the website deconstruction questions in Worksheet 7.3 can be applied to analysing and constructing the music artist websites.

Analysis of a range of CD covers helps students to identify genre specific conventions and so enrich their controlled assessment outcomes. Analysing image and brand identity in short activities using such print promotional material is a manageable preparation for the more complex analysis of an artist's website. It also enables more thoughtful exploration of the key differences between print, electronic print and video to address 'how the product has been adapted to suit a particular platform' ('Guidance Notes', AQA 2009: 13).

Class group analysis of a range of music video case studies is followed by individual analysis of a chosen artist. Working in peer groups exploring artists in a similar genre further supports student engagement and achievement. Critical distance can be a problem when students evaluate favourite stars, so it is acceptable to narrow case study options, and to vet videos for suitability and richness of material, to enable target grade attainment.

Key Questions Assignment 2 – Promotion of music

- What impact have the internet and social networking sites had on the consumption and production of popular music by both institutions and fans?
- How might a music artist achieve *synergy* in their promotion across different media platforms?
- What gender and racial stereotypes exist in music promotion? Why? What is the impact?
- How important is *intertextuality* in audience response to music video?

Figure 7.7 Key Questions Assignment 2 – Promotion of music

Scheme of Work 7.3 Assignment 2 – Promotion of music		
Week	**Learning objectives/ Lesson focus**	**Activities**
1	Research the origins, conventions and messages and values of musical genres.	Play 5 tracks from different decades and ask students to identify the genre and era. Research a genre of their choice: **Worksheet 7.9**.
2	Evaluate different types of promotional photographs. Introduce the concept of navigation; focal points through contrast/lighting.	Five tips you would offer a photographer about how to shoot some promotional shots of a musical artist or band (offer different genres). Analyse pin-ups, location shots, mood shots, live-performance and surprise shots. Choose one image: describe and interpret the framing, composition, body language, facial expression dress codes, iconography; and suggested lifestyles, attitudes, values, behaviour.

Scheme of Work 7.3 Assignment 2 – *continued*		
Week	**Learning objectives/ Lesson focus**	**Activities**
	Compare representation of gender in different genres.	CD cover analysis: **Worksheet 7.10**. Create an annotated representation collage of music genre/gender images. Present findings.
3/4	Evaluate the impact of the Web and social networking on the music industry. Controlled assessment task: Analyse artist promotion across different media.	How do you reach young people? Class survey of media use. What is synergy? Allocate groups a musical genre. They list the different media used to promote a particular musical artist and how they are used (e.g. Fatboyslim *The Greatest Hits: Why Try Harder*, The Prodigy *Music for the Jilted Generation*, Rihanna *Good Girl Gone Bad Reloaded*, and 50 Cent *Get Rich or Die Tryin*). What are the advantages of different forms? E.g. music magazines, promotional events and public appearances, sponsorship deals, radio, internet, TV programmes, news media. Create a plan for your artist to be promoted across the Media over a twelve-month period. Explain which media you would use and why. Analysis of an artist's website: **Worksheet 7.11** and **Worksheet 7.3**. Annotate web pages and write up as PowerPoint presentations with screen shots.
5	Analyse music videos. Explore representation of gender and race.	Beyoncé *If I Were a Boy* and a chosen case study: **Worksheet 7.12**. 1,000 word analytical piece: written report or PowerPoint presentation.
6/7/8	Promote an artist across two media.	Devise a MySpace webpage and storyboard for a music video (hand drawn or photographic): **Worksheet 7.13**. Organise photo-shoot of artist. Plan framing and composition of shots, facial expression, body language, dress codes.
9	Re-draft assessment tasks.	Ensure storyboard is fully annotated with action, audio, shot types, edits, transitions.

Worksheet 7.9 Popular music research task
1. Where did the music come from? (a particular country or area, urban or rural environment).
2. What decade did it come about? What is the music about? (Love, romance, violence, war, politics, fun, friendship, other).
3 What are the fashions and symbols associated with the genre? What do they represent?
4. Describe the type of fan that would enjoy this music (age, gender, attitudes and values).
5. Why do you think they would listen to it? In what ways might the music appeal to the fans?
6. Where is the music enjoyed? Live, at home alone, in a club?
7. What messages, attitudes and values are suggested?
8. What are the typical conventions for a music video in your chosen genre? Support your points with specific examples from your research.

Worksheet 7.10 Compare CD covers

Music is promoted through genre and/or star image.

What genre of music do you think these CD covers might be? How do you know?

What are the connotations of each cover? How do they represent each artist?

Who is the target audience and how might the cover appeal to them?

What are the similarities and differences between the covers? Explain why.

What do the covers illustrate about the career development and brand identity of your artist?

Worksheet 7.11 Music promotion case studies

UK Indie band: Arctic Monkeys: famously capitalised on social networking and the role of audiences in sharing circulating media texts and their success was attributed to the internet as they gave away demos, and the process of fans file sharing.

Record label: www.dominorecordco.com/

Video: *The View from the Afternoon.*

www.arcticmonkeys.com/videos.php?s=wLKWwSHpUr4#player

Representation: masculinity/youth/the North.

Representation of the artist on the Web: www.arcticmonkeys.com/

Further reading: Have Arctic Monkeys changed the music business?

www.guardian.co.uk/music/2005/oct/25/popandrock.arcticmonkeys

Male UK Garage/grime artist: Dizzee Rascal.

Record Label: www.xlrecordings.com/dizzeerascal/

Video: *Bonkers/Holiday.*

Representation: Race/crime/urban/London.

Collaboration: Wiley/Calvin Harris.

Further reading: www.cbc.ca/arts/music/grimewave.html.

Representation of the artist on the Web: www.myspace.com/dizzeerascal.

US Female R&B artist: Beyoncé.

"Known for writing personally driven and female-empowerment themed compositions" (Wikipedia).

Record Label: Columbia Records. Owned by Sony US one of Big Four major labels.

Video: *If I were a Boy.*

Representation: Gender, femininity, glamour, race.

Collaboration: Jay-Z/Lady Gaga.

Representation of the artist on the web: Official website:

www.beyonceonline.com/uk/home, www.myspace.com/beyonce.

I Am . . . Sasha Fierce alter ego concept album http://whoissashafierce.com/

www.myspace.com/sashafierce.

Worksheet 7.12 Music video analysis guide (adapted from Fraser 2005)

Students should choose their own videos, but have some available in case of problems, e.g. Wu-Tang Clan *Protect Ya Neck from Legend of the Wu Tang: The Videos* (2004), Chicane *Poppiholla* (2008).

1. Does the song/music belong to a particular genre? How do you know?
2. Is it performance based or narrative?
3. What is the relationship between the visuals and the lyrics? (Illustrative, amplifying or contradicting.)
4. What settings are used? What is the effect? (On stage, location, acting.)
5. How is/are the performers shown? What are the connotations?
6. Does the video tell a story? If so what is it?
7. How are men and women represented?
8. What other texts does it draw on? (The album cover, films, adverts, other pop videos.)
9. Describe the overall visual style (colour, camera techniques and editing).
   - Performance
   - Close ups of artist
   - Direct address
   - Symmetrical framing
   - Animation/computer graphics
   - Cross-cutting
   - Cuts on the musical beat
   - Repeat shots
   - Lip synching
   - Freeze shots
   - Fast motion
   - Slow motion
   - Intertextuality

Worksheet 7.13 Brief: Music promotion controlled assessment

Task 1: Construct a webpage for an original artist in the genre you have researched.

Task 2: Devise a storyboard for a music video (hand drawn or photographic) to promote the same artist. Annotate your storyboard to explain how you have represented your artist and used music video conventions.

Other tasks:

Organise a photo-shoot for your artist to create publicity shots or a music video photographic storyboard.

Plan framing and composition of shots, facial expression, body language, dress codes and connotations. Consider how you are representing them including any possible gender or racial stereotyping issues.

Produce a flat plan for your web page including interactive features and links.

Annotate your web page. Explain how you have represented your artist and how the site will promote your artist? Explain how you have you appealed to your target audience through content and style. Analyse and interpret your choice of layout, use of images, links, interactive elements, fan blogs, audio and video clips.

How do your two products complement each other?

Year two

Assignment 3: Practical production and evaluation – advertising and marketing: campaign adverts (12 weeks)

Assignment Bank 3: Practical production and evaluation (individual or group)

Key concepts: Media language, audience, representation and institution

Topic option: Advertising and marketing

Production tasks: Three print adverts, or three 30-second television adverts;

700–800 word evaluation (see 'Guidance notes' AQA 2009: 15–16).

Marks total: 45 (AO3–15), AO4 (30).

Figure 7.8 Assignment Bank 3 – Practical production and evaluation

This assignment can be adapted for OCR Media Studies B324: production portfolio in Media Studies option 12 cross-media marketing a new album, and WJEC external assessment (2011) Section A: Music video.

Students address all four key concepts in equal depth through creating an advertising campaign and written evaluation. Campaign advertisements (charities, health education, public information) offer rich texts to investigate audience impact, persuasion techniques, and diverse social and moral issues that are directly relevant to students' lives. Modelling analysis is still necessary at this stage to focus students' independent issue and product research. Stimulating resources include the *'THINK!'* website archive of road safety campaign adverts, the NSPCC's *Ventriloquist* and British Heart Foundation adverts, which are on the organisations' websites. Other examples can be found on *YouTube*, and an extensive section of Grahame's (2008) *Doing Ads*.

Allowing students to choose their own issue promotes the high levels of personal engagement, independence and varied creative outcomes necessary for the highest grades. Students can focus their issue research by identifying a problem and possible solutions; this in turn helps them to identify the target audience (whom the problem affects), campaign objectives (how the problem could be resolved) and hard information such as statistics (features of the problem).

The sequence of lessons structures students' thinking, and helps to evidence the development of their ideas and critical decisions through planning sketches, charts and an ongoing production diary or blog that can be drawn upon for the evaluation. Students can be reluctant to plan, partly through impatience but also because they find drawing difficult. This can be circumvented through mock-ups, thumbnails or collages. There is high expectation for quality production outcomes in Assignment 3, and the scheme of work gives students the opportunity to extend the basic Photoshop skills initiated in Assignment 1 to more creative image manipulation.

At the task-taking stage students must explain how their campaign planning has been directly informed by their research, how they identified and tailored their products to their audience, complied with the Committee of Advertising Practice (CAP) Code, and assess the overall success of their outcomes in meeting their campaign objectives. Regulation is

Scheme of Work 7.4 Assignment 3 – Production and evaluation		
Week	**Learning objectives/ Lesson focus**	**Activities**
1/2	Evaluate advertising techniques Apply the CAP Code	Explain context/brief Analysis of print and video road safety campaigns: **Worksheets 7.14 and 7.15**. Read the CAP Code and apply to adverts: **Worksheet 7.16**.
3	Primary and secondary research	Evaluate other students' campaigns, e.g. Lurhs 2008. Research tasks/see brief: **Worksheet 7.17**.
4	Plan for the production process	Summarise research findings. Chart audience and campaign objectives for each advert. Prepare an advertising pitch to present to the class (see *Doing Ads* p. 102). Explain the problem, what needs to change, and how their advert will address this through AIDA: Awareness-Interest-Desire-Action. Create sketches/mock-ups.
5	Develop skills in image manipulation to create meaning Pre-production tasks	Model techniques for creating charity adverts using Photoshop. Planning/agree roles and responsibilities. Create sketches/storyboards.
6	School mock exam schedule	Mock exam pre-release that requires students to write up pre-production planning as a pitch.
7/8	Pre-production recording	For video: organise equipment (video camera, tripod, tapes), record and log shots. Storyboard to plan framing, lighting, sound, mise-en-scène, editing. For print: photograph original images with digital cameras. Plan framing and composition.
9/10/ 11	Post-production work/editing	Upload and review footage, prepare an edit schedule; editing, add graphics and rendering. Post-production (print) apply image manipulation techniques and digital effects to integrate image and text. Ensure slogan, logo, original image, charity name and web or telephone link are included.
12	Evaluation	Write evaluation: **Worksheet 7.18**.

often challenging for students to understand, but role-play is an effective learning strategy such as reading and applying brief extracts from the CAP Code to judge the compliance of case studies. Advertising case studies can be found on the Advertising Standards Authority (ASA) website, which administers CAP, and the *Doing Ads* DVD regulation activity.

The Scheme of Work 7.4 for this assignment is on page 128 and the worksheets follow below.

Key questions Assignment 3 – Campaign advertising

- What are the advantages and disadvantages of campaign advertising techniques? E.g. humour, 'ah' factor, shock tactics, celebrity endorsement, statistics, direct address and viral advertising.
- Are shock tactics justified?
- What kind of advertising strategies reach young people?
- How is advertising regulated?

Figure 7.9 Key Questions Assignment 3 – Campaign advertising

Worksheet 7.14 Road safety print advert analysis

1. What is the purpose of the advert?
2. Who is the target audience? How do you know?
3. What are the connotations of the dominant image?
4. Describe any people in the advert. How are they represented?
5. What is the slogan? What does this suggest?
6. Describe the logo. What does this represent?
7. Describe the use and effect of colour and lighting.
8. What advertising techniques are used – humour, wish fulfillment, shock tactics and glamour?
9. How have media technologies been used for digital image manipulation? What is the effect?
10. What is the impact of the advert on the target audience? Is the advert successful? Justify your opinion.

Worksheet 7.15 Moving image analysis questions

Jot down your first reactions to the advertisement. How does it make you feel? Explain why.

Is it effective?

Whose **point of view** is presented? What is the effect?

Summarise the **story**, main **characters** and **themes**.

How are the characters represented? What is the impact?

Describe aspects of the **mise-en-scène** that are significant including setting, props, acting, costumes, make-up and lighting.

What **advertising techniques** are used? What is the effect?

What are the connotations of **dialogue, music, voiceover** and **sound effects**?

Comment on any significant aspects of **camerawork** including **framing, angle, distance, camera movements, editing** and **transitions**.

Worksheet 7.16 Regulation of advertising

Task: Read Section 4 and Section 5 of the CAP Code: 'Harm and Offence' and 'Children' with particular reference to paragraphs 4.2 and 5.1.2 below.

4.2 Marketing communications must not cause fear or distress without justifiable reason; if it can be justified, the fear or distress should not be excessive. Marketers must not use a shocking claim or image to merely attract attention (CAP Code Section 4, p. 28).

5.1.2 Children must not be shown in hazardous situations or behaving dangerously except to promote safety. Children must not be shown unattended in street scenes unless they are old enough to take responsibility for their own safety. Pedestrians and cyclists must be seen to observe the Highway Code (CAP Code Section 5, p. 30).

1. How might these restrictions inform your planning for your advertising campaign?
2. Check for any other rules in these sections that you will need to consider when planning your campaign.

Worksheet 7.17 Brief: campaign adverts production

Produce a charity, public information or health education campaign based on one of the following issues: road safety, smoking, fair trade, global warming, homophobia, racism, animal welfare, homelessness, gun or knife crime.

Group project: An advertising campaign realised as three 30-second television adverts. (Group size must not exceed four and individual contributions must be clearly identified.)

Individual task: Three magazine or billboard advertisements.

Research:
- Similar texts and advertising techniques.
- Audience questionnaire.
- Background information and statistical evidence to back up findings.

List your sources with an explanation about why each was useful. You can present your research findings as a PowerPoint presentation, annotations, charts, bullet points, continuous prose or a combination of these.

Planning:
- Decide on your target audience.
- Your aims/campaign objective/call to action or intended response.
- Create mock-ups for print adverts or a storyboard for moving images.

Worksheet 7.18 Evaluation guide (700–800 words)

Institution
Have you achieved your aims in your production?
Explain the purpose of your products and how successful they are.
When and where would your product be shown? Explain why. How would this fit into your overall promotional strategy?
Explain how you have made sure that your advert complies with the CAP Code and any issues arising from positioning or scheduling.

Audience
Describe your intended audience and how you have appealed to them?
What impact will your adverts have on the target audience?

Representation
How have you represented your artist or people and places in your products? Explain why.

Language
Which codes and conventions have you used? Explain why.
Explain what advertising techniques you have used and why.

Evaluation
What are the main strengths and weaknesses of your campaign?

Unit 2 Extension tasks for Double Award Unit 3: Exploring media industries

In Unit 3 students are assessed externally on their knowledge of two media industries chosen from a prescribed list (AQA 2009: 19), in this case Popular music, and Advertising and marketing. These extension tasks target them by building on Unit 2's Assignment 2 (music promotion) and Assignment 3 (advertising practical production). Studying the organisation and production processes in these industries should include, where possible, engagement with local media based firms and professional practitioners. The sector skills council for media arts (www.skillset.org) is a good central resource for contact advice and for student research about industry organisation, practices and job roles. The areas of prior learning developed in the extension tasks include:

- How the industry creates a range of products to sell to particular audiences.
- How the industry and the products they make are influenced by ownership and control.
- The job roles and working practices within the organisation.
- How the organisation is financed and regulated.
- The effects of developments in technology within this industry.

This knowledge and understanding also supports students' extended responses to the Unit 4 brief, a weighty controlled test practical task for which students build on their planning and production skills for a campaign across two media platforms. Professional practice can be explored through music industry simulations, for instance at http://uk.blastbeat.org/about. It should be noted that the Unit 4 brief changes annually but though the requisite industry knowledge changes the areas of learning are a constant framework.

UNIT 3 learning outcomes (AQA 2010: 18)

AO1 Recall, select and communicate their knowledge and understanding of media products and the contexts in which they are produced and consumed. 10%.
AO2 Analyse and respond to media texts/topics using media key concepts and appropriate terminology. 10%.

Figure 7.10 Unit 3 learning outcomes

Worksheet 7.19 Exploring the music industry

There is a tension in the music industry between music as an art form and music as commodity. Conflict can arise as a musician's desire for authenticity conflicts with the expectations of industry professionals who are mediating their image.

Audiences: Visit Project Phoenix for research into how music is consumed and audience segmentation www.bauermedia.co.uk/Insight/Project-Phoenix/.

Production process: Examine how different types of artists' careers might develop. Research the different stages of a musical artist's career from forming a band and writing songs, to signing a record deal and releasing a single or album and promotional video. Consider the importance of live performance and web promotion to build a fan base. Look at biographies online.

Ownership/control/finance: Find the major record labels. What is an independent record label? What is a subsidiary label? How are they different? Choose three artists you listen to. Which record label are they signed to? How might the type of record label impact on creative control and how the artist is represented?

Industry roles: Find out how the following contribute to the career development of a music artist and creating a star image: A&R, manager, events manager/promoter, stylist, choreographer, record producer, music journalist, online promoter, photographer, sales and marketing manager.

Regulation: Find out about product placement in pop videos, explicit lyrics, music copyright, or royalties.

New technologies: What is the impact of internet piracy; social networking sites such as www.myspace.com and music downloads on the music industry?

Worksheet 7.20 Exploring industry constraints

Agree or disagree with the following statements? Explain why:

Musicians need to appeal to as wide an audience as possible to maximize profits.

Sex sells, therefore it is ok to represent an artist in a provocative way, it's not hurting anyone.

Giving fans what they want is important.

Genre conventions must be followed so fans will be able to recognise the music that they prefer.

Gender stereotypes are important to attract the target audience as fans can relate to them.

So what if rappers are represented as thugs, as long as the image sells records and makes a profit what harm could be done?

Worksheet 7.21 Exploring the advertising industry

Advertising is a cross-platform industry, selling lifestyles, and generating emotions in a global market place. Changes in how young people consume media provide opportunities and challenges for advertisers seeking to reach the teenage market.

Audiences: Psychographic profiles, socio-economic grading, social networking sites.

Production processes: For an introduction to marketing browse the Chartered Institute of Marketing site www.cim.co.uk/ as their *Marketing Knowledge* section interactive guides provide detailed information, models and diagrams about branding.

Ownership/control/finance: Visit www.bartleboglehegarty.com, the global agency responsible for the Levi's jeans campaigns, for insight into their company ethos, their 'Graduates' section for information on advertising agencies at work, frequently asked questions about how adverts are produced, and links to recommended journals and web-sites.

Industry roles: The Advertising Association Information Centre www.adassoc.org.uk has briefing papers and articles for students on the advertising industry: agencies, careers, audience research and regulation, as well as statistical data on trends in advertising expenditure.
www.skillset.org the sector skills council for the audio-visual industries offers an insider perspective on training and employment opportunities in advertising.

Regulation: Visit www.ofcom.org.uk and www.asa.org.uk/asa/ for an introduction to regulation. The Advertising Standards Authority (ASA) 'Schools and Colleges' section has downloadable pdfs with extensive case study examples. The 'Adjudications' section of the ASA site includes outcomes of complaints against controversial campaigns such as Barnardo's. The English & Media Centre's *Media Mag* online archive has an informative article on Barnardo's *Child Poverty* campaign: 'Too Shocking for Words', Steve Connolly, April 2004.

New technologies: Investigate the following advertising methods: viral advertising, guerrilla and ambush marketing. Find out what is meant by 'shareability', 'Digg', 'buzz up/down', 'seeding' and 'driving views and traffic' at www.viraladnetwork.net/.

Suggested viewing for investigations into the impact of technologies

BBC CLICK http://news.bbc.co.uk/1/hi/programmes/click_online/default.stm
The Virtual Revolution www.bbc.co.uk/virtualrevolution/
Charles Leadbetter interview www.open2.net/digitalrevolution/web_2_0.html
History of magazines www.magforum.com/index.htm
Lady Gaga Official website: *Telephone* video www.ladygaga.com/telephone/
Viral advertising slideshow www.rubberrepublic.com/blog/blog/2010/02/shareability-and-virals/

Articles

www.telegraph.co.uk/culture/music/rockandpopfeatures/7466152/Lady-GaGas-Telephone-
   video.html
http://uk.playstation.com/games-media/news/articles/detail/item232497/Dizzee-Rascal-to-
   launch-the-SingStar-Rooms-VIP/
www.xlrecordings.com/

Chapter summary

Media Studies GCSE 2009 brought specifications that are responsive to, and increasingly utilise, contemporary media. They provide opportunities to plan courses that equip students as critical readers and with transferable skills to confidently participate in contemporary communication systems, and employment. This course endorses and builds on students' personal media experience, enabling them to develop a wide range of skills such as primary and secondary research, creativity in video and print production, and the ability to evaluate and make critical connections between practical and theoretical work. The chapter offers a model, adaptable for all specifications of how to address, and creatively interpret, highly directive controlled assessment requirements. A range of stimulating texts, focused resources, guided research and production activities manage and engender students' increasing sense of ownership and independence. Teachers who frame learning experiences in this way and accommodate their students' seemingly superior knowledge of digital media as another learning resource and talent pool to draw on can evolve the strong facilitator and partnership elements typical of media pedagogy and not only meet the rubric of the specifications, but also their implicit spirit.

Further reading

AQA has an extensive range of online resources to support the GCSE Single and Double Award; and there are AQA approved or targeted publications for teachers and students containing detailed explanations of the courses, appealing case studies and classroom activities:

Esseen, M., Phillips, M. and Wisson, L. (2009) *AQA GCSE Media Studies,* Portsmouth, Heinemann:
   student book with ActiveBook CD-ROM.
Morris, R., Varley, D., Robinson, K. and McInerney, J. (2009) *AQA Media Studies*, Cheltenham,
   Nelson Thornes. Awarding Body exclusively endorsed book linked to online student resources at
   www.kerboodle.com.
Wisson, L. (2009) *AQA GCSE Media Studies*, Portsmouth, Heinemann: teacher's resources, Lesley
   Wisson is the AQA Chief Examiner.

Recommended resources

AQA Awarding Body Specification (2009) web-based resources

AQA Teacher Resource Bank: www.aqa.org.uk/qualifications/gcse/english-and-media/media-studies/
media-studies-key-materials.php.
AQA GCSE Specification, version 1.4 (2009) http://store.aqa.org.uk/qual/newgcse/pdf/AQA-
4810-W-SP-10.PDF.

AQA GCSE Media Studies productions on YouTube

www.youtube.com/results?search_query=AQA+GCSE+Media+Studies&search_type=&aq=f

Industry Resources for the AQA Double Award

www.bbc.co.uk/schools/websites/11_16/site/english.shtml hosts the BBC annual school report
event and supporting educational material.
www.channel4.com/learning/breakingthenews/index.html contains an online course for KS3-KS4
with tutorials by Channel 4 professionals to produce news programmes.
www.guardian.co.uk/newsroom/map/0,12104,735562,00.html is the Guardian Visitors Education
Centre.
The Sector Skills Council (www.skillset.org) for the audiovisual industries offers an insider perspective
on training and employment opportunities.

Chapter 8

Media Studies A level

An introduction

Elaine Scarratt

Introduction

A level Media Studies appeared substantially later than the first formal media assessments of the late 1970s when Oxford and Cambridge and Royal Society of Arts Examinations (OCR) established the first course in 1990 with 60 candidates. Current A level Media Studies Awarding Bodies are: Assessment and Qualifications Alliance (AQA); Oxford and Cambridge and Royal Society of Arts Examinations (OCR); Welsh Joint Education Committee (WJEC). Following OCR's initiative, versions of A level Media Studies were developed by WJEC then AQA, and by 2010 there were 23,792 entries for A2. This total is taken from the provisional data in the Awarding Bodies' Examiners' Reports Unit 4 statistics, as indicating course completion.

The specifications following the 2008 A level review have highly distinctive and stimulating versions of Level 3 specialist media study, and so offer genuine choice for preferred teaching and learning styles. They are, however, quite complex with some detailed precise demands in places. The main purpose of this chapter is to outline and compare the key features of each specification, linking these features to the rationales for them in the context of the overall ethos of each specification, prevailing political concerns and consequent QCA requirements, in order to explain their purpose and help to focus teachers' learning aims. The comparisons will be useful as another illustration of the field's diversity, and an aid to choosing specifications most suited to teachers' own pedagogical styles, their students and their institution's policies.

The comparative exam cohorts' sizes for each Awarding Body continue to reflect the historical order in which the specifications appeared. There has been some movement of entry across specifications as centres 'tested the water' of the 2008 specifications, but overall there has been much closer parity as Table 8.1 suggests.

The data in Table 8.1 comprises the first AS entry in June 2009; the numbers for that cohort and its subsequent entry for A2 in June 2010 are shaded. The information is approximate as the effect on June numbers from January entries cannot be indicated in this context, and OCR supply only rounded numbers. Because of the relative closeness in preferences, extensive amount of published Awarding Body teaching material and the idiosyncratic natures of the A level specifications, this chapter aims for a broadly comparative overview.

Table 8.1 Approximate Awarding Body entries for Media Studies A level

AS/A2	Unit	AQA	WJEC	OCR
2009	1	11,370	13,087	15,000
	2	11,699	13,393	16,000
2010	1	10,325	13,794	15,000
	2	10,790	14,582	16,000
2010	3	7,307	8,793	9,000
	4	7,345	8,447	8,000

Sources: AQA, OCR, WJEC Examiners' Reports for June 2009, and June 2010

Getting started

A level Media Studies teaching often stimulates new media teachers and motivates them to specialize in it. However, the levels of theoretical knowledge and technical skills required at A level Media Studies can be even more disproportionately demanding than GCSE for the non-specialist teacher getting to grips with its demands while teaching. Schools can be eager to set up A level Media Studies courses because of their popularity among students and the money that follows post-16 students. It is not unreasonable though for those teachers establishing an A level Media Studies course to request a preparation year: after all, there is an issue of quality assurance. While there are plenty of resources (noted below) research shows that the most productive CPD is face-to-face contact. There are several sources, which, although short, are high quality and, combined, give good preparation and networking opportunities. These opportunities include Awarding Body annual training days and conferences (AQA in mid-July, OCR in March, WJEC two days in September/October). Awarding Body focused content is included among broader media education perspectives in other annual conferences: *CP3* Film Education, June; A level Media and Film Studies British Film Institute (BFI), July; Media Education Association, November. Additionally, making contact with, and visits to, successful media departments is highly beneficial – as is setting up a local partnership with colleagues in such departments.

A level course structures

The 2008 A levels comprise two discrete courses leading to qualifications: an AS, which if successfully followed by an A2 course gains an A level qualification. However, the A level is designed as a continuous course to be developmental over two years: AS level enables the acquisition of knowledge and skills, while A2 applies and extends them through engaging with theory. Both units in AQA and WJEC A2 directly elaborate their AS counterparts, whereas OCR's A2 exam is markedly different, integrating reflection on coursework and academic work.

The 2008 specifications were informed by the Tomlinson Report (DfES 2004), which found the 'legacy' versions of A level specifications too 'assessment heavy'. The two examinations were reduced to one with shorter overall duration than the previous two combined times. However, the amount of content for the exam was retained and compressed into one unit instead of two. Online specification Teacher Guides include exemplar models of broad course structures, for example, details of how to organize linear or parallel teaching of the two units. However, courses need to be tightly planned to ensure the required range of content is covered: this is particularly so for WJEC and AQA AS courses that have to marshal a wide range of media. Time should be given to develop well-focused exam responses, especially for the very short AQA MEST 1 paper. The WJEC AS course, shown in Figure 8.1 below, illustrates one way to manage the timeframes involved. It is offered as a stimulus to discuss other approaches, and as a starting point for such planning. Students should be in no doubt they have to be 'on-task' from day one and having their own copies of the course plan will encourage responsibility for organizing their learning. AS is a very short two-term dash and time losses, for instance students taking other subject exams in the January exam period, have to be factored in.

Because of their content demands, the courses have effectively become linear end-of-course assessments. It is a challenge for students to be adequately prepared for first time entry in January, so it is advisable to use this exam period primarily for re-sits. However, it is not impossible for students to develop to suitable standards for first-time entry in January, and the experience may be a useful 'dry run' for them. Where necessary, they can re-sit in June and be awarded the higher mark. The detailed accounts of national cohort student performance in Examiners' Reports on January entries enable teachers to make informed decisions about their own students' entries. OCR incorporates Disability Discrimination Act (2005) requirements by offering a choice of audio or audio-visual texts for the AS exam topic – currently radio or TV drama. Changing technology is not only a subject topic, but also the means by which the Awarding Bodies operate, so teachers also need to be alert to online developments in exam procedures, and coursework administration.

Teacher support

All the Awarding Bodies are highly supportive and in effect provide all the materials and training needed 'to pass the test'. As noted above, they have annual training days to review exam performance, advise on practice and disseminate materials such as exemplar assessed exam scripts and production work. Their annual conferences (which also support GCSE courses) include topic workshops, specification sessions, and opportunities to buy resources and share ideas. All specifications have student-friendly Awarding Body endorsed books (see *Further reading* on page 153). They are written by experienced media teachers and examiners, and provide a wealth of teaching and assessment advice, stimulating case studies, assignment and assessment criteria tailored activities that, in AQA's and OCR's cases, are linked with additional online resources.

OCR and AQA have extensive online support. However, WJEC, a much smaller organization, makes up for any lack of parity in this regard in availability for direct contact. AQA also has a system of regional teacher support. All the specifications are online and linked to support documentation such as teacher guides, FAQs, mark schemes, past examination papers, exemplar marked scripts, sample students' work and Examiners' Reports. The latter are essential advisory reading for teachers to review their courses and strategies as the reports itemize strengths and shortcomings in student performance, and note texts and strategies that have worked well to meet specification requirements. These WJEC resources are on the Media Studies A level home page, while AQA's Teacher Resource Bank is reached via the 'Key Materials' link from its home page and OCR's Support Materials

AS level Autumn Term

This is the provisional schedule for the Autumn term of your Media Studies course. There may be a small number of late changes to accommodate trips etc. However, students must note that deadlines are final and that failure to submit coursework will result in the withdrawal of exam entry.

Week commencing	Teacher 1	Teacher 2
8/9	Intro to media studies/key concepts (hw: intro assignment – which one's pink?)	Intro to media language – iconography/image comparison of print texts across three genres
15/9	Intro to media language – editing/ mise-en-scène (hw: understanding editing)	Intro to media research – representation across comparative texts – spy films/tv
22/9	Television spy drama – codes & conventions (prepare recce)	Representations – across range of media cont. (hw: produce display – write report)
29/9	Production Exercise – camera skills – practical (PRACTICAL SKILLS)	Production Exercise – location recce (layout shoot/evaluate shoot)
6/10	Production Exercise – storyboarding (PRACTICAL SKILLS)	Production Exercise – layout and presentation (PRACTICAL SKILLS)
13/10	Production Exercise – stills shoot **(6th Form Assessment 1 – report)**	Production Exercise – layout and presentation **Storyboard display (MS2)**
20/10	Production Exercise – group work	Production Exercise – select sequence to shoot
Half Term		
3/11	Production Exercise – recap conventions camera exercise/evaluation (PRACTICAL SKILLS)	Production Exercise – planning
10/11	Production Exercise – shooting **DEADLINE: PROJECT – shooting**	Production Exercise – shooting
17/11	Production Exercise – editing/tutorials	Representation of gender – range of texts advertising – concept of target audience
24/11	Production Exercise – editing/tutorials	Representation of gender – range of texts comics – audiences
1/12	Production Exercise – editing/screening	Representation of gender – newspapers **(6TH FORM ASSESSMENT –** representation of gender essay)
8/12	Production Exercise – re-editing / tutorials **DEADLINE: FINAL EDIT/PROJECT (MS2)**	Representation/narrative – longer text
15/12	Production Report tutorials	

Figure 8.1 Example of an AS course plan

AS level Spring Term

This is the provisional schedule for the SPRING term of your Media Studies course. There may be a small number of late changes to accommodate trips etc. However, students must note that deadlines are final and that failure to submit coursework will result in the withdrawal of exam entry.

Week commencing

5/1	PRODUCTION REPORT (hw: report MS2)	Key theories – i.e. audience/ideology market research/demographics
12/1	Print texts – codes and conventions (hw: research task)	Audience/representation/ideology – text preferred/negotiated/aberrant readings
19/1	Range of print/web texts DEADLINE – PRODUCTION REPORT	Narrative theory in print / a/v
26/1	Factual media – across media news stories – codes and conventions	Narrative theory in print / a/v
2/2	Industry – ownership technologies – convergence assignment	Exam practice
9/2	Industry – ownership professional practice – economics & audience	(mock exam) **(6th FORM Assessment 3)**

Half Term

23/2	Range of texts	Case studies in genre/representation set up student research/presentation tasks from list of representational groups
2/3	Range of texts video games	Range of texts
9/3	Range of texts radio formats	Range of texts **student presentations**
16/3	Range of texts exam practice	Range of texts **student presentations**
23/3	Range of texts technologies/convergence	Range of texts
30/3	Genre films/tv	Range of texts
6/4	Genre film/tv	Range of texts
13/4	Exam practice	Revision

Figure 8.1 continued

are reached from its home page using the 'View all Documents' link. Additionally, the OCR materials include training day presentations, videos demonstrating camerawork, teacher-produced schemes of work with sample lesson plans and exemplar student coursework, including PowerPoint evaluations. OCR has several other online sites such as a *Get Ahead* blog with postings and archived e-community threads, and a *weebly* (a type of blog) for its annual conference. Both AQA and OCR have online teacher communities: AQA's Teacher Forum is accessed via the A level homepage, and following free subscription to mediastudies-a@community.ocr.org.uk, OCR compiles posts into email alerts to subscribers.

Commonalities and differences

The chapter now considers the rubric and key informing principles to be found in specifications. Page numbers refer to the latest online editions of the specifications at the time of writing in 2011: AQA (2009), OCR version 4 (2009), WJEC (2009). All AS courses echo the structures and key interests of their GCSE courses (AQA cross-media texts, OCR representation and production, WJEC's formula of Text, Narrative and Genre). So progression is straightforward, 'brand loyalty' encouraged and a spiral model of learning sustained.

Assessment weightings

The current broad structures of 50 per cent examination and 50 per cent coursework at both AS and A2 have parity as required by the Qualification and Curriculum Authority (QCA) to ensure standardized quality. The higher weighting of coursework from 40 per cent in the legacy specifications to 50 per cent was lobbied for to reflect the integration of practical and academic study. This was agreed because, unlike GCSE, A level coursework was thought to be more under the control of teachers. All specifications have production as part of the coursework for A2, whereas previously it was only OCR – where the production element remains the dominant feature. The legacy A2 coursework of an extended research essay for AQA and WJEC has been translated into a shorter, but still extended, research *Investigation* for the production.

Ethos

All the specifications now share explicit incorporation of digital media; however each has a strongly distinct ethos. The specifications illustrate, though not exclusively, the 'creative tensions' between 'text-based' study and 'people and processes' study noted in Chapter 2. AQA focuses on cross-media study, which is a requirement in three units. Extended research also features in three units as a means to develop students' 'critical autonomy' and personal engagement. OCR has shifted more than the other two Awarding Bodies towards a 'Media 2.0' ethos at A level. At A2 in particular it has closer integration of practical and academic work; and the examination's 'Contemporary Media Issues' section is 'interested in how people, in cultural contexts, use the Media at the end of the first decade of the twenty-first century' (McDougall 2009: 42) rather than a 'media and texts' structure. Students are expected to prepare case studies informed by preferred theoretical approaches associated with 'Web 2.0'. McDougall's *MediaMagazine* article provides a student-friendly explanation and the prelude to the OCR A2 textbook has a rationale for digital media literacy (McDougall 2009: 1–13). WJEC took a 'back to basics' approach familiar to teachers with concept led units, holding back *Institutions* to A2, and focusing on text as the main engagement for students.

Levels of prescription

OCR has the most heavily prescribed of the specifications with a pre-set AS exam topic ('TV Drama' at the time of writing). Production tasks are chosen from a menu of set briefs at both AS and A2. Production evaluations must be electronic at AS and A2, and the research and planning electronic at A2. Making 'writing' with such technologies a requirement moves OCR smartly towards Media 2.0. Pre-set options may limit choice but, as some centres have struggled to set appropriate practical tasks, it is a means to ensure standards. The option range on offer increases dramatically from four at AS to 13 at A2, and any appropriate content can be chosen to tackle the A2 'Contemporary Media Issues' paper.

As noted above, AQA requires a cross-media focus for three units. The range of choice in its pre-set options is narrow: three briefs for AS production work (Creating Media), and two topic areas for A2 'Critical Perspectives', from which students select one brief and option respectively. However, the aim is to coax centres and students to extend the repertoires of genre and form, and there is flexibility within the options. While AQA and OCR allow repetition of media form from AS to A2, WJEC does not. Nevertheless, WJEC is the least prescriptive Awarding Body and is quite straightforward to navigate. It gives more freedom for teachers to choose content and rely on their own professional expertise. Of course, this approach may be challenging for inexperienced teachers.

Engagement with digital technology

Digital media are at the heart of all the specifications but they focus on different aspects, and have differing degrees of compulsion. All centres are expected to have adequate hardware/software for coursework and to incorporate digital technologies as the means and objects of production and study. Habitually, WJEC employs the term 'audience/user', digital media are integral to all unit content and electronic media are options (though limited compared to OCR) for production evaluations. AQA's key theme of cross-media study enabled by digital media is noted above. Both WJEC and AQA strongly promote study of convergence. AQA also provides the option for students to present their 'Critical Investigation' as a DVD commentary or 'wiki-based investigation of at least four pages with links, analysis, comparisons and visual materials' (AQA: 17).

OCR has the most substantial commitment to using digital technology for both production and 'writing'. E-media are compulsory for both AS and A2 evaluations, and for research and planning in the latter. The rationale here is both a broad one of media education adjusting to the ways people are writing and communicating now, and a specific one of choosing the most effective format for conveying content. As these processes refer to, or use, images, audio, video and links to online resources, then blogs, PowerPoint presentations, DVD commentaries and such like, more efficiently enable shared media planning, development of ideas and related reflection. The specification states the potential of the chosen format should be exploited (OCR: 12), a point strongly repeated in the *Examiner's Reports*.

Stretch and challenge

As all specifications now have a strong element of coursework, it is expected that the wider range of skills will enable more students to achieve Grade 'A'. However, the requirement to reach good levels in all skills, especially at A2 will mean fewer 'A' Grade achievements. Annual improvements in students' achievement and concerns about apparent 'dumbing down' at A level has led to requirements for all Awarding Bodies to provide identifiable elements to 'stretch' students. OCR has markedly greater expectations of production skills than previously for both the Foundation and Advanced Portfolios, and 'considerable' theoretical requirements for the A2 examination (January 2010, *Examiners' Report*: 5, 20, 23). For AQA (p. 23) and WJEC stretch and challenge is in 'extended writing' for their A2 *Investigations*; 'extensive research' for AQA's *Critical Perspectives* case study; and the range of media industries and texts required for WJEC's A2 *Media – Text, Industry and Audience* unit.

All specifications expect explicit understanding and application of cultural theory. OCR requires students to be up to date with the latest perspectives, and there are detailed case studies in McDougall and Potimis (2010). There was some reluctance to be too prescriptive here, but helpful suggestions have been put on the *Get Ahead* blog, and recommended theorists are regularly noted in Examiners' Reports. AQA usefully indicates the established theories with which students should engage (AQA: 16) and groups them as 'Analytical' – semiotics, structuralism and post-structuralism, postmodernism and its critiques. The 'Politics and the Media' group are – gender and ethnicity, Marxism and hegemony, liberal pluralism, colonialism and post-colonialism. Audience and genre theories are characterized as 'Consumption and Production'. WJEC's open approach to trust teacher expertise means that such information is not stated in the specifications, but the case studies in the Connell (2010) and theory section in the Bateman *et al.* (2010) A2 WJEC book are similar.

Assessment objectives

Assessment Objectives (AOs) are standardized across the specifications (AQA: 22–23; OCR: 44–45; WJEC: 9). They summarize the breadth of skills to be acquired, and are the guiding principles for teacher planning and student learning. The weightings are similar in all specifications, but minor variations of wording and weightings indicate Awarding Body ethos. Figure 8.2 compares the weightings allocated to each AO in each of the four units across the specifications. The unit orders of AS OCR and A2 AQA have been reversed to enable direct comparison. The AOs show that production coursework is not just about technical skills: 15 per cent (OCR and WJEC) or 20 per cent (AQA) of the production units develop knowledge and understanding through research (AO4) and evaluation (AO2). WJEC and AQA have more emphasis on meaning construction (AO2) and research (AO4) respectively at the expense of production, whereas OCR favours production (AO3).

There are four specification *aims*, which are also standardized (AQA: 22; OCR: 6; WJEC: 8). They reflect the '3Cs' (critical, cultural and creative) of media literacy (see Chapter 2), and additionally 'enjoyment and appreciation' of the media, knowledge of production related processes and contexts, and acquisition and application of research skills are specified. The only variation is the absence of students becoming independent 'in developing their own views and interpretations' in OCR's version of the last aim, though this aspiration may be implicit.

ASSESSMENT OBJECTIVE	AQA AS and A2 Units				OCR AS and A2 Units				WJEC AS and A2 Units			
AO1 Demonstrate knowledge and understanding of media concepts, contexts and critical debates. (OCR . . . using terminology appropriately and with accurate coherent written expression).	Investigating Media	15	Critical Perspectives	10	Key Media Concepts	15	Critical Perspectives	10	Representations & Responses	15	Investigation & Prod.	0
	Creating Media	0		30%	Foundation Portfolio	0		30%	Production Processes	0	Text, Industry & Aud.	15
	Research & Production	5			Advanced Portfolio	5						30%
AO2 Apply knowledge and understanding to show how meanings are created when analysing media products and evaluating their own practical work.	Investigating Media	10	Critical Perspectives	15	Key Media Concepts	10	Critical Perspectives	10	Representations & Responses	10	Investigation & Prod.	8.75
	Creating Media	5		30%	Foundation Portfolio	5		30%	Production Processes	5	Text, Industry & Aud.	15
	Research & Production	0			Advanced Portfolio	5						38.75%
AO3 Demonstrate the ability to plan and construct media products using appropriate technical and creative skills.	Investigating Media	0	Critical Perspectives	0	Key Media Concepts	0	Critical Perspectives	0	Representations & Responses	0	Investigation & Prod.	11.25
	Creating Media	15		25%	Foundation Portfolio	15		30%	Production Processes	15	Text, Industry & Aud.	0
	Research & Production	10			Advanced Portfolio	15						26.25%
AO4 Demonstrate the ability to undertake and apply appropriate research.	Investigating Media	0	Critical Perspectives	0	Key Media Concepts	0	Critical Perspectives	0	Representations & Responses	0	Investigation & Production	5
	Creating Media	5		15%	Foundation Portfolio	5		10%	Production Processes	5	Text, Industry & Audience	0
	Research & Production	10			Advanced Portfolio	5						10%

Figure 8.2 Comparison of specification assessment objective weightings

Quality of written communication

The Quality of Written Communication (QWC) criterion is written into the levels of assessment mark schemes see (AQA: 22; OCR: 45; WJEC: 20). While students learn a range of 'writing skills' in different technologies, essays are the main form of assessment. Students need guidance to be adept at the range of writing styles required for the various examination formats, evaluations forms and research tasks. They have to be succinct, fluent and clear in the now shorter examination responses at AS when they have to write 'sharp focused scripts at speed' (Shea, OCR e-community post 22 October 2010). AQA and WJEC research *Investigations* require sustained complexity amalgamating argument, textual analysis and theory. All Examiners' Reports note the severe hindrance to students' achievement caused by poorly structured writing, notably through reliance on 'dumping' chunks of unrelated or unexplored information instead of selecting and shaping it to structure arguments and analysis.

Advanced Subsidiary (AS) Courses

Undoubtedly, students enjoy the range of learning in A level. As advised in Chapter 12, it is worth ensuring that students are well informed about what to expect of A level Media Studies. Criteria for accepting students for AS are at the centre's discretion and should be flexible, as the range of skills in the course means there are several routes to achievement – but A2 is significantly more demanding than AS. Bright students who are taking Media Studies as an 'extra' subject can find production work too demanding. While less academically able students may like the idea of practical production work more than written work, they may well find that they have to work even harder to manage productions efficiently. The specifications have slightly differing perspectives about prior learning. All agree that a GCSE Media Studies qualification is not a pre-requisite for A level study, but AQA 'recommend that candidates should have acquired the skills and knowledge' associated with such a Level 2 course (p. 23), WJEC perceive any formal or informal media learning and curricular skills achieved at KS4 as transferable (p. 5), of which OCR recommend attainment of 'communication and literacy skills at a level equivalent to GCSE Grade C in English' (p. 6). Therefore, 'taster lessons' organized in Year 11 are usefully informative for students, and setting a pre-course task in such sessions for students to bring to the first lesson of the course will give teachers useful indicators of attitude and ability. While course time might be limited, it is worth having an introductory task during the early AS days of students settling their option choices, for them to be clear about the range of skills and content they will be undertaking.

Figure 8.3 summarizes the content and assessment of the two units that comprise AS level Media Studies across the Awarding Bodies. OCR foregrounds production by having it as the first unit, but it is placed second for the sake of simpler comparison of the requirements.

AS coursework

All specifications strongly make clear that there should be adequate equipment, software and staff training, otherwise candidates will be seriously disadvantaged.

It is advisable for classes to do the same production task, as there is not time to teach all the practical skills. This strategy also supports consistency of marking. Practical skills

AQA	WJEC	OCR
MEST 1 AO1, AO2	MS1 AO1, AO2	G322/3 AO1, AO2
Investigating Media 1 hr 15 mins, exam inc. viewing/reading time	**Media Representations and Responses** 2 hrs 30 mins exam inc. viewing time 3 compulsory questions	**Key Media Concepts** 2 hr exam, inc. 30 mins. screening and note making time.
Section A: Unseen Textual Analysis 4 compulsory short questions on all 4 concepts. Answer booklet.	Texts, Representations and Audiences Unseen Analysis Q.1 Technical codes, visual codes, genre, narrative	Section A: Textual Analysis 'Unseen' analysis of a TV Drama extract. Language and Representation
Section B: Cross-media topic 1 essay question from a choice of 2. Students apply their case study topic using all 4 concepts, features and issues	Q. 2 & 3 Audience and Representation issues drawing on students' case studies.	Section B: Institutions and Audiences Contemporary case studies
MEST 2 AO2, AO3, AO4	MS2 AO2, AO3, AO4	G321 A02, A03, A04

Creating Media
Select 1 from a choice of 3
set cross-media briefs.
Portfolio:
Produce 2 linked artefacts
across 2 media from 2 of the
3 media platforms
 	
5 production stages
Pre-production:
– Research
– Intentions
– Planning
Production
Evaluation: 1,500 words,
must be word-processed
	**Media Production
	Processes**
	3 pieces of linked work
	
	– Pre-production reflecting
	  research and demon-
	  strating planning
	  techniques
	– Production
	– Report: 1,200–1,600
	  words: illustrated report,
	  essay, or suitably
	  edited blog
		Foundation Portfolio
		Choice from:
		4 Set Tasks each with a
		preliminary task:
		Print, video, audio, web
		
		Planning & Research
		Construction
		Electronic evaluation
		answering 7 questions (p. 12)
		using full potential of the
		chosen format

Figure 8.3 AS Media Studies units

development is essential before embarking on assessed production work (see Chapter 11). OCR has formalized the intrinsic value of such preparation into preliminary tasks paired with the set tasks of its foundation portfolio. Although not assessed, marks are lost if the preliminary task is not done, and it is referred to in the *Evaluation* and A2 synoptic examination to reflect on technical skills progress.

The *Evaluation* comprises seven set questions, based on the key concepts and skills progress, which should be given to students before they embark on any coursework. As noted in 'Engagement with Technology' above, the *Evaluation* has to be electronic.

The AQA (cross-media) Production Tasks should evolve out of a Unit 1 (cross-media) topic, so, in effect, planning has to work backwards from the choice of production options (AQA: 8). There are specific areas to cover in the 'five stages'. All the specifications have given a higher profile to planning in the 2008 specifications as essential to successful outcomes in the production process, and encouragement for research to be very focused. WJEC has a planning artefact as part of the assessment, and the reflective 'Report' considers how it was informed by product research. See the *Spy* materials in Chapter 11 for an example of managing WJEC production coursework: digital storyboard and a television sequence. Both AQA and WJEC retain lengthy reflections, whereas the OCR questions in the context of electronic presentation encourages more succinct and manageable responses.

AS examination

Textual analysis skills using specialist terminology are expected to be acquired and are recognized, but the main learning rewarded in assessment is for recognizing how technical codes and strategies create meaning in particular contexts; how they create specific representations of groups, events and places and, at deeper levels, values and ideologies. Asking questions about other media concepts helps to develop deeper levels of textual analysis:

- Whose point of view is dominating and how?
- How is the audience kept in suspense at this point in the narrative?
- How is the webpage constructing a relationship with its user?

Although higher order analysis is certainly the aim, observant, well-articulated description is also a skill. The more detailed and precise the observations are, the easier it will be to reach worthwhile connotations and develop more complex and subtle analysis. So it is worth pushing students to note and consider more than *to say* 'he's wearing a normal shirt' but *to ask* and thereby extend the quality of their response – for example asking themselves: – 'normal' for what? – inside/outside of the trousers? – smart/crumpled, clean/dirty, well/ill fitting, colour? and so on. Hendry's (2008b) textual analysis guide is useful for all specifications.

OCR takes an in-depth approach to learning about meaning construction through examining representation in a genre: contemporary British TV Drama. This hybrid genre offers a wide variety of texts from literary adaptations to soap opera so students encounter a good breadth of styles, narrative strategies and representations. Active group analysis can be undertaken by students using computers to examine 'Quicktimes' (video extracts using Quicktime or other media players). Resources such as Grahame (2009) and Points (2006) have further teaching ideas and stimulating case studies with analytical guidance.

WJEC and AQA's broad approach to analysing meaning construction across a range of texts aims for student confidence in applying this repertoire to any text. Covering such a range can also help to recognize socially significant meaning. However, WJEC has a list of eleven media forms, four socio-cultural groups and events and issues to cover, and a focus on ways audiences and users respond to texts. AQA has all four key concepts (see Chapter 2), though institution is less significant, and the macro influence of platforms on meaning. The concern is to avoid superficial treatments. Case studies of a rich main text and two subsidiary texts give depth and breadth, and students gain personal engagement from giving class presentations. There were concerns about AQA's short exam time and pre-set space to answer four concept questions, but it is suggested that the questions act as prompts to ensure even and relevant coverage of all concepts.

In addition to the 'unseen' preparation, which is the sum of the WJEC course, AQA has a cross-media study in which students investigate the growing interdependence of media texts, how producers seek synergy where possible, and how choice of form influences the nature of a product. Students construct a cross-platform case study within a loose 'genre' topic (see AQA: 7); however there will need to be class modeling and support at this stage in their development. Figure 8.4, for example, is a conceptually based investigation into the 2010 *Sherlock Holmes* television series and website, which can also be adapted for WJEC.

Hendry (2009), an AQA Senior Examiner, outlines key issues, approaches and describes the impacts of technologies with stimulating case studies. The breadth of cross-media and research demands in AQA Unit 1 lay the groundwork for the two extended independent research elements at A2. The 'topic' constructions in both AS units also promote a broader perspective approach to media study as characterizing the AQA course. OCR's *Institution and Audience* section addresses similar territory but takes a self-contained in-depth approach of an industry organization case study in one of six specified areas. OCR (pp. 19–20) provides prompt points and approaches to case studies, and there are schemes of work on the website.

From AS to A2

The significantly higher expectations of theoretical, practical and independent work at A2, need to be established quickly. However, the summer term when A2 begins will be disrupted by university visits, subject trips and so on. A judgment will need to be made about the best way to move students forward, but approaches could include:

- short courses such as self-contained mini-*investigations* (AQA, WJEC) to develop research and presentation skills, followed by summer research;
- more open self-directed research and initial planning for advanced productions to be further developed over the summer.

A2 courses

Figure 8.5 *A2 Media Studies Units* outlines the key content and forms of assessment at A2. AQA position their examination unit first at A2 as it includes a durational research section that students need to start early in the course. However, the order has been reversed for the purpose of more direct comparison.

Learning objective: To analyse the production context, consumption, promotion and reception of Sherlock (2010)

Sources:
Sherlock site www.bbc.co.uk/programmes/b00t4pgh

Background information:
http://en.wikipedia.org/wiki/Sherlock_(TV_series)

Viewing figures:
www.barb.co.uk/

Task: Create a Powerpoint presentation in response to the questions below. Use screen dumps from the website to support your answers.

Secondary research
Find out when and where the show was first broadcast? Why?
How else can the show be consumed?
When was the show released on DVD? Why?
Who is the audience for the show? (Age/gender.) What type of fan might enjoy this type of show? How do you know?
What kind of viewing figures did the show receive?
What kind of critical reception did the show receive? How do you know?

Website analysis
Describe the home-page and entry to the site. What do you notice about the content, layout, use of colour and interactive features.
Who produced the site? Why?
Who do you think the target audience is for the site?
How does your website appeal to the audience? In what ways is the site informative and entertaining? What is the best feature? How might the audience use the site?
What adverts are included? Why?

Fan response
In what ways have fans been able to respond to Sherlock (2010) critically and creatively? Find examples of reviews in fan sites, discussion forums, social networking groups, parody by creating their own video responses.

Marketing and promotion
In what ways has the show been promoted; find at least three examples across different Media platforms (print, broadcast, the Web). Describe the benefits to the producers of each example and which you think is likely to be the most successful in raising awareness and encouraging the target audience to view.

Key words: Home-page; Icon; Interactive

Figure 8.4 Sherlock Holmes cross-curriculum case study

AQA	WJEC	OCR
MEST 4 AO1, AO3, AO4	**MS3** AO3, AO4	**G324** AO2, AO3, A04
Media: Research and Production	**Media Investigation and Production**	**Advanced Portfolio in Media**

AQA	WJEC	OCR
Critical Investigation 2,000 word report or equivalent in a 10-minute DVD commentary, or 4-page wiki. Textually focused: Text, theme, issue or debate relevant to the contemporary media landscape. In-depth 'autonomous research', encourages broadening of opportunities.	**Investigation** 1,400–1,800 words written independent investigation into texts based on one or more of: Genre, Narrative, Representation. The Investigation is direct research for the production. Students working in groups should focus on different concepts to enable full conceptual research across the group.	**Media Portfolio** One brief chosen from a menu of 13 set briefs. One Main, two ancillary tasks in different media. Combination of two or more media. **Presentation of research, planning and evaluation** In electronic format. All stages may be group or individual work
Linked production piece This can be any form including the same form as AS.	**Production** Informed by the investigation. Students must make a different form from AS, but otherwise are free to choose the product.	

AQA	WJEC	OCR
MEST 3 AO1, AO2	**Evaluation** Brief evaluation, 500–700 words or equivalent; explores how the research informed the product. Choice of form: essay, digital slide presentation, or suitably edited blog.	
Critical Perspectives		
Section A: 1 hr, 15 minutes exam inc. 15 mins reading/viewing time		

AQA	WJEC	OCR
Unseen textual analysis 3 compulsory questions Focus on: – Media concepts – Wider contexts – Media issues and debates	**MS4** AO1, AO2 **Media – Text, Industry, Audience** 2 hr 30 mins written paper 3 questions	**G325** **Critical Perspectives** 2 hour written exam 2 sections, 3 questions
Section B 1 hr **Pre-set topics:** – Representations in the Media – The Impact of New/Digital Media Answer one question from a choice of open-ended questions.	Section A: 1 question from a choice of 2 on Media Texts (Genre, Narrative **or** Representation). Section B: 2 questions from a choice of 4 (Industry **and** Audience).	Section A **Theoretical Evaluation of Production** 2 compulsory questions 1a) Evaluate skills development, question on 1 of 5 possible topics. 1b) Evaluate one production in relation to 1 of 5 media concepts.
This is an invitation for students to apply their synoptic knowledge and understanding through using the texts they have studied throughout the course.	Candidates study 3 industries chosen from a list of 8, through 3 texts in each industry. Two of the texts must be contemporary and one must be British. Each question must be addressed through a different industry.	Section B **Contemporary Media Issues** 1 question from a choice of 6 topic areas.

Figure 8.5 A2 Media Studies units

A2 coursework

Although they appear very different in structure these are all holistic production work units. All Awarding Bodies expect substantial progress from AS in the productions reflecting confident use of technology, exploration of media concepts and even 'aesthetic credibility' (AQA). All Awarding Bodies have 'creativity' as one of their performance descriptors; it is a tricky area and teachers should be clear what they are looking for (see Chapter 2). OCR's detailed Marking Criteria (Foundation Portfolio: 57, Advanced Portfolio: 70) are very useful in specifying types and levels of skills. They can be usefully used for skills development with students. (See above for comments about using electronic planning.)

OCR is entirely based on production processes and foregrounds use of technology throughout, so very high production standards, and substantial progress aimed for, and it is quite an immersive experience. There is a wide choice of 13 briefs. Each has a substantial main text with three related ancillary texts, from which two are chosen. The evaluation, guided by key questions in the specification, reflects upon student experience of the creative process, and is delivered as presentations – similar to practice in Higher Education and the workplace. There is no formal essay, but as students reflect on this and the AS production in the essay, they should make notes in relation to key concepts learning for that question.

AQA and WJEC's (Critical) Investigations serve a double purpose of developing extended independent research skills and writing, and as product research for their linked productions. AQA has a very broad scope for students to pursue any contemporary media interest subject to Awarding Body approval. This is seen as a dialogic process rather than rubric checking. WJEC students investigate an area of study by focusing on genre, narrative or representation. If working in a group, AQA students can pursue similar research studies; WJEC students must focus on different concepts so that there is a broad theoretical basis for the production. WJEC students produce a formal essay, which can be demanding to structure (although at time of writing the Awarding Body, like AQA, is aiming to move away from this requirement); AQA has the option of a wiki or DVD commentary option, which makes the 2,000 words more manageable.

Such work offers a chance for students to be fully engaged with an area of personal choice. However, they will need to be taught research skills, how to evaluate sources and to have a timetable with key moments in the process, such as pitching ideas, shared presentations, tutorials, drafts and so on. OCR's required use of electronic media for research and planning is worth trying for the *investigations*. Blogs, wikis, *inter alia*, are also an efficient and dynamic way for teachers to monitor and aid progress. They also enable students and teachers to share information and ideas, including visual and audio images and links on information pages, for instance through messaging features on wikis. Uploading to YouTube for audience response research is another appealing feature of this approach and a means for teachers and students to view model material.

Examinations

The three examination structures are markedly different. AQA and WJEC focus on the academic. OCR's innovation in Section A is to interweave the practical as an element in its own right to reflect on course duration skills development. A second question considers how practical work has aided conceptual understanding, thus embedding an underlying principle of media pedagogy. It is a challenge for students to evaluate in this open way, and a supportive response framework was recently put on the OCR *Get Ahead* blog. The thematic structure of OCR Section B is also a fresh perspective inviting direct engagement with the technological changes brought by the contemporary media landscape and how people experience it. The WJEC exam places texts in their industrial landscapes and students take a broad view of the institutional factors across market sectors that shape media texts and audiences' interactions with them. AQA's unseen paper builds on its AS concepts to incorporate similar wider industrial and cultural contexts and media issues. Its characteristically wide field of enquiry is focused in its final section, in which students respond to an open question within a chosen pre-set topic utilizing the texts and analytical understanding they have accumulated throughout the course.

Summary

The A level review occurred at a time when digital media technologies very quickly became a ubiquitous part of daily life. It was an opportune moment for a subject predicated on cultural change, to start shaping new discourses, and test the resilience of old ones. The new A level specifications offer coherently plotted routes through their interpretations of current media 'events', and a genuine choice of pedagogical approaches to stimulate and engage students in issue that have interest to them. Furthermore, a wealth of high quality materials, resources and support for teachers and students are readily available.

As this chapter has shown, whatever Awarding Body is chosen A level Media Studies is quite complex and includes some detailed, precise demands. Similarly, the sustained workload for both teacher and student needs to be acknowledged from the outset. Nevertheless, with a considered approach to choosing the most appropriate set of specifications, careful planning and preparation, A level Media Studies teaching and learning can be an extremely interesting, stimulating and rewarding experience for teacher and student alike.

As well the 'Further reading' below, 'Recommended resources' contains details of many useful books, materials and resources.

Further reading

Branston, G. with Stafford, R. (2010) *The Media Students' Book* (5th edition), London: Routledge. Targeted at KS5, this book provides a wealth of subject knowledge and incisive analysis of media concepts, issues and debates with fully developed and applied case studies. The regular new editions are testament to its quality and usefulness. A supporting website, at www.mediastudentsbook.com, has chapters from previous editions, extra case studies and further resources and links to the book's blog at http://msb5.wordpress.com/. Roy Stafford's http://itpworld.wordpress.com/ site is another rich source for his global and erudite perspectives on cinema.

Clark *et al.* (2007) *Media & Film Studies Handbook*, London, Hodder Arnold. This is an essential glossary of all technical, cultural, industrial and theoretical terms. It is very accessible to students who will, therefore, have little excuse for not using specialist terminology habitually.

Lacey, N. (2009) *Image and Representation: Key Concepts in Media Studies* (2nd edition), London: Palgrave Macmillan. The book provides a very thorough explanation of the theoretical underpinnings to textual analysis and representation, and narrative and genre theories.

McDougall, J. and Potamitis, N. (2010) *The Media Teacher's Book* (2nd edition), London: Hodder Education. This book targets KS4+; it provides an accessible account of a range of academic theories (with suggestions for further reading) lesson outlines, stimulating teaching strategies and assessment advice. It establishes a case for Media Studies 2.0 approaches and, as one of the authors is Principal Examiner for OCR provides a background rationale for the innovations in the OCR specification.

Recommended resources

Dictionary

Probert, D. (2005) *AS/A Level Media Studies Essential Word Dictionary*, London: Philip Allan
   A dictionary for AS and A2 students directly relevant to AS/A level Media Studies. Entries are cross-referenced to related terms and concepts and include guidance from David Probert, an experienced examiner.

Awarding Body endorsed/partnership books

AQA

Andrews, M. *et al.* (2009) *AQA Media Studies: A2 Media Studies*, London: Nelson Thornes.
Burton, J. and Stephenson, E. (2008) *AQA Media Studies: AS*, London: Nelson Thornes.

OCR

McDougall, J. (2008) *OCR Media Studies for AS* (3rd edition), London: Hodder Education.
McDougall, J. (2009) *OCR Media Studies for A2* (3rd edition), London: Hodder Education.

WJEC

Connell, B. (ed.) (2010) *Exploring the Media: Text, Industry, Audience* (2nd edition), Leighton Buzzard: Auteur (see Specialist Media Studies Publishers below).
   Additionally, the following is a WJEC specification targeted book written by experienced examiners and teachers:
Bateman, A. *et al.* (2010) *Media Studies: The Essential Introduction for WJEC A2*, London: Routledge.

Specialist Media Studies Publishers

English & Media Centre, 18 Compton Terrace, London N1 2UN. Tel: 020 7359 8080. Fax: 020 7354 0133, Email: info@englishandmedia.co.uk. Website: www.englishandmedia.co.uk/.
The Centre's quarterly *Media Magazine* is a subscription publication targeted at A level students and is essential reading. It has clear focused informative articles on case studies, issues and debates for all specifications written by experienced teachers, examiners, media professional and students. There are archived articles and further resources on its website. Subscribe at: www.englishandmedia.co.uk/mm/subscribe.html.
Auteur Publishing, The Old Surgery, 9 Pulford Road, Leighton Buzzard LU7 1AB. Auteur publishes books on Media Studies topics and media texts written by experienced teachers and examiners. Contact: www.auteur.co.uk/.
British Film Institute and BFI National Library, 21 Stephen Street London W1T 1LN. Tel: +44 (0)20 7255 1444. Website: www.bfi.org.uk/. BFI Education produces the *Teaching Film and Media Studies* series (series editor Clark, V.). Although the series list of titles is no longer growing, there are many existing titles with content that continues to be useful. BFI Publishing books are now managed by publishers Palgrave Macmillan: see: www.palgrave.com/bfi/education.asp and www.palgrave.com/resources/catalogue/pdfs/2010/palgrave_bfi_catalogue.pdf.

Webography of Awarding Bodies' Resources

AQA online support documents:
  www.aqa.org.uk/qualifications/a-level/english-and-media/media-studies.php
AQA Teachers' Media Studies and Communication and Culture Forum: http://services.aqa.org.uk/
  forums/media_studies/index.php
OCR online key documents: www.ocr.org.uk/qualifications/type/gce/amlw/media_studies/
  documents/index.html
OCR online community: mediastudies-a@community.ocr.org.uk
OCR Media Blog *Get Ahead*: http://getaheadocrmedia.blogspot.com/.
OCR Annual Conference: http://ocrmediaconference2011.weebly.com/.
WJEC online resources: www.wjec.co.uk/index.php?subject=22&level=21.
Sign up for email alerts: claire.radley@wjec.co.uk
Annual National Media Studies Conferences
British Film Institute: A Level Media and Film Studies: www.bfi.org.uk/education/conferences/
Film Education CP3: www.cp3.org.uk/.
Media Education Association: http://themea.org/.

Chapter 9

Creative and Media Diploma

Jon Wardle and Emma Walters

Introduction

In 1985 Routledge published *Teaching the Media* by Len Masterman. He identified many of the key issues in media education and offered a blueprint upon which subsequent important contributors such as Buckingham (2003), Burn (2007), Gauntlett (2007), Jenkins (2008) and McDougall (2006) built a more nuanced understanding of, and rationale for, subject discipline. There have been moments of agreement: the introduction of A level Media Studies legitimized the work of the secondary media teacher (now more students do A level Media Studies than Physics); and times of disagreement – the value of sector-related so-called 'vocational' courses. Such diverse views are articulated more comprehensively in McDougall (2006). However, a quarter of a century on it is clear that there is a broad consensus in the theoretical framework for Media Studies that:

- media representations are not reality;
- the media are produced by organizations and individuals and therefore can and should be read critically;
- the media are now not only received, but also reinterpreted by audiences.

There is still some way to go in identifying a comprehensive teaching and learning framework for media education, which seems ironic as recently media educators have articulated a clearer outcome for much of their work – media literate consumers and creators. The key question then is – how important is the connection between consuming and creating?

The tensions that exist have in part been smoothed by books and articles that detail teaching and learning strategies such as David Buckingham's (2003) *Media Education*, which outlines 'a repertoire of teaching techniques' including *textual and contextual analysis, case studies, translations, simulations* and *production* that enable subject knowledge and analysis. This repertoire, in varying degrees, informs most media courses whether they are GCSE or A level Media Studies, or, say, a National Diploma. At first glance it seems that agreements have been built upon and disagreements overcome.

However these strategies, although presented as a portfolio of approaches to media education, have largely been interpreted and enacted in *silos* and segregated the subject rather than supported it. It would seem that the subject has been 'Balkanised' into small groups based on small differences. For example, it is common in most larger media departments for one teacher to focus upon production (practice) and another textual analysis (theory) with the assumption that students, by osmosis, will make the interconnections, which on the whole they do not. Alternately, some smaller departments with minimal staff may be required to deliver both theory and practice, but there is no requirement, and certainly no guarantee, that making connections between the two ends of the theory–practice spectrum should occur.

It is also true that agreements and disagreements between media educators have become more complex. A level and GCSE Media Studies have embraced production more fully, and production-orientated courses have seen the benefit of theory in supporting their students' *cultural capital*, which is seen as attractive to employers and universities alike. All this might suggest that academic and vocational aspects of media education are on a collision course for the middle ground, which would be excellent news as long as it is not simply an 'accommodation'. Clearly, the subject is still experiencing some significant growing pains as a discipline, and two key areas of teaching and learning are still to be fully worked out. The 'how to teach' divide therefore seems to be in two parts:

- It is commonly understood that both theory and practice have a place, but it is less clear what role each takes and what their reciprocal relationship should be. Which, if either, should lead the agenda? Should practice inform theory or should theory lead practice? There is certainly no agreement that they have to be taught and learnt together.
- New media are widely regarded as something to be studied but the impact on the traditional areas of media education – film, television radio, newspapers etc. – is unclear. Are new media forms such as video games, social networking and peer-to-peer file sharing as important as film and television? Can the same theory be used to explore them? (See Chapter 3 for a discussion of these issues in relation to games and Web 2.0.)

Perhaps these two divides, although seemingly different, are actually the same issue: how people learn and what roles teacher and student play.

This chapter seeks to negotiate a possible route through these two debates while also seeking to offer practical help and advice on how to approach media education more holistically. It argues that students' understanding of the discipline is closely aligned to the teaching and learning strategies employed, not simply the material covered through the curriculum. It should be said that many of the core ideas explored in this chapter build upon the dialogic approach to teaching and learning summarized in Chapter 9 of Buckingham (2003).

The not-so-deep divide

Masterman stated that production, although worthwhile as an activity because it allows students to read texts *from the inside*, is not in and of itself media education. He suggested instead that 'the link between practical work and analytical activities needs to be consciously forged by the teacher' (1985, p. 26). Masterman warns of the technicist trap where production work becomes reductionist, first through media education becoming a series of technical operations, and second by students producing work that naturalizes dominant practice through cultural reproduction.

A quarter of a century on it is clear that prioritizing 'kit' – software and hardware – is dangerous if it becomes in and of itself the focus of study as opposed to the means of realization. The boundary between two seemingly opposite worlds of media education is in part caused by the mechanics of how they are delivered. Almost 20 years after Masterman, Buckingham makes similar points about the relationship between analysis and production, asserting 'media production work needs to be effectively integrated with the kinds of critical analysis students are undertaking elsewhere in their courses' (2003, p. 83). Perhaps the telling word here is 'elsewhere': due to administrative and practical difficulties media educators were coming to accept that these things are taught separately. This type of division within media teaching and learning is also evidenced by William Merrin and David Gauntlett in the new versus old media debate: *Media Studies 2.0* (see Chapter 3 for an outline of this debate) in their posts online at twopointzeroforum.com.

David Gauntlett (2004) referred to the late twentieth century as a 'stodgy period' when Media Studies was 'nearly dead'. However, resuscitation arrived in the form of the Web, which marked the beginning of a new phase in media education and radically transformed the role of the audience to one of participation. It presented a platform for audiences to be creative producers from their PCs, and thus impart something of themselves. The *digital era* adds a new dimension to theories of passive and active audiences, and signifies the rise of a more personalized engagement, which paradoxically also celebrates the collective.

Surely these types of activities – planning, production, creation – are the very things many media educators would recognize as the characteristics of what is commonly understood as *media production* and yet, in their posts, Gauntlett and Merrin are talking about Media Studies. Therefore, perhaps a new term is required that neither bias – study nor production, the academic nor the vocational, new media nor old media? This chapter proposes that the term should be *Applied Learning,* and further proposes that the subject should be called *Media Practice.*

For the purposes of this chapter the term Media Practice requires clarification and assertion. The practical application of learning (theory) in a real life context (practice) appears less radical and more logical when considering how pervasive and global the media has become. *Media Practice,* therefore, focuses on developing critical thinkers in practical scenarios. The acquisition and application of knowledge forms its nucleus.

Perhaps more critically the chapter extends this definition to include media facilitators as active participants in *Media Practice.* The media educator's own exploration and engagement should be clearly demonstrated and integral to planning and delivery, thus inciting a culture of applied learning in Media Practice. It is not intended as a displacement of traditional Media Studies (aka Media 1.0), but rather the term signifies its extension. Moving away from the language of yesteryear could help to overcome the division between these two worlds that comes neither from the discipline itself, nor from the student's view of Media Studies, but from the background and cultural traditions of the media educator and subject delivery within a particular institution.

Perhaps as media education has sought to move beyond being seen as an extension of the English department and more recently to reinvent itself for the networked world, some key characteristics of the academic toolkit have been abandoned, while other elements have been overemphasized. For example, in a poetry lesson nobody would question if students were asked to both study the rhyming couplets of say Alexander Pope and to construct some using a theme of their own or one set by the teacher. In fact one activity would be seen to be mutually supportive of the other. Hopefully, poetry teachers would not be tempted to spend hours debating together whether the class described above was vocational or academic and which of the activities was most critical to the students' learning.

To extend the analogy further, it could also be envisaged that the poetry teacher would have no problem looking at both Chaucer and T.S. Eliot in the same lesson, since both are innovators in technique though writing in different styles in different centuries, in different social and political contexts, and for different audiences. Neither is better nor worse, but one does inform the other.

Ultimately, viewing the subject through existing lenses divides educators between academic and vocational, old and new and by virtue, unfortunately, into teacher, practitioner, researcher all of which seems rather narrow and unhelpful. Yet these debates persist, so it is perhaps helpful to identify the spectrums of opinion and the boundaries that exist.

All of the items in Figure 9.1 are important to a greater or lesser extent, but broad shifts can be seen, which must not be resisted, that comprise a move:

- from reception to participation;
- from a small number of big media texts to a larger number of niche texts
- from celebrating a small number of key texts to an acceptance and celebration of a wider range of media.

Others might argue for other shifts such as changes in power. Gauntlett, in a series of YouTube videos (www.youtube.com/user/davidgauntlett01), argues that big media organizations have diminished in importance because of the Web. However, this seems overly simplistic when there is still a licence fee and massive audiences for BBC content. Furthermore, the Web can be a very corporate space – News Corporation owned MySpace and its sale shows that corporations are vulnerable to the effects of change as much if not more than newer smaller players. To both sustain mass audiences and to cater for an increasingly fragmented media landscape the BBC has restructured its activities and remodelled the value it offers licence fee payers from old broadcast quantitative measures to including a platform-based model focusing on quality of engagement. It is perhaps truer to say that big media institutions and smaller less well-resourced producers, bloggers, tweeters etc. are all part of a more complex media ecology.

Aligning the old and new is not easy within existing structures and systems. Friedman (2005) cites the difficulties in upgrading high-speed networks in the UK and US, which would have been structured differently if new web systems had been foreseen, whereas developing countries such as India have a clean slate on which to begin. Perhaps the Diploma in Creative and Media offers a clean slate.

Old	New	Academic	Vocational
The press	Internet	Mass	Personalised
Film	Video games	Critical theory	Niche
Radio	Medium Non-	Audience studies	Production
Television	Specific/Agnostic	Media effects	Participation
Newspapers		Reception	
Magazines			

Figure 9.1 Divisional boundaries in media education

Diploma in Creative and Media: an opportunity for change

The 2008 introduction of the Diploma in Creative and Media (the Diploma) marked a crystallizing moment in the debate between different biases in media education as a means of bridging the gap between vocational and academic learning. The course structure represents an amalgamation of Higher Education (HE) and media employer thinking, each having identified key areas of learning that were not being sufficiently addressed in the education system, which was consequently not preparing learners adequately for either HE or twenty-first-century employment demands.

The employers are represented by Skillset, the Sector Skills Council (SSC) for Creative Media, which is co-funded by industry and government. Its remit is 'to support the improvements to the productivity of our industry to ensure that it remains globally competitive' (www.skillset.org/skillset). It makes explicit the impetus behind the Diploma:

> The aim is to develop critical thinkers, not specialists in a certain area. It is a new way of learning in the context of the creative and media industries and brings learners closer to the reality of the workplace. Students will also develop skills such as communication, teamwork and critical analysis.

Skillset describe the learning philosophy of the Diploma as 'applied', so perhaps this qualification can bridge the academic/pre-vocational gap and be a gateway to the type of learning discussed above. An example of combining academic and pre-vocational approaches can be found in McDougall (2006), in which a detailed lesson integrates theory and production, old and new media – though it should be noted that it is not presented in this case as applied learning:

> Rather than teach about semiotics first and then require students to consider their own production in relation to the theory at the end-point why not teach semiotics through digital image manipulation?
>
> (ibid., p. 52)

Applied learning also means engaging with a very broad list of sector-related disciplines, ranging from television to computer games, and footwear to drama.

> This mixture of discipline headings is not intended as a comprehensive or mutually exclusive list of areas for study or jobs to be trained for, but rather an indication of the possibilities for providing the context for exploring creativity and learning about the realities of working in the creative and media industries.
>
> (Diploma Companion Document, www.skillset.org)

Such variety poses a serious problem for any media teacher, whether from a theory or practice background. Even training HE institutions such as Bournemouth University with 150 staff in the country's largest media school does not have a broad enough academic footprint, so selection is inevitable and tangential areas such as textiles, dance and fashion may be sidelined. The danger is that teachers in school simply choose two or three sector-related disciplines and focus on those, delivering them in the same way that 'traditional' media courses are delivered.

Conversely, such an extensive matrix free of media (and curriculum subject) specificity can easily stimulate experimentation, risk-taking and innovative teaching and learning. The flexibility engendered by the Diploma's more ecological environment, and its focus on themes and issues across media rather than standards and quality mean that technicist and cultural reproduction traps can be avoided, and changes in markets can be adapted to. The interdisciplinary nature of the qualification also strengthens the focus on Personal Learning and Thinking Skills (PLTS) and the four underpinning themes (www.skillset.org/uploads/flash/skillsetcm.html).

Parallels can be drawn with the US, where the New Commission on the Skills of the American Workforce about how 'to better prepare learners for the global economy' had 'a remarkable consensus among educators and business and policy leaders' to bring the content and method of teaching 'into the 21st Century' (Wallis 2006). Twenty-first-century skills identified by Wallis include:

- Knowing more about the world. Kids are global citizens now . . . and they must learn to act that way.
- Thinking outside the box. Jobs in the new economy – the ones that won't get outsourced or automated – 'put an enormous premium on creative and innovative skills, seeing patterns where other people see only chaos' (quoting Marc Tucker, president of the National Centre on Education and the Economy).
- Becoming smarter about new sources of information. 'It's important that students know how to manage it, interpret it, validate it, and how to act on it' (quoting Dell executive Karen Bruett).
- Developing good people skills. She stresses the importance of emotional intelligence for success in the workplace.

These skills are strikingly similar to those at the heart of the Diploma – processing information, reflective practice, capitalizing on strengths, identifying and overcoming challenges, working as a team, problem-solving, thinking critically and innovatively when working with clients and industry. Such transferable skills can also be applied to teaching. Projects can be recorded, say audio-visually, and disseminated to teachers and students across Diploma consortia and beyond and, in the process, break down an 'enculturated' institution-based model of learning (Claxton, 2002, p. 119).

However, much of this is aspirational. Such capabilities are difficult to 'teach' students and, as McDougall has indicated, cannot be learned in a purely conceptual manner through production. Instead the following should characterize the applied curriculum.

Cross media

If an idea is worth discussing as part of a media programme it is only worth discussing in the context of multiple media, and with appreciation of the impact of a wired world. This is not the accepted view. Masterman (1985) argued that 'local analysis', a term he borrowed from Leavis, was the starting point for much media education. Once analysis and criticism had taken place and principles had been established around a single text then those ideas could be broadened out to other texts. In today's cross media world, where everything is networked and interconnected, that no longer seems sensible. Masterman was obviously writing prior to the internet and Web, but even so, others such as McLuhan would have disagreed with him.

For example, it seems counterintuitive to discuss a concept such as narrative by only looking at film or television programmes. A comprehensive approach would include video games, alternate reality games and Web-based dramas as each of these media enable learners to understand that the discourse around narrative is very much alive and that different media, such as these electronic forms, push the boundaries of existing thinking and writing on the topic forward in different ways. Surely learners come to understand the concepts more fully if they make their own narratives to show that they can *apply* their learning from the texts they have studied across media. It perhaps even offers them insights, which allow them to challenge pre-existing thinking and standards. For example, using techniques from film in video games or vice versa.

McDougall (2006, p. 3) argues for something similar by stating:

> My own view is that ideally we would 'do' Textual Studies and move away from academic boundaries that separate poems, paintings, websites and films from one another. This would, for example, create parity between creative writing and video production, as well as Shakespeare and *The Sopranos*.

However, to date this approach is uncommon as Media Studies and production are an agglomeration of largely medium-specific ideas, which rely heavily on teachers having a broad and deep understanding of these topics, and on the curriculum being structured in such a way as to allow it. The Diploma presents the opportunity for a more open and integrated approach. The examples of Diploma units below are for a Level 3 course.

Capture, Unit 1, Edexcel specification (2008, p. 277) presents an opportunity for learners to conduct live consumer profiling of viewer 'uses' of media. It neatly provides a basis for a spectrum of audience theory to be explored alongside the outcomes as they

---

Capture: record via various video and audio sources, log and analyse the data.

Monitor use: What type of media is accessed or engaged with, e.g. internet, web, gaming, mobile phone/iPhone/Blackberry, television, radio, downloading music and video? For how long? In what context, e.g. isolation, with friends, family, as a wider community? For what purpose, e.g. leisure, entertainment, information, social networking, escapism?

Research: Advertisements attributed to each media – the nature of consumer targeting.

Evaluate: Tabulate and analyse data; use comparative analysis to draw out similarities and differences between learners' profiles.

Compare: Different demographics. Select an additional three consumers (of varying age, gender, status, socio-economic background, etc.) and repeat the same activity. This equates to one cohort providing 60 consumer profiles.

Figure 9.2 Student examples of integrated cross-media activities: capture

emerge. A group of say 15 learners can undertake the activities in Figure 9.2 with the aim of developing a deeper understanding of their own and others' consumption and related behaviours.

Once captured, logged and compiled learners discuss: current consumer uses and trends of media in relation to earlier reception theories such as the Uses and Gratifications Theory (Blumler and Katz, 1974), consumption (Baudrillard, 1972) and participation in the construction of identity such as Gauntlett (2007b).

Learners, therefore, use and act upon their findings to prompt theoretical relevancies. The data can be used as a premise to explore the roles of audiences as meaning-makers and the personalization of one's assertion of the self. This live task embeds the wider footprint that now belongs to 'creative media' in practical and theoretical activities.

Process-oriented *and* product-orientated

Since the 1970s, when media education programmes started to experiment with production as a part of the media curriculum, there has been a tendency for the final production artefact to become fetishised by both teachers and learners. In part this is due to media education becoming more employment-sector focused and many students signing up for media programmes because they want to work in a related industrial field. The problem is often exacerbated through assessment procedures that bias final product over the 'working out'. Yet employers and universities alike want students who can work in teams, think critically and creatively, and who demonstrate initiative and tolerate uncertainty. Therefore, it seems ironic that more credit is given to the final product, when it is the *process* of getting to that product that needs to be visible enough for universities and employers to identify the necessary capabilities in candidates for further study or employment.

Claxton identifies process-driven learning as fundamental to the rethinking of pedagogic practice:

> The problem is that, for all this flurry of activity and innovation, the experience of many young people in schools and classrooms has not changed dramatically in generations. The emphasis has remained firmly on the content to be learnt rather than the processes of learning.
>
> (Claxton, 2002, p. 51)

In addition, he believes that in order for facilitators to move into the twenty-first century, they need to realize that:

- Students can learn to learn more effectively.
- Many of their difficulties are actually opportunities to strengthen their learning power.
- Strengthening learning power is what education for the twenty-first century should centrally be about.

> (ibid., p. 52)

Ironically, media educators might better facilitate learning from the processes encountered if they themselves explicitly share and deconstruct the processes at the heart of their pedagogic planning and allow learners to respond and inform future direction. However alien it may seem, it is interesting, and perhaps more realistic, to set projects or tasks that teachers may have difficulty with in terms of the predictability of the actual outcome. The idea of stretching learners inevitably involves a stretching of pedagogic practices. The suggestions offered in Figure 9.3 invite elements of risk, experimentation and uncertainty. The learning process therefore can be viewed as far more fluid, responsive and ultimately demonstrating applied learning as a two-way process based on the conditions of co-existence.

Valuing the learning process does need more than words however, it requires a change in our assessment methods. The rise of peer and self-assessment indicates a promising development as does the re-emergence of the workbook and the 'crit' as a means of digging below the surface of the production. Certainly, Claxton's principles above would enable educators to pay proper attention to these activities.

Audience-focused

Apart from the *Evaluation* unit, all of the principal units on the Diploma, including *Capture, Show, Interaction, Commission* and *Investigation,* are anchored by some aspect of the concept of *Audience,* such as client, partner, target audience. Therefore, close consideration of what is meant by the term *Audience* is required.

The specification lacks detail and reference to the changing role of the *Audience,* as we have traditionally understood it, to one that is participatory. This represents a key area of exploration (for both learners and facilitators equally). Teaching and learning about *Audience* ranges from: production, students being asked to target a particular demographic group, through to traditional models of investigation around the study of the flow of information from producer to receiver. Some of this work is still valuable but it is a much more complex picture now that audiences are more fragmented and becoming producers as well. At the heart of this work, though, is still the notion that the socio-cultural determinants around a text are not fixed, and that individuals make meaning out of these texts and their associated determinants in ever more complex and sophisticated ways beyond that articulated by Ang (1985), Fiske (1987) and Hall (1981) to something nearer to Barthes (1973) and Gauntlett (2007).

It still appears that conversations about audience take place around the work of third parties. A variety of new and creative methods are emerging that seek to allow media practitioners and researchers to interpret audiences' beliefs and understanding in ever more authentic ways: Gauntlett (2007), for example, illustrates the power of these more creative methods in his book *Creative Explorations.* However, the starting point for students should surely be their own practice, such as the News project in Figure 9.4. Whatever form is used for self-evaluation, reflection on and analysis of their own artefacts enables students to more effectively understand the factors that shape other people's products.

The teacher as facilitator

In *Psychology and Education,* Bentham (2002) discusses how Rogers (1977) identified a 'person-centred' approach as a means of unlocking the learning experience. He describes 'non-directive pedagogy as the opposite to didactic instruction' (Bentham, ibid., p. 31). Kolb's *Learning Cycle* (Bentham ibid., p. 11), Claxton's (2002) notions of *Building Learning Power* and Gauntlett's (2007) *Creative Explorations* are extensions of Rogers' educational philosophy.

Evaluation, Unit 5 in the Edexcel specification (p. 369) presents the opportunity to make explicit the processes encountered as a result of the learner journey as he/she progresses throughout the course.

The project suggested here is entitled *Multiple Faces* with each face representing a principal unit on the course. The idea is that each face (a relevant metaphor, a photograph or image selected by each learner) has a 'process capsule' attributed to it that identifies and represents how each process contributed to decision-making. It is important that learners make visually explicit all processes undertaken (e.g. photographs of mind maps, of people interviewed, of meetings attended and/or mobile footage of testing ideas out, animation, blogs, video diaries or audio diaries with a bank of *Flickr* photographs to support the emerging narrative) in order to communicate their thoughts and ideas to the viewer. All non-electronic evidence (2D, written work, mind maps, role-play etc.) should be clearly labelled, photographed and stored in a designated Flickr file.

There is a multitude of ways to present the capsules and other ideas should be discussed with learners. Providing the evidence is tangible all formats and styles should be encouraged. This offers learners the chance to experiment with new equipment and techniques – itself integral to their learning process.

The practicalities and potential modes of creating the capsules add a further dimension to the notion of process and reflective practice. The methods by which learners *choose* to represent themselves opens up opportunities to explore theoretical underpinning issues, such as identity and representation, at the core of the activities. Learners engage in the construction of reality in the selection processes of capturing the evidence. The interpretation of such decisions and behaviours opens the floodgates to questions of truth, context, performance and subjectivity, etc. A semiotic self-reflexive examination can then support and accompany the capsules created.

It is advisable to apply basic criteria to video diaries (e.g. What am I doing? Why am I doing it?), and to include learner responses to interim feedback. Blog entries are useful tools for self-reflection but establishing criteria is essential for assessment purposes; e.g. learners could identify where PLTS are used, and include how their reflections are relevant to unit outcomes. Blog evidence can demonstrate independent thinking, detail the strengths and challenges of working collaboratively, and ensure that any work that is not their own is referenced).

Most critically, the Evaluation Unit involves a four-hour externally assessed examination at the end of the two-year course. The word count is set (*Unit 5*, p. 383) and electronic files of such visual methods will assist the recollection of events and better prepare learners for the specified exam requirements.

Figure 9.3 Student examples of process-driven activities: *Multiple Faces*

Interaction, Unit 3, Edexcel specification (p. 325), involves reflecting community or minority group interests or concerns. One way to tackle such a project is to devise an interactive news site specific to a selected community, in this case the learners. The benefits of a news site are three-fold:

1) It places the audience as the key driver of content, therefore shifting the control to the user not an editorial team/producers.

2) It is designed around the active participation of the voices/ narratives within the community of learners. Members of the community can be represented in many forms – as interview subjects, initiating and uploading their own stories, or simply commenting via email or on a designated blog or forum. Therefore the production practices serve to reiterate learner understanding of a participatory culture in a very real context. It is a practical exploration and application of how the Web repositions ideas of democracy (extending Habermas' notion of the 'public sphere,' 1989). This suggested approach presents a clear platform to introduce discussion on collective intelligence, convergence culture (Jenkins, 2008), and the potential power of a networked audience.

3) An interactive news site can be applied to all disciplines affiliated to the Diploma. It is generic because news can be applied to all fields of interest.

The relevant disciplines would need to collaborate on editorial/production considerations (e.g. content, style, layout, participatory capacity, photography, etc.), and adapt the agenda as stories develop.

The idea is process-driven, positions the audience as central and demonstrates a vital theoretical underpinning. Arguably more importantly it places 'applied learning' – the nucleus of Media Practice as fundamental.

Figure 9.4 Student examples of audience-focused activities: news site

Of equal importance is the concept of *scaffolding,* based on Vygotsky's *zone of proximal development,* 'a process whereby, through language of a shared communication, a more skilled individual is trying to impart knowledge to a less skilled individual' (Bentham ibid., p. 11). Scaffolding enables various types of support to assist the learning process. However, in the context of a converging culture, and a qualification such as the Diploma that demands alternative approaches, it becomes more difficult to define the boundaries between the skilled and unskilled as in the teacher–learner dynamic *both* require scaffolding.

Furthermore, Considine (1997, p. 253) cites Masterman's (1989) statement of 20 years ago that 'the teacher was no longer the arbiter of taste, but a co-partner or investigator in what was now a much more open ended process'. The co-existence Considine describes is extended by Merrin (2009) who places the idea of co-existence within the context of a converging world, hence the requirement to upgrade media education. Such an upgrade is being referred to in places as 'Media 2.0':

Today we can't expect that generation to move into our media. Instead we're having to move into theirs. Either way their current media use isn't a phase: it's too integrated into the structure of their lives, experiences and relationships and succeeding generations will only bring with them new patterns of media use.

Ultimately, perhaps, it is the critical scaffolding that needs to be revived using the skills of the teacher to address issues for students such as: collaboration, problem-solving strategies, face-to-face communication, taking responsibility, improving performance, developing drafts, re-edits, time-management, pitching ideas, interpreting and validating information sources, seeing links between reality and fantasy, adapting to challenges and audience needs and understanding their role in the production of meaning.

It is the role of media educators to support learner understanding of the social ramifications in a culture they take for granted. Quin and McMahon (1997) highlight the need for learners to become more critical and analytical about the media they view and 'use', and to assess the cultural values and ideologies that emerge from this interaction. They state that, 'part of a teacher's task is to make students aware that they do have positions, attitudes and values that they bring to bear in their interaction with the media' (ibid., p. 312).

The Diploma heralds a time for rethinking the media educator's role more broadly. The changes and challenges entailed do not have to be daunting; they can only serve to enrich and diversify media practice itself, and to advance and invigorate the teacher–learner dynamic. Attempting to close the gap between the learners' media world and that which media teachers might define for themselves means teachers stepping into the 'new' territory of the learners' world, as Merrin (2009) suggests. At the dawn of experimentation media education is arguably at the cutting edge, and media practitioners of the twenty-first century need to actively participate in exchanging ideas that challenge traditional structures. Roberts (2006, p. 46) states that the successful implementation of practice will 'involve teachers and leaders collaborating and devising solutions across curriculum areas, or beyond the boundaries of the institution'.

Summary

Connecting the distances between media production and Media Studies, and *new* and *old* media, can be problematic at times for several reasons – cultural tradition, curriculum structures, and teachers' individual aptitudes and pedagogy. This chapter has focused on possible ways, and their potential, to bridge those divides; and proposed a new language to encapsulate the attendant pedagogy: Applied Learning and Media Practice. The chapter also considered how the divides can be bridged in practical ways combined with ideas for moving the discipline forward – in particular by outlining four key areas for future focus: cross media teaching and learning, the importance of process, the role of the audience in refocusing student learning, and implications for the teacher's role. Applied Learning, therefore, should come to be seen as the nucleus of Media Practice, which advances and better aligns media pedagogy to twenty-first-century learners' needs.

Such a standpoint is not about making media education sexy, nor about sensationalizing technological changes. It is about placing the process of learning as central to experiences of the technological environment, and about teachers reconnecting with learners in a culture we share. It is not about technological determinism but about using new communications devices that by their nature challenge traditional methods of understanding, and offer more to explore. In preparing this chapter we have come to sympathize with many of Merrin's and Gauntlett's ideas about upgrading the subject by moving it from spectatorship to immersion, from interpretation to experience, from centralized to ubiquitous media. Such ideas provide theoretical ways to put into practice our belief that *how* we teach is just as important as *what* we teach – something Media Studies 1.0 never fully embraced.

However, we approach this upgrade from a slightly different angle by suggesting that the application of Media Practice is not solely based on the viewer as a 'user' of media in a networked world. Rather Media Practice engages with how phenomena such as consumption impact on the nature of learning and thus can also contribute to advancing the teacher–learner dynamic. Media Practice as proposed here acknowledges pedagogical challenges in the scale, fluidity and complexities of a converging culture, but requires investigation and experimentation in real contexts. Above all, Applied Learning in Media Practice is a responsibility and requirement that both the teacher and learner now share, and forms the nucleus of media education as a stable yet flexible entity to withstand the challenges the future presents.

Further reading

Claxton, G. (2002) *Building Learning Power: Helping Young People Become Better Learners,* Bristol: TLO Ltd. The book is integral to developing the role of 'teacher-as-facilitator' and fundamental to the idea of 'applied learning' as the bedrock of media practice. Substantiated by scientific evidence and elucidated examples, the ideas of resilience, resourcefulness, reflectiveness and reciprocity (aka the four Rs) offer practical ways to enhance the teacher–learner dynamic to one based on co-existence.

Jenkins, H. (2008) *Convergence Culture,* New York and London: New York University Press. This readable and engaging academic text with a plethora of contemporary examples provides the foundations for understanding the meaning(s) behind the term convergence.

Potamitis, N. (2009) 'Play / Make / Learn: creativity and well-being in 14–19 education', in *PoV: The Journal of the Media Education Association*, Summer 2009, vol. 1, no. 3. A stimulating range of activities and equipment for an introductory Level 3 scheme of work for the Higher Diploma in Creative and Media that also addresses the 'Every Child Matters' agenda producing written, oral, web-based and moving image outcomes.

Edexcel Specification – www.edexcel.com/quals/diploma/creative-media/Pages/default.aspx

DP019916 – *Guidance and Units – Edexcel Diplomas* June 2008.

Edexcel Level 1, Level 2 and Level 3 *Principal Learning in Creative and Media*, Edexcel Limited.

Recommended resources

Websites

David Gauntlett's website is extremely practical and informative. It succinctly defines and illuminates 'Media Studies 2.0', and differentiates between traditional pedagogic approaches with a more contemporary perspective that is inclusive of converging cultural practices.

David Gauntlett's and Ross Horsley's website 'Web. Studies': www.newmediastudies.com/intro2000.htm (accessed 24 July 2010).

David Gauntlett's *YouTube* Channel: www.youtube.com/user/davidgauntlett01 (accessed 24 July 2010).

Diploma Companion Document: www.skillset.org/uploads/pdf/asset_13790.pdf?2 (accessed 1 August 2010).

Skillset flash graphic of Diploma / PLTS composites: www.skillset.org/uploads/flash/skillsetcm.html (accessed 9 June 2009).

Skillset remit: www.skillset.org.skillset/ (accessed 9 July 2010).

Time Magazine (online): www.time.com/time/magazine/article/0,9171,1568480,00.html (accessed 24 May 2010).

William Merrin's Blog: http://twopointzeroforum.blogspot.com/ (accessed via May – July 2010).

Chapter 10

Media and citizenship

Elaine Scarratt and Jon Davison

> The Media are undoubtedly the major contemporary means of cultural expression and communication: to become an active participant in public life necessarily involves making use of the modern media.
>
> (Buckingham 2003: 5)

> Citizenship . . . helps pupils make sense of the world today and equips them for the challenges and changes facing communities in the future.
>
> (QCA 2007a: 32)

Introduction

Media and Citizenship education have strong common topics and pedagogical characteristics: both subjects focus on contemporary social issues of interest to students and thereby stimulate their engagement with broader perspectives beyond their immediate world; both share a pedagogy that favours active and critical enquiry. This chapter focuses primarily on introducing the field of Citizenship education to media teachers. Additionally, Citizenship specialists should also refer to Chapter 2 for an analytical framework, as acquaintance with basic media education terminology and media concepts will help planning and learning to focus on, and articulate how, the Media create meaning in addition to textual content. The British Film Institute (BFI) resources in 'Further reading' outline several classroom techniques for those less familiar with moving image teaching.

Teachers are encouraged to look beyond the literal Citizenship Programme of Study (PoS) rubric. The KS3 and KS4 'Curriculum Opportunities' sections (item j) cites 'work on the Media in English and ICT' as a link with 'other subjects and areas of the curriculum'. This is another welcome entitlement for media education, but it is essential to use media education pedagogy to ensure equal subject rigour, rather than the constricted English PoS version. ICT tends to focus on technology processes, and the apparent divorce of meaning-making from choice of technology is reinforced by the separation in the 'Explanatory Notes' of 'Media and ICT'. However, there is much potential in cross-curricular co-operation with ICT. Bazalgette (2009) and anecdotal evidence of ICT teacher attendance at media conferences point to increasing awareness in ICT of meaning-making in 'texts and textual practices', and interest in the media literacy 3Cs – creativity, culture and criticism, as well as aesthetics, and engaging audiences.

This chapter's background to, and summary of, Citizenship education includes suggested media resources for news and documentary, which aim to amplify its non-fiction media element. Citizenship highlights the Cultural Studies aspects of media education through shared interests in identity formation, multiple identities, social diversity and social inclusion. A brief background to the government education policies for these areas, including Britishness, is followed by representations of second generation British Asian Muslims. The films in the case study illustrate how media education can address diversity as well as History and RE, the cited link subjects for this topic in the Citizenship PoS (QCA 2007a: 34). The Citizenship focus here complements the 'Identity and diversity' section in Chapter 4 of this book and employs its theoretical outlines of character typing and identity politics.

Citizenship Education

The New Labour Government's agenda for the social development of students was located within Personal, Social and Health Education (PSHE) and since 2002 in a new curriculum area: Citizenship Education. In November 1997 the Advisory Group on Citizenship Education, chaired by Professor Bernard Crick, was established to provide advice on effective education for citizenship in schools. The resultant 'Crick Report' contained recommendations relating to the development of the knowledge, skills, understanding and values necessary for 'active citizenship' (QCA 1998: 10). The authors of the Crick Report were keen to move beyond the model of *functional citizenship* that had underpinned earlier civics education curricula in favour of promoting *critical citizenship* characterised by active participation.

The Report highlights three 'mutually-dependent' aspects believed to underpin an effective education for citizenship: 'social and moral responsibility, community involvement and political literacy' (1998: 11–13). However, while the school plays a role in this development, it can, in the words of the Crick Report, 'only do so much' (QCA 1998: 9). Such development is the product of complex interactions between children and their homes, and between children and the wider community in which they grow: a community that of course includes a variety of media. Key aspects of the specification have been extrapolated for the purposes of this chapter; the full specification of the National Curriculum order for Citizenship is online at the Qualifications and Curriculum Authority (QCA) web-site: http://curriculum.qcda.gov.uk/key-stages-3-and-4/subjects/key-stage-3/citizenship/index.aspx.

The sub-headings below follow the structure of the PoS.

Importance of Citizenship

Study for both KS3 and KS4 Citizenship are premised on principles of effective citizenship education in the importance of citizenship section, which states that study of the subject provides students with:

- knowledge about their rights, responsibilities, duties and freedoms, and about laws, justice and democracy;
- skills that enable them to participate in decision making and to play an active role in the life of their schools, neighbourhoods, communities and wider society as active and global citizens;
- understanding and respect for different national, religious and ethnic identities.

Citizenship education 'equips students to engage critically with and explore diverse ideas, beliefs, cultures and identities and the values we share as citizens in the UK' and 'develops in them interest in topical and controversial issues and to engage in discussion and debate' (QCA 2007a: 41).

Key Concepts

The Citizenship programmes of study at KS3 and KS4 comprise three *Key Concepts* (QCA 2007a: 42–43):

- democracy and justice;
- rights and responsibilities;
- identities and diversity.

As well as developing knowledge and understanding about the political and judicial systems in the UK and in other countries, students are expected to explore concepts of fairness, justice, power, authority and accountability. Central to this exploration is an understanding of the necessity of active participation in order to scrutinise, test and challenge authority where appropriate in a democracy. Students are also expected 'to explore contested areas surrounding rights and responsibilities, for example the checks and balances needed in relation to freedom of speech in the context of threats from extremism and terrorism' (QCA 2007a: 43).

In 2007 the DfES *Diversity and Citizenship Curriculum Review* was published. This independent review, led by the former headteacher of Deptford Green School, Sir Keith Ajegbo, made a series of recommendations aimed at promoting diversity across the curriculum, and in the curriculum content of Citizenship education. The key proposal was inclusion of a new element entitled *Identity and Diversity: Living Together in the UK*, which became the third Key Concept in the revised 2007 National Curriculum Order for Citizenship. This third key concept requires that 'all students, regardless of their legal or residential status, should explore and develop their understanding of what it means to be a citizen in the UK', and 'the multiple identities that may be held by groups and communities in a diverse society, and the ways in which these identities are affected by changes in society' (QCA 2007a: 43). An Explanatory Note in this section sums up the third Key Concept agenda:

> Community cohesion: Citizenship offers opportunities for schools to address their statutory duty to promote community cohesion.
>
> (QCA 2007a: 43)

Key Processes

The three *Key Processes* (QCA 2007a: 44–45) include:

- critical thinking and enquiry;
- advocacy and representation;
- taking informed and responsible action.

Understandably, many of the skills and attributes to be developed in students through the key processes relate to critical thinking, enquiry, analysis of evidence, synthesis, advocacy and debate through the exploration of social, political and ethical issues, including those that are controversial. The skills and attributes are seen as foundations of active citizenship. One might also say that they would be the perfect foundations for the highest quality journalism. However, although a related Explanatory Note promotes 'lobbying and communicating views publicly via a website, campaign or display; setting up an action group or network' (QCA 2007a: 45), surprisingly, there is no explicit link to the Media within this section.

Range and Content

The *Range and Content* of the KS4 PoS comprise the very stuff of daily media output in all its manifestations including, *inter alia*,

> political, legal and human rights and freedoms . . . contexts from local to global . . . civil and criminal law and the justice system . . . how laws are made and shaped . . . the work of parliament, government and the courts . . . actions citizens can take in democratic and electoral processes to influence decisions locally, nationally and beyond . . . other forms of government, both democratic and non-democratic, beyond the UK . . . the development of, and struggle for, different kinds of rights and freedoms in the UK . . . the impact and consequences of individual and collective actions . . . impact on the environment . . . rights and responsibilities of consumers, employers and employees . . . origins and implications of diversity and the changing nature of society in the UK . . . the impact of migration and integration on identities, groups and communities . . . the UK's role in the world . . . the challenges facing the global community, including international disagreements and conflict, and debates about inequalities, sustainability and use of the world's resources.
>
> (QCA 2007a: 46–47).

It would be no exaggeration to say that comprehensive examples of all of the items listed in *Range and Content* may be found in the media output of any week in any year. It is, therefore, particularly disappointing to look at the PoS in relation to the Media. There are only a few direct mentions to be found: one of the fourteen items in *Range and Content*, and one of the ten items in *Curriculum Opportunities*.

Curriculum Opportunities

The variety of Curriculum Opportunities comprise what might be expected in a programme of study intended to promote Sir Bernard Crick's 'active citizenship' (QCA 1998): discussion, debate, individual and group work, school- and community-based citizenship activities, participation in collective action, including campaigning and working with community partners and other agencies to address issues and problems in communities. The rubric about the media – 'how different media inform and shape opinion . . .' suggests a broad range of media; but the content – 'public debate', 'policy formation', 'pressure and interest groups', 'those in power' – invokes only news and current affairs forms. The implied focus on non-fiction also unhelpfully reinforces the strange conflation of 'media and non-fiction' in the English PoS.

KEY STAGE 3 (QCA 2007a: 32–33)	KEY STAGE 4 (QCA 2007a: 47–48)
Range and Content	**_Range and Content_**
d. freedom of speech and diversity of views, and the role of the Media in informing and influencing public opinion and holding those in power to account	**g.** how information is used in public debate and policy formation, including information from the Media and from pressure and interest groups
Curriculum Opportunities	**_Curriculum Opportunities_**
i. use and interpret different media and ICT both as sources of information and as a means of communicating ideas	**i.** use and interpret different media and ICT both as sources of information and as a means of communicating ideas
Explanatory Notes	**_Explanatory Notes_**
Media and ICT	**Media and ICT**
This includes: using different media and ICT to communicate ideas, raise awareness, lobby or campaign on issues; using and interpreting a wide range of sources of information during the course of enquiries and research; and learning how different media inform and shape opinion. Pupils need to evaluate the extent to which a balanced or partial view of events and issues is presented.	This includes: broadcast media, print media and ICT as a means of disseminating information. Students should examine the extent to which the Media reflect, distort and create opinion; the use that politicians make of the Media in communicating with the public; and the use of the Media by other groups wishing to influence public opinion and those in power.

Figure 10.1 Media in the citizenship curriculum

As noted in the introduction, the separation of Media and ICT is also misleading. There may have been an intention to highlight digital media, for example there are stimulating internet models sych as 38 Degrees (http://38degrees.org.uk/) for organising campaigns; and interesting issues are raised about comparative effectiveness, for instance why the UK 'youth' electorate responded to the 'traditional' media of prospective prime minister TV debates in 2010 rather than electioneering via social networking sites. Given the speed of changes in the ways audiences use new technologies to access news, a more accurate approach would be to indicate the '360 degree' (cross-media) content and distribution of news provision. The same story appears in: print and online newspapers, terrestrial and satellite television, radio, RSS feeds to laptops, mobile text messages, podcast subscriptions, journalists' blogs, user-generated content, alternative news websites and so on. This will help students to understand the influences of context (producer, media form) as well as text in meaning construction.

News

> Our journalistic training tells us to go for the most dramatic story.
>
> (Roger Harabin, BBC Radio 4, *The Today Programme*, 26 August 2010)

> The news has an authoritative voice, but it never says 'we had a big argument in the office, this is the best we've got at the moment so we're going to run with it'.
>
> (Jimmy Wells, Founder of *Wikipedia*)

News stories are rewarding for language and ideological analysis, but knowing about production processes and institutional constraints gives fuller understanding of news stories and their political implications. Questioning news sources, the reasons for selecting and discarding stories, how they are presented and so on prepares students for informed critical citizenship.

Evaluation is essential for this outcome, but the analysis implied in the *Explanatory Notes* assumes a passive effects audience model – how the media 'inform and shape opinion' (KS3), 'extent . . . the media reflect, distort and create opinion' (KS4). Crick (1989: 59) adopted a 'defensive' approach for students to be 'adequately equipped with ideas and information which counteract those they get from the media'. Institutional knowledge means that students know that newspapers are politically partisan by nature; their targeted audiences choose them, journalists' blogs, TV channel news, and so on according to their own world-views. More substantial representational differences are available through digital TV channels such as *Al Jazeera* (www.freeview.co.uk/Al-Jazeera, http://english.aljazeera.net/) that can challenge 'naturalised' Western assumptions and reflect those of the middle-Eastern British population. Small-scale qualitative primary audience research by students can find out people's reasons, pleasures and uses for their choices of news sources.

Public Service Broadcasting (PSB) in the UK is required to be impartial but, as the BBC Editorial Guidelines imply, realistically it is a sincere aim, not a description of achievement: 'we should do all we can to treat . . . subjects with due accuracy and impartiality'. Meanings can be perceived regardless of conscious intent. The BBC's refusal to broadcast an appeal for Palestinians in Gaza after the Israeli invasion because it might imply political empathy was strongly criticised (*Telegraph.co.uk*, 24 January 2010); whereas an appeal following the Haiti earthquake, a 'neutral' natural disaster, was but students can consider whether it also added to the negative stereotypes of victimhood in poor black countries. News is 'therefore inevitably "biased"' (Grahame, 2006: 7); investigating the nature and sources of the inherent bias is more informative than trying to assess the 'extent' to which the media reflect, distort and create opinion.

All this is challenging learning, especially for non-specialists. Grahame's account of an interesting and ambitious English/Media/Citizenship KS3 CPD news project outlines some difficulties, but also imaginative outcomes (2008/09: 23), such as ownership role-plays. There are several comprehensively informative resources with stimulating pedagogy for KS3-KS5 such as Grahame (2006), a cross-media pack for Citizenship, PSHE, Sociology and English as well as specialist media study. For instance, an editorial team simulation to choose news stories leads into discussions of news agendas and values. In *A Window on the World?* (BFI), students, for example, explore meaning construction for different media forms and audiences in a generic translation activity for a news story across broadcast, online and written texts, and plan its presentation for a proposed news programme targeting young adults.

The best ways to explore production conventions and constraints is through practical work and critical reflection. The BBC's *School Report* is an established annual event, supported by extensive website materials in which KS3 students gather local news stories to broadcast online. They benefit from working with professional practitioners (and their work ethic). Critical reflection can discuss the imperatives of established conventions, how production processes affected the stories, comparison of the BBC's journalist news values with academic versions (Grahame, 2006: 154–157), what alternative approaches there could be. Models of such work can be short-lived but at the time of writing *Listen Up!* (http://listenup.org) is a global network of youth-made media about political and personal issues. *Current TV* (http://current.com) is an online one-third viewer-generated content initiated by Al Gore in 2005 to 'provide a different outlet for independent points of view and young adults, and to democratise the Media' (David Eschalany, Brunel University/BFI Television News conference, 2007).

Channel 4's *Breaking the News* (KS4 and KS5) site is a legacy from its *Newsday* project with a similarly high level of educational resources. Smaller scale projects are achievable in the classroom through podcasts. The *Euronews* satellite TV channel has 'No Comment' sequences with only images and ambient sound of an event; students can consider how they would apply the 5Ws journalist questions, and the role of mediation. Buckingham (2000) provides a strong empirical and theoretical underpinning from his research about how young people interpret and respond to political stories on television news.

Documentaries are of course useful for single-issue investigations, and for assessing mode of address and audience positioning. Benyahia (2008) is a useful guide and her case studies include the politics of food in *Supersize Me*. The *Blood, Sweat and T-Shirts* (2008) series on the BBC3 youth channel has extracts on *YouTube*. It is an accessible resource for 'local and global' issues in which fashion conscious young adults work in developing world sweatshops that produce their clothes, and react to camera accordingly. *Black Gold* (2006) is a documentary film about Tadesse, the Manager of an Ethiopian coffee cooperative, trying to get fair trade prices for his farmers (www.blackgoldmovie.com). Their impoverished lives are contrasted with high-end Western coffee culture and commodity dealing in New York.

Citizenship resources include a discussion forum about Fair Trade and a 'Take Action' link to campaign groups; the film's distribution and promotion extras make a useful media industry case study. The DVD is available via the website, and from *TV Choice* with an education pack.

Identity and cultural diversity

Media has a narrow remit in the Citizenship PoS but the Ajegbo Review advocated a fuller role for critical media literacy. The following extracts from it also provide a rationale to the case study on second-generation Muslim Asians below.

> Even though the white population who live in predominantly white areas might be removed from the immediate personal experience of ethnic diversity, it is still likely to be an issue for them because they encounter diversity through media representations; and in a world of increasing mobility, their experience of diversity in their own context may well change.

(p. 31)

In this 'media generation', where information from all over the world is available at the click of a mouse, we cannot stress too highly the importance of critical literacy, which must be enhanced in schools in all areas of the UK, regardless of demographics. Pupils need to be able to interpret reports and develop skills to interrogate and make judgments about how their meaning is constructed and conveyed. While different localities may have different contexts, the Media, especially the press and TV, are universally available and afford all pupils opportunities to explore diversity and its representations. Critical literacy is crucial: if you are white, for example, living in a white area, how do you relate what you see on the television to your idea of being British and the nature of British society? If you are black, how do you interpret programmes on AIDs and famine in Africa, or inner city issues in America? If you are Muslim, how do you cope with the barrage of media images about terrorism or the veil? Schools must play their part in recapturing the middle ground for groups who are misrepresented.

Stereotypes are an insult to an individual's identity and can lead to frustration and demoralisation. These are likely to have a considerable impact on the individual and the wider community, which in turn knocks on to achievement levels. One of the black boy pupils we spoke to thought society saw black boys as 'hanging around streets, not clever, mucking around', and a Muslim pupil felt that 'everyone thought Muslims were terrorists'. The 2005 MORI report states that young people in England and Wales rely on TV for most of their knowledge of the world – 80 per cent of them said this was their main source (p. 70). Issues about refugees and asylum seekers have been much reported in the Media; the Refugee Council produces some invaluable resources for schools. Clearly such resources cannot be used without clear thinking by the school about where and how; but they provide useful support (p. 109).

The Citizenship PoS focus on non-fiction media overlooks how fiction can prompt deeper and more detailed engagement with social and personal issues. Much audience research shows that soap operas are a catalyst for reflective discussions that would otherwise be difficult to initiate both inside and outside school. Comedy sketches such as 'Going for an English' in *Goodness Gracious Me* (see YouTube) benignly invite challenges to stereotyping. TV dramas such as *Criminal Justice* make abstract concepts more tangible (see *Doing TV Drama*, English & Media Centre). Fiction films are important social documents as they reflect the contemporary social, cultural, historical, political and economic conditions in which they are made. For Amnesty International films can be affectingly informative:

> Film – used with integrity – is a very powerful medium. It often expresses complex issues in a more direct way than is sometimes possible with several thousand words.

> It also potentially provides access to these issues for large audiences, including young people, who would not consider them otherwise.
>
> (Tom Hedley, Chair Amnesty International, launch
> of National Schools Film Week, 2006)

The great claims for films are their humanity and transformative potential. Further rationales for using film can be found in the BFI and Film Education resources below.

Multiple identities

Identity and cultural diversity raise questions about how far towards the sociological and ethnographic theory of Cultural Studies media education should go. Exploring these issues quickly reveals the complexities of 'identity formation'. Hall (1994: 225) describes continuing processes of unity and commonality ('being'), and discontinuity ('becoming'). Friere (1972, 1976) sees human beings in this process of 'becoming' as active historical and cultural agents in a process of reflection upon their own and others' actions. 'Becoming' is achieved through a process of 'dialogue' between the discourses of social institutions – the family, schools, churches, clubs, ethnic groups and so on. Discourses are cultural activities (Lankshear 1997: 17) involving use of language, ways of thinking, believing, valuing and behaving, which offer new and different ways of seeing the world. As the Media proliferate and target young people, they are increasingly cited as the primary discourse in identity formation:

> The media, it is often argued, have now taken the place of the family, the church and the school as the major socializing influence in contemporary society.
>
> (Buckingham 2003: 5)

However, social and discourse theorists (Freire 1985: 45–49; Mercer 1995) clearly differentiate between family as the primary discourse and the remainder as secondary.

National identities: Britishness

Complex personal, cultural, national, global identities overlap and shift. National identities are cross cut by transnational identities (European, Commonwealth) and their secondary discourses (political systems, economic, social class, religions). These identities interweave and shift with 'different intensities of affiliation and allegiance at different times' (Crick 2008: 33). If humans live in a state of constant mutability but creating social inclusion entails belonging to an identifiable entity, such as the British nation, how is a sense of social inclusion achieved on such a large scale?

Impressed by America's strong sense of common national identity and values, former Prime Minister Gordon Brown attempted to transplant similar attitudes in Britain. Arthur (2007) points out the fragility of assuming that being British means having a national identity as we have no clearly defined sense of nationality like the Americans and French. Politically, the four nations of the United Kingdom of Great Britain and Northern Ireland (England, Northern Ireland, Scotland and Wales) were not a national entity until the Acts of Union in 1707 created this constitutional monarchy, many argue, to resist Catholic Europe. There is also a debate about being British at a time when increasing numbers are choosing to describe themselves as English, Scottish, Welsh and Irish. Since the Northern Ireland Assembly in 1998, there has been further devolution into the sub-national governments of the Scottish Parliament and the National Assembly for Wales. According to Crick, Britishness accommodates a sense of dual nationalities that are not necessarily mutually exclusive: Welsh/British, Scots/British. The Northern Irish Unionists are decidedly British, the duality is an ethnic divide between the Protestantism that defined Northern Ireland's separation from the rest of Ireland, and its 20 per cent Catholic population. The Celtic nations have confident cultural identities, if there is a national identity 'problem' it is the use of British/Britain when English/England is more accurate. Arthur argues that Britain is increasingly fragmented and many of the sub-cultures within multi-ethnic Britain have been turning inward. In the context of the relentless individualism of a consumerist society this puts the concept of Britishness at risk.

Anderson (2002) catalogues the inherent unreliability of standard markers such as geography, politics, biology, race, ethnicity. A nation is far too vast an entity for all its members to know each other, yet 'vital to the sense of a nation is that its members form a unified community of people with shared interests and concerns and institutions'. Politicians therefore promote identity based on shared 'British' values, but as Arthur points out, this is also problematic. Characteristics cited by Brown (*Britishness*, BBC Radio 4, 3 April 2009) as distinctively British – tolerance, fairness, liberty, democracy, the law, even football – are shared by many other nations. (Also see 'Ten core values of the British identity' *Telegraph.co.uk*, 27 July 2005, and 'Politeness? Reserve? Stiff upper lip? Not bloody likely', *TES Connect*, 5 March 2010). Britishness, as the BNP activity below illustrates, is too often built on myths of selective historical moments – Gloriana, Empire and so on. Anderson proposes that:

> unification of people in the modern nation is achieved . . . by cultural means . . . in particular the role of the national media and the education system in enabling a nation to imagine itself as a coherent, meaningful and homogenous community.

The complexity of historical and modern Britain has shifted the focus in education to valuing diversity as a significant key to social cohesion and thus a means to actively maintaining a 'sense of nation'. It is argued that homogeneity does not necessitate single identity; accommodating diversity is equally integral to a unifying sense of identity.

Historically minorities have not fared well in the national media, but representations have broadened over time through lived experience and through equal opportunities and public service policies. Such policies, particularly in media with PSB remits, include the BBC's to 'engage the totality of the UK audience' (www.bbc.co.uk/info/policies/ diversity.shtml). The advent of Channel 4 in 1982 brought a remit for visibility and access for minorities, now articulated as a promise to 'reflect the diversity of Britain; culturally and geographically': (see 'Statement of Promises': www.channel4.com/about_c4/promises_ 2001/promises_intro2.html). The internet has of course played its part in democratic access for people to represent and disseminate their own 'voices'. Research by Ipsos MORI (2007) into16–21 year-olds' attitudes to nationality provides useful statistical and qualitative classroom material.

Classroom activities

Exploring personal identity

Starting with the personal and local is an accessible way into the complexities of this concept, and understanding why diversity is perceived as a social value. Students make identity maps in any visual format. Brett (2002: 5) suggests two multi-ringed diagrams starting with personal information in the centre and opening out to broader spheres: place identity (home, street, town, region, etc) and social and cultural identity (family, ethnicity, local activities, religion, accent, languages, football team supported, etc.). Discussions in groups and then as a class quickly reveal their common and many different characteristics.

Constructing British identity

The simplest strategy, and clearest way for students to see the construction of British identity operating, is through propaganda. It is often produced at times of national crisis like *Island People* (1940) during the Second World War. Part of the BFI DVD compilation *Essentially British? Exploring Citizenship &'Britishness' Using Film*, it has related resources at: www.screenonline.org.uk/education/id/1265832/classroom.html. *Island People* uses the uniting metaphor of the family through four groups of images: industries and businesses, jobs and who does them, leisure, and family activities. Students can identify the content of each category, and how audio-visual techniques such as camerawork, music, voice over, editing (especially juxtaposition of images) reinforce the national unity message. They could follow up with a proposal for how they would represent Britain today. Students could also research the origins and meanings of symbolic national images such as Britannia, John Bull, the British bulldog and political constructs such as 'Cool Britannia', then suggest one of their own.

Ideological challenges

The title of the British National Party (BNP) magazine, *Identity*, is a reminder of how discourses are sites of ideological struggle for ownership. The term 'diversity' according to the BNP's website mission statement means 'indigenous' early settlers since the Ice Age such as the 'Celts, Anglo-Saxons, Danes, and Norse'. Using a selection of *Identity* magazine covers accessible at: www.identitymagazine.org.uk/archive.html students can deconstruct the versions of Britishness they promote. It is worth pausing here to differentiate between patriotism and nationalism. Crick (QCA 1998: 35) sees the love of one's country, its familiar common customs, language and traditions to which one has implicit of explicit allegiance as patriotism that can 'appreciate, value and respect complexity and diversity', whereas nationalism is invariably 'unthinking patriotism' that lays a 'claim to superiority over some other'.

Case study

Representation of second generation British Asian Muslims in fiction film

The choice of the case study theme addresses state schools' statutory duty to promote community cohesion and to prevent violent extremism. (See DCSF [2009]) *Learning Together to be Safe*, www.dcsf.gov.uk/violentextremism/toolkitforschools.) The policy encompasses all cultures in Britain but includes a specific focus on promoting understanding of Muslim communities. Fears for national security following the 7 July 2005 London bombings and disturbances in Oldham and Bradford add a political element to this focus in aiming to pre-empt predatory extremist indoctrination of young Muslims. The strategy echoes a comparative process to prevent black youth disaffection and social unrest following the black youth inner city riots in the early 1980s.

Since the 1980s there have been several successful films made by or with British Muslim Asians. The three films selected here represent very different experiences in this broad collective identity. *Yasmin* has the 'cultural schizophrenia' (screenwriter Simon Beaufoy) of the eponymous protagonist challenged when she feels compelled by the aftermath of the Twin Towers attack to choose where her strongest cultural loyalty lies. *Ae Fond Kiss* features a similar choice for Glaswegian British Muslim Casim when he falls in love with Northern Irish Catholic Roisin and tries to gain his family's acceptance of her. Casim's younger sister Tahara however celebrates her multiple allegiances. In *My Beautiful Laundrette*, writer Hanif Kureishi dissolves social group boundaries through the fluidity of personal identity – the white working class and middle class gay Pakistani lovers, the middle-aged mistress's dependence on men derided by a younger woman's fight for independence, the left-wing academic and Thatcherite capitalist brothers, and so on.

This case study aims to challenge stereotyped views of social groups through a variety of representations. As noted in Chapter 4, studying a diversity of texts aids empathetic understanding more productively than the 1970s–1980s politically defensive approach of seeking positive images to counteract negative representations. 'Meeting' a range of individuals on the screen is more akin to lived experience of getting to know individuals rather than social groups en masse. The films' common theme is the relationships between immigrant Pakistani Muslim parents and their children born and brought up in Britain, with which they identify. The children's conflicts as ethnic Britons include wanting to integrate into 'Western' British ways with their peers while retaining loyalty and respect for their parents' and community's values and traditions.

The case study also identifies how a unit of work can address several curriculum requirements:

- *The National Curriculum* (2007: 5): contribute to community cohesion.
- *Whole Curriculum Dimension*: identity and cultural diversity.

Citizenship:

- *Importance of Citizenship*: respect for different national, religious and ethnic identities.
- *Range and Content*: origins and implications of diversity and the changing nature of society in the UK . . . the impact of migration and integration on identities, groups and communities.
- *Key concept*: identities and diversity.
- *Key process*: critical thinking and enquiry.

Media education:

- *Media language*: meaning constructed through narrative, technical codes and mise-en-scène.
- *Representation and values*: challenging stereotypes; social groups (British Muslims, gender, families, sexuality, social class); issues and ideologies (identity politics, cultural diversity, racism, religion, capitalism, extremism); political and historical contexts (1980s Conservative economic policy Thatcherism, 9/11, net immigration concerns).
- *Audience*: how are audiences positioned to empathise with the Muslim protagonists?

One approach is to use *Yasmin*, relatively short at 82 minutes, for a full screening as the main text with comparative extracts from the other two. All the films have 15 certifications due to sex scenes but the extracts below are suitable for KS3–KS4. The films are also suitable for GCSE and A level Media Studies, for instance the textual element of 'Media and Collective Identity' in OCR A2.

Yasmin (2004), Director Kenneth Glenaan, UK/Germany

The production context for *Yasmin* suggests authenticity as it was developed through workshops with local people some of whom appeared in the film; it had regional financial support from Screen Yorkshire, and distribution through Channel 4. The film is set mostly in the Yorkshire Dale mill town of Keighley prior to, and post, the 9/11 attack on New York's Twin Towers. The story follows a young woman, Yasmin, coping with the changed attitudes of colleagues whose lifestyle she has mostly adopted, her family duties as a female, trying to end the marriage of convenience arranged by her father, and the police who arrest her innocent husband and then her under anti-terrorist laws. There are criticisms (Mirza 2005), of unconvincing relationships and cliched victims (Muslims) and antagonists (white working class). Although the film failed to gain a theatrical release it won critical acclaim for tackling raw issues empathetic to the Muslim viewpoint. The following activities are a choice of using short extracts – the opening and ending – to look in detail at media language and citizenship issues, or discussion of the themes in the whole film using textual evidence.

Yasmin: *film themes*

The many issues in the film can be broadly grouped into four areas:

- *Identity*: what it means to be British Asian Muslim in twenty-first-century northern England. The mixture of languages and dialects; re-evaluating faith, culture and relationships; events that test loyalty; representations of Muslim and 'local' women.
- *Race and racism*: prejudice and discrimination in a background of poverty, fear and unemployment; racism within ethnic minorities ('import', 'banana boat'); denial of one's own ethnicity.
- *Culture*: how communities that live with each other know very little about each other; the role of community leaders (Yasmin's father); stubbornness and pride within cultures (family respect and Muslim traditions); the machismo of young Asian men; potential difficulties for partners from different cultures.
- *The impacts of significant external events*: justice versus retribution; the Draconian anti-terrorist rules relying on vagueness ('I can hold you as long as I want to'), innocent phone calls used to condemn Faisal. How trust between communities can be destroyed by war; society using hatred, fear and scapegoats to blame; how it feels to be ostracised by colleagues or society.

My Beautiful Laundrette (1985), director Stephen Frears, UK

The plentiful resources for this film are a mark of its cultural significance – which is the structuring theme in Geraghty (2005). BFI Classroom resources include Chanda with several clips, and Andrews and Clark (2009: 88–92). Chapter 4 cites this film's importance as breaking the conventional typing of British Asians and raising their visibility as an established part of British society. As a 'bold exploration of issues such as sexuality, race, class and generational difference' (Chanda) it is a rich text for Citizenship and representation. There are complex portrayals of characters with both unpleasant and appealing facets such as Omar, his uncle Nasser and Johnny. For some the film reinforces stereotyped prejudices 'about Asians . . . that they are money-grabbing, scheming, sex-crazed people' (Jamal 1985). Writer

A. Opening sequence

Watch the opening sequence to where Yasmin leaves with John in the social services minibus. The film's marketing strapline 'One woman, two lives' captures Yasmin's duality and invites analysis of the dramatic and ideological tensions in her story through the narrative structure of binary opposition. Students can work in expert groups to consider the following questions; the notes in brackets underneath some of the questions are initial pointers for teacher use.

B. Mise-en-scène

What pairs of opposites do we see in the mise-en-scène, what do you think they symbolise?

(Consider youth and age; town and countryside; Yasmin's clothes; the men walking and Yasmin's flashy VW Golf car; the way she speaks and the call to prayer; and so on).

C. Technical codes

How do the technical codes (camerawork, sound, editing) show the split in Yasmin's life; position the audience as empathetic if slightly disorientated observers; create close engagement with Yasmin?

(The audience meets Yasmin's father and brother in the first shot positioned on the street like a watching neighbour; the first encounter with Yasmin is a series of intriguing fast cut close up fragments of her as she reconstructs herself. The contrasting music, the traditional call to prayer and Yasmin's Yorkshire accent and consumerist gloating over her car. The opening has slower paced cuts from long shots to extreme close ups to overhead shots, low positions and movement into the frame.)

D. Narrative prediction

There are several enigmas and unexpected moments that set up later developments. Who is the man in the bed? Who had we expected to perform the call to prayer? Why is the racist graffiti shown twice in close up? Is there more to Yasmin's relationship with John . . . ?

E. The final scene

Is the final scene a satisfactory (logical) resolution to Yasmin's and her brother's stories?

(The resolution is the strongest indicator of a film's values. The conventional resolution for binary opposition is a wish fulfilment in which the conflicting opposites are reconciled – usually with the dominant ideology restored. Yasmin has been politicised by her experiences: she rejects her brother's extremism but decides to reintegrate into her minority community.)

Figure 10.2 Yasmin Activity 1, short extracts

After watching the film expert groups discuss, with textual references, one of the following questions, and feedback to the class:

- What is the wider symbolic significance of Yasmin's journey to work across the Yorkshire Dales and dress codes both to Yasmin and the film as a whole? Consider writer Simon Beaufoy's view that Yasmin encapsulates the 'cultural schizophrenia' of her generation.
- What Western cultural experiences does Yasmin participate in, how is her identity shaped by them? How does her identity and role change during the film?
- 9/11 is the central event that develops the narrative; discuss its impact on Yasmin with her friends and colleagues, within her family (particularly the men) and community.
- What do you think the filmmakers wanted to say with how they represented the police during Faisal's and Yasmin's internments?
- How does the film explore the tension between the younger and older generation of Muslims in the light of the wider political and international developments?

Figure 10.3 Yasmin Activity 2, whole film themes

Hanif Kureishi however refuses the racial 'burden of representation'. Fixed identities illustrated by Cherry's complaint that she is fed up with mixed race 'in-betweens' like Omar, is precisely the film's dispute, pointedly symbolised in the superimposition of Omar's and Johnny's faces in the laundrette mirror. Kureishi favours of a state of the nation allegory critiquing Thatcherite free market capitalism in which profit justified the means by which it was achieved, generated 'materialism and selfishness' (Hill 1999: 211), and hastened the decline of traditional manufacturing industries and trade unions. Johnny, as the defeated indigenous white working class of this process, depends on the favours of the new entrepreneurial class and its fresh energies brought by motivated immigrants.

Scene 10 in which Nasser employs Johnny to 'unscrew' – get rid of a tenant – has challenging representations and issues for students to explore, not least their responses to their audience positioning. The scene shows Nasser's business methods; racist dialogue; the significance of the tenant's ethnicity; the tenant being a poet (in a climate that scorned culture other than High Art); and Nasser's comment 'I'm a professional businessman, not a professional Pakistani. There's no question of race in the new enterprise culture'.

Ae Fond Kiss (2004), director Ken Loach, UK/Belgium/Germany/Italy/Spain

This film offers strong emotional engagement for students to understand the conflicts of straddling cultures. It has the conviction of Ken Loach's social realist credentials and occasional polemic alongside the fairy tale wish-fulfilment of a traditional love story. The film opens with rousing performance of a young woman celebrating the multiple identities she embodies, and could be used as a stimulus for the multiple identities activity above. Tahara, the youngest child in the central family is speaking against a school debate motion:

'This house believes that the West's campaign against international terrorism is fully justified'. She rejects the homogenous representation of 'one billion Muslims in 50 different countries and hundreds of different languages in countless different ethnic groups' and:

> above all I reject the West's simplification of a Muslim, I am a Glaswegian, Pakistani teenager woman – woman of Muslim descent [removes her tie and school shirt to reveal a football shirt] who supports Glasgow Rangers in a Catholic school because I'm a dazzling mixture and I'm proud of it.

Scenes 10–12 plot out the split cultural dilemmas for Casim and Tahara. Casim is told by his seemingly Westernised friend Hammid why he must choose his family not a 'nobody' (Roisin), and culminates in Tahara breaking the news to her parents that she has been offered a place at Edinburgh University 30 miles away and wants to leave home for the full student experience. The scene fully exploits the power of sustained close ups as she expects support from Casim but he is frozen with distress. The scene illustrates the depth of anguish that cultural collision creates for these good and sincere people of both generations.

Using fiction and non-fiction texts

The three films' humanitarian perspectives can be compared to public policy debates and issues, such as the current agenda about net immigration figures, in non-fiction texts such the news. Rothschild's (2008) challenge to the warning by 'politicians and broadsheet newspapers' to focus on facts rather than overly politicising immigration is that such a strategy discards 'political principle and morality from the immigration debate' and fosters a dehumanised view of migrants as 'numbers on a spreadsheet'. Articles such as 'Immigrant baby boom helps to push Britain's population to 62 million' in *The Daily Express* (Little 2010) illustrate how use of media language turns apparently neutral statistics into political bias and exploits public fears of terrorism – why choose three women in full niqab for an accompanying photo? A press version of such a story makes the point more strongly as the online versions are tamed down. The print photo is in stark black and white, the women are pushing prams, and their three heads threateningly break out of the top of the frame, above which are three circle shapes containing apparently alarming statistics, thereby implying a direct causal link.

Summary

Although the logistical challenges of interdisciplinary work are not to be underestimated (Grahame 2008/09: 23), given institutional commitment especially adequate time for detailed planning and reviewing, such cross-fertilisation offers mutual subject enhancement and a sustained impact on students' learning. Media education and citizenship are both subjects that aim to take students beyond their own experiences to become informed, active and critically aware citizens. Combining media education and Citizenship disciplines helps to avoid simplistic analysis of the Media as inherently untrustworthy. Understanding that all texts are selected versions of the world enables productive engagement with how issues are presented and the meanings thereby constructed. Comparing and producing news stories across a range of media forms demonstrates how their meanings are modified by the different attributes of technologies, forms, production and other institutional processes and constraints.

Using the flexibility of Curriculum 2007 to plan beyond its literal guidelines invites the use of fiction texts as effective ways to engage students with challenging and demanding issues. As products of the culture and society in which they are made, films are informative social documents and revealing metaphors for social issues. They can dispel views of social groups as homogenous and restricted stereotypes and the unknowable 'other'. Well-constructed individuated characters alongside the privileged access that film language brings to their thoughts, feelings and motivations help audiences to empathise with their lives and viewpoints.

Diversity and change are integral to the notion of collective identity in confident cultures, rather than sets of behaviours and the preservation of selective moments in history. Instead of clinging defensively to fixed restricted notions, strong senses of unity and identity can be gained through perceiving the self, others, cultures and nations as evolving interplays of multiple identities and diversity as a concept with rich possibilities, rather than a threat to the selective familiar.

Further reading

Andrews, J. and Clark, J. (2009) *The World in the Movies*, BFI, www.bfi.org.uk/education/teaching/pdfonlyresource/world_in_the_movies.pdf (accessed 2 April 2010).
This free, downloadable resource includes institutional contexts about the film industry including regulation, and classroom techniques for using film. There are suggested extracts, analytic and practical activities for 16 films, including *My Beautiful Laundrette*. All are mapped to aspects of citizenship at KS3 and KS4; although it was written before Curriculum 2007 the range and content are similar and easily adapted.

Clayton, G., Randell, F. and Dyja, E. (2009) *A Window on the World? A Teachers' Guide to Studying Television in the Context of the Citizenship Curriculum*, BFI, www.bfi.org.uk/education/teaching/tvcitizenship/pdf/window_on_the_world.pdf (accessed 2 April 2010).
This free downloadable resource includes, as with the film resource above, a discussion of representation and realism. Extensive institutional information is related to its effects on programmes, and Television News is a key case study throughout. Lesson plans for KS3 and KS4 address several topics in Curriculum 2007 with a range of stimulus texts and hotlinks to further resources.

Film Education: www.filmeducation.org/staffroom/film_in_the_classroom/film_and_citizenship/
Contains a collection of free downloadable units for Citizenship with informative background materials, investigative approaches; most have embedded clips with related activities. Case studies include *Persepolis*, *The Boy in the Striped Pyjamas* and *Kite Runner*. National Schools Film Week has a Citizenship strand of films and materials with strong political themes – *Tsotsi*, *The Road to Guantanamo*, *The Wind That Shakes the Barley* (accessed 7 September 2011).

Recommended resources

Websites

CitizEd – www.citized.info – A citizenship education project funded by the Training and Development Agency. The website contains a vast wealth of resources, materials and links for teachers and student teachers of Citizenship.

engagED – http://engagED.educ.cam.ac.uk/ – Based at the University of Cambridge, the project aims to build the voice, citizenship action and learning of young people. *engagED* is investigating the ways in which young people express their civic identities and engage with their communities at a local, national and global level.

Association for Teaching Citizenship (ACT) – www.teachingcitizenship.org.uk – The website of subject association for teachers of citizenship education contains resources and materials.

Chapter 11

Practical media production

Rob McInnes

Introduction

This chapter explores some approaches to practical work in Media Studies. While not offering an exhaustive account of the debates and rationale that underpin the status of practical work, it nonetheless acknowledges from the outset that practical work has experienced a troubled history and that different attitudes and approaches towards it, together with a very wide range of teaching contexts can result in radically different experiences for students, which in turn produce different notions of what media education is.

The chapter examines the now inevitable centrality of media and information and communications technology (ICT) to the development of students' media literacy through not only viewing, listening to and reading of, a wide range of mass media forms, but also through 'writing' their own media texts. The assumption is made throughout that media education characteristically uses active pedagogy to develop both technical skills and theoretical understanding. The chapter provides examples of both 'low-tech' and 'high-tech' pre-production, production and editing activities in a range of media including desktop publishing, video, photography and website design. Ultimately, the chapter aims to help teachers locate the practical work they ask students to undertake within appropriate theoretical and institutional contexts.

Creativity at the margins?

> In fifth grade I remember sitting at the back of the class with a paperback dictionary in my hands and using the side margins, where there is no writing, to draw in little stick figures on each page, creating my own little flip cartoon movies. Since I wasn't paying attention to the teacher, I had the entire day to draw my movies, giving me the patience and attention to detail I could never have now. The elaborate cartoons featured invincible characters bouncing around and off the pages, battling evil, and blowing up everything in sight. I wasn't very good in math, science, history . . . in anything really.
>
> (Robert Rodriguez, 1996, *Rebel Without a Crew*)

> Media Studies is a subject with little intellectual coherence and meagre relevance to the world of work.
>
> (Chris Woodhead, *Sunday Times*, 8 March 2009)

The rationale for practical work in Media Studies may seem self-evident to media education practitioners, but this has not always been the case. The status of production work has in the past been fiercely contested, but it has also been the focus of much of the critical attention that the subject has attracted over the years. Film director Robert Rodriguez's attitude to formal education (above), caricatured in the very entertaining and enlightening account of the making of his low-budget independent Mexican feature *El Mariachi* (1992), nevertheless exemplifies a particularly prevalent view of practical media production and film-making – in particular, in its suggestion that it is more fulfilling and satisfying creatively to work outside or on the margins of 'industry' as opposed to within its mainstream. It is a view echoed by many filmmakers. In an era when many media courses have embraced the 'industry ethic' of practical work by adopting many of its organisational practices (along with its forms of planning documentation and incorporating these into their assessment procedures) it is nevertheless apparent that the maverick approach favored by filmmakers such as Rodriguez retains a particular appeal to students and teachers alike. This may be in part because it echoes the historical status of many art and media departments in secondary schools where the subject's pleasures have tended to include a degree of rule-breaking, guerrilla activism and counter-cultural pursuit. One imagines, therefore, that the fifth grade teacher mentioned by Rodriguez was not an art or media teacher – first among those educators more likely to have encouraged his marginal activities than to have disapproved of them. On the other hand the apparent (and illusory) 'ease' involved with picking up a camera and creating something meaningful or worthwhile as a learning activity has been seen by some to work against the ethos of Media Studies as a 'serious academic subject'.

Rodriguez's position opens up other areas of debate that ought to interest any current or future media teacher. One such debate concerns the degree of originality and creativity that one might seek to encourage in students' production work. This is an area where different media courses originating from different cultural contexts can bring about an apparent conflict of intentions and methodologies. Courses that have tended to incorporate the word 'studies' in their title have in the past used practical work as a means to exemplify students' understanding of media concepts (genre, narrative and representation, being the most common). On the other hand, courses that have emerged from industry agencies such as Skillset or that have been written with the involvement of industry practitioners (the Creative and Media Diploma being the most recent and high-profile example) have tended to focus on production skills as ends in themselves and as an (indirect) route to future employment in the creative industries.

The 'problem' with both these contexts (even as somewhat simplified positions here) is that whereas one appears to prioritise intellectual understanding, the other conversely appears to prioritise what might be seen as craft skills. One might almost see these as a binary opposition between *critical* and *functional* media literacies. The other issue is that although neither approach *apparently* foregrounds creativity, both presumably take for granted that a degree of creativity must somehow be inherent in the process of shaping a media text from 'scratch'. Interestingly, the issue of 'creativity' is also at the heart of the government's latest 'reforms' of the National Curriculum, which in many ways have had the result of bringing into other subjects many of the learning styles and strategies that English, Media and Art teachers have taken for granted for years as being good practice. These include the integral use of collaboration and negotiation in guided practical activities and stress the importance of having specific goals and conceptual frameworks, together with an understanding of the importance of audience in small-scale production work.

From the work of Grahame (2003), Fraser (2005), Burn and Durran (2007), and McDougall (2006), it is possible to identify approaches to practical work that encourage in students a robust interrogation of media concepts together with a creative and nuanced understanding of audience and institutional process. McDougall (2006), for instance, suggests there should be no essential difference between production technologies available to students on prevocational and applied courses than those used in the more 'academic/ theoretical' courses. Fraser and Oram (2006) shows how the industry's requirements for efficient organisational practices should be reflected in the ways students' productions are managed, including the imposition of deadlines and the presentation of artifacts to real audiences. Grahame (2003) suggests approaches to production work that de-emphasise the technology through activities that require minimal technology, but help hone the collaborative and creative skills required for effective production work.

Technology and power – who is in control?

> A computer lets you make more mistakes faster than any other invention in history – with the possible exception of handguns and tequila.
>
> (Mitch Ratcliffe, *Technology Review*, April 1992)

A crucial issue that has shaped the history of practical work in media education at every level is the availability of, and the significant advances in, the *technologies* of production. The question of what is taken for granted that a media teacher should have access to in a media classroom remains as pertinent now as it ever has. However, to read and experience some of the literature surrounding media education these days might easily lead one to believe that we have entered an educational Nirvana regarding the potential of technology in schools. It is certainly true that the ratio of computers to students in secondary classrooms has dramatically increased, and that many students have significantly greater access to a much wider range of equipment and software than has previously been the case. What is not so clear is precisely what the benefits of such investment have been. Technology allows us to carry out tasks with enormous speed and efficiency, but may also inhibit the motivation to *reflect* upon the process of learning. As Buckingham *et al.* (1995) point out:

> 'Older' technologies establish barriers at many stages of the production process, not least to do with the skills that are required. For many years, these barriers certainly prevented school students from producing media work with which they themselves could be satisfied. Yet on the other hand, these barriers also represented points at which students were forced to be explicit about their aims, and to reflect upon what they had achieved thus far.
>
> (Buckingham, Grahame and Sefton Green, 1995: 73)

It has been observed that the rapid integration of computers into almost every aspect of schoolwork has led to a situation where, arguably, the speed of some learning activities has outpaced the ability of teachers to reflect on the value of such activities. The arguments here might be likened to the gradual introduction of and accommodation of pocket calculators into the mathematics curriculum, where resistance was often contingent on the fact that calculators empowered students to carry out tasks instantaneously that had previously taken several minutes, coupled to a requirement to show 'working'. Calculators have now been around for many decades and in the time since their introduction, the mathematics curriculum has evolved considerably and raised questions about what mathematical concepts remain important enough for students to engage with. Similar challenges continue to raise questions around what constitutes a demonstration of conceptual understanding in the media education curriculum, both in Media Studies and its manifestation in other subject areas such as English (see Chapter 5), a subject that has traditionally been constructed around activities – reading, writing, speaking and listening, rather than concepts.

Buckingham (2007a) points out that although cheaper and more powerful digital technology appears to offer clear advantages to media educators, we cannot take for granted that IT learning is automatically improved merely because of its power to motivate students. As he suggests, computer use has a strong tendency to *individualise* learning when it is often far more desirable to construct situations where collaboration is likely to occur. This is particularly true in media education where almost every product, or text, a student might encounter is likely to have come about through an intensive series of collaborations and is likely to provoke multiple meanings from a range of audiences.

Most importantly, perhaps, Buckingham reminds us of the need to support the use of any technology with an active pedagogic framework of intervention and reflection.

> It could be argued that the new range of choices made available by digital technology does not *necessarily* make the act of constructing an image any more conscious or deliberate. In the case of digital still cameras, for example, the ease with which filters and manipulations can be applied encourages the production of stylized images, but these may well continue to be seen as distinct from pictures presented as 'evidence' of reality. Unless these basic questions about selection and manipulation are built into the process, and made the focus of conscious reflection, these new choices may well become merely an excuse for arbitrary experimentation.
>
> (Buckingham, 2007a: 171)

Technology will clearly continue to change and offer new and innovative solutions to creativity, and clearly offers many solutions to the *tabula rasa* phenomenon well known to teachers. Templates, exemplar work and structured tuition aids can all be set up easily in a range of software applications, upon which students can more easily model their own work. However, we need also to guard against the banality that can so easily emerge from such support. A well-designed practical learning activity is one in which the student outcomes are varied and imaginative and lead organically to debates about both form and meaning. The ability of a Nintendo Developer's System (DS) hand-held, dual-screen games console to capture facial images and morph them into something resembling the underside of a glass pudding bowl, or the potential of Apple's *Garageband* to create a serviceable tune using off-the-shelf rhythm loops may ultimately offer their human end-users a kind of experience analogous to solving a Sudoku puzzle, or building a construction toy. And it can be soul-destroying at the assessment stage to wrestle with the meaninglessness of the work of students who have not engaged with either the process of construction or the potential of the technology at its deeper levels.

In terms of course management, it is also worth remembering that *whatever* you plan for using technology at some point either: the batteries will fail; the microphone will not work; the memory card will become corrupted or the hard drive unreadable; the power will cut out; the operating system will crash; the screen will go blank or freeze; the keyboard will jam; files will go missing; the memory stick will be stolen; or there will be gum on your seat. Always have a (possibly low-tech) contingency activity to hand and remember that students also need to be able to cope with the management of these kinds of failures, so backing up files and management of their workflow (particularly for older students) are essential components of their learning.

Research

Research has become more inextricably linked with production work as media courses have evolved, and there has been an increasing expectation that not only will projects reflect the results of students' understanding of the codes and conventions of products they are creating, but that such understanding will be reinforced by a disciplined approach to the acquisition of knowledge that underpins such understanding.

An inevitable feature of curriculum development has been that what teachers undertake with students in the classroom has tended to be driven by changes in Awarding Bodies' Media Studies specifications. For instance, in the past, they differed substantially in the amount of practical work offered and the specifications tended to reflect the different axis of the debate around practical versus theoretical study, and to a certain extent all now still separate practical work from theory for the purposes of assessment – though OCR's A2 examination paper is one of the few exceptions. Research frequently takes the form of primary research into forms and content (critical analysis of relevant media texts) or primary research into, for example, the popularity of particular texts within the production genre. However, it is worth avoiding the trap of allowing research to take up more time than necessary and neglecting the time required to allow students to develop production skills. Research can be undertaken simultaneously and, in an effective collaboration, shared (specification assessment requirements permitting, of course). Ultimately, research can be time-limited far more easily than can production work, so it is worth building this into course planning. The following camera exercise, *A Rendezvous*, can be undertaken for skills development during the research and pre-production phases of production work.

The true purpose of research should of course be to enhance students' conceptual understanding of the kinds of narrative, genre (or whatever) they are themselves producing. McDougall makes the point that even the 'big concepts' (in other words those that would be normally be taught) are far more likely to come alive for students when considered *during* the production process. As an example he considers summarising the 'narrative codes' of Roland Barthes, by asking key questions such as 'How does the text use images and meanings which tap into already held oppositions and responses to symbols?' He argues strongly that theory is only of use to students if they can reinvent it in their own way and apply it meaningfully to learning situations with a degree of autonomy.

> I would encourage students to consider those questions about their production activities during production rather than before they start (in which case you end up with a rather artificial attempt to 'evidence' conceptual understanding through making a film) or after they have finished (in which case you can end up with some less than heartfelt claims, as in: 'my video has lots of images and is postmodern').
>
> (McDougall, 2006: 130)

CAMERA EXERCISE

Aim

This camera exercise is designed to help you prepare for your coursework production and to help you develop your camera skills. You need to consider how the camera can be used to frame and compose shots and consider the range of shots you need to record in order to construct a sequence in which meaning is apparent to the viewer.

Pre-production and production

Storyboard, stage and film this sequence, taking care to include as much invention and originality as you can to make it dramatic and interesting.

Try not to rely on dialogue (it will be better to make it dialogue free if possible). Aim to create **narrative interest** visually through the **positioning** of your performers and objects in the frame, through **camera angles** and a range of shots, and through **character performance.**

Use the **full range of shot types** to film the *Key actions* below. You must clearly convey the *Key actions*, although you can add other character and narrative details if you wish.

Remember, the audience needs to know and possibly **identify with** at least **one** of the characters.

Key actions
1. Character A is to meet Character B in 'plain sight' yet surreptitiously.
2. Some object is secretly passed between them.
3. Unknown to A or B, Character C is keeping them under surveillance (either visually or aurally).

Figure 11.1 A rendezvous (1) camera exercise

Arguably, the same is true of research (and, to a certain extent again, teaching) into professional production practices. If research can be a dry process for some students then it is only highly motivated ones who are likely to read extensively about how George Martin recorded the Beatles or how Kubrick lit his sound stages. DVD extras can provide quite accessible information on how films and television programmes are made. As can the ten-minute film schools made by Robert Rodriguez, which are not only entertaining, but also can motivate students to innovate and think outside the box. There is also no substitute for students meeting media professionals first hand – although, of course, they will probably need careful preparation in order to know what to ask.

Pre-production

Considerable confusion appears to exist around the different kinds of planning that a student might undertake for a project and this has often differed radically depending on the

Awarding Body and specification. For instance, the latest version of the Welsh Joint Education Board's (WJEC) specification for A level Film Studies has replaced the 'traditional' storyboard with a 'digital' version that requires still images to be produced by digital cameras, whereas other specifications and other levels may still have a use for a paper drawn storyboard as a valid pre-production tool.

This notion of a pre-production task that increasingly resembles a production task highlights developments within the media industries themselves and also problematises a crucial aspect of most Media Studies courses in which the pre-production activities must be 'documented' and form part of the assessment. For applied courses (such as the Creative and Media Diploma, or the BTec Nationals) the emphasis on assessment may substantially depend upon evidence of the students' ability for 'production management'. On such courses, the business and administrative side of the media industries are heavily emphasised: for example, location *recces* are rigorously supported by health and safety risk assessments; a production is fully budgeted on spreadsheets; minutes of production meetings are kept; and the hours spent on each production task counted and audited.

The pre-eminence of storyboarding among pre-production tasks has tended to mask (or perhaps highlight) a central problem of pedagogy and assessment in Media Studies, in that one element of the pre-production process has acquired a particular elevated importance and that the notion of the ideas that fuel a visual medium must also, therefore, be represented in visual form.

The status of the storyboard in the film and television industries has shifted considerably over the years. Many productions do not routinely use storyboards and would have no real need of them, whereas for major studio films involving large crews and complex staging or special effects, storyboarding has evolved from paper drawings (which still take place) into elaborate pre-visualisations and *animatics* that run still or animated images in real time with temporary (temp) soundtracks. A further complication of storyboards was pointed out by Buckingham, Grahame and Sefton-Green (1995) who noted that in order for them to form a useful part of the pre-production process they require students to have a pre-existing understanding of the components of framing and composition, among other things.

> In fact, it requires a high degree of 'visual literacy'; and unless students are already experienced film or video makers, aspects such as shot time or camera angle are rarely meaningful.
>
> (Buckingham, Grahame and Sefton Green, 1995: 67)

The other aspect of pre-production that tends to be sidelined in the rush for cameras, field-recorders and the fastest computer with the latest version of Adobe Photoshop photographic package, or Adobe Dreamweaver website design software, is that a huge part of the pre-production process is the generation of ideas and their effective commitment to a shareable medium, such as paper. Although the documents of pre-production such as a screenplay or a *flatplan* (a map of a publication in production), the drafts of copy for a magazine article or a stick-drawn animatic, may or may not be necessary as part of the assessment, they are undeniably important, and time spent on their development and appropriate interventions for teacher and peer feedback are essential. Figure 11.2 suggests in some detail how to guide the pre-production stage of making a magazine cover to ensure focus on the conventions and development, working out and recording, of ideas.

What you will learn:
- Some of the basic techniques of image creation and manipulation.
- 'Modeling' skills through analysis of professional products.
- Basic use of a digital camera and an introduction to Adobe Photoshop.
- Simple use of a page grid to aid design and layout.
- Creation of appropriate image and text for a specified target audience.
- Some basic aesthetic principles of page design and introduction to desktop publishing.
- Software (eg. Microsoft Publisher).
- Skills of both collaborative and independent working.
- Simple project management.
- To maintain appropriate documentation to support assessment and evaluation such as accompanying planning notes and print-outs of your work-in-progress with annotation.
- To use appropriate subject-specific terminology in evaluative comment and analysis.

Task 1 Pre-production

Step 1
Choose one of the magazine covers selection featuring either a full facial close-up or a partial close up.

Step 2
Make some brief notes about who you think the intended readership is and why you think the editors and designers made the cover that way. Then work out who you want the readership for your product to be and begin thinking about content you could develop.

Step 3
Using the 15 square grid, sketch out a version of the cover you have chosen. Use the grid to help you measure the correct proportions of image, text and graphic elements.

Step 4
You will be designing a cover using the same design components but with different content. **Note**: you will need to use your imagination here. You do not need to produce a straight copy of the original.

Step 5
Now use a second grid to sketch your own version. Use the same proportions, but vary some elements, such as the facial expression, colours or background.

Step 6
Using a word-processor, write out equivalents to all the text elements on the original cover. Again, use your imagination here – this activity is not about slavishly copying – it is about 'borrowing' the design proportions of a professional product to aid your own sense of aesthetic awareness and to suit your purpose and target audience (which may be different). Create your own title and 'splashes'. When you paste these into your DTP application, you will need to match the size and typestyle of the original.

Figure 11.2 Magazine cover pre-production: 'Faces' (1)

The *Spy* project below was conceived for WJEC AS Media Studies (2008), in which students individually complete a stand alone planning task assessed separately from the production. The production, depending on the individual or group's choices, may or may not be used to plan the separate production task. Figures 11.3–11.5 (*Spy* Project 1–3) demonstrate the type of rigour with which students should be guided to storyboard and, along with Figure 11.9, how research, theory and practice can be integrated. The *Spy* storyboard task is easily adaptable for any Level 2 or 3 Media Studies specification for which judgments can be made about requisite levels of 'finish'.

Aim: This pre-production exercise is designed to help you prepare for your coursework production. For this assignment you will need to produce a detailed storyboard comprising of 24–36 still photographs. The photographs can, if necessary, be augmented by drawings. You need to consider how the camera can be used to frame and compose shots and how lighting and iconography affect representation.

This pre-production task must be devised and finished **individually**.

You may collaborate on some shots (no more than six – but it's better if they are all your own). You may help each other with the practical aspects of production or as performers, etc.

The production brief

You have been asked to storyboard a sequence of a new Spy/Thriller programme targeted either at the junior audience (9–11 years old) or at an older teen/adult audience.

The shots in your storyboard need to demonstrate your ability to represent:

- Character
- Mood
- Setting
- Awareness of target audience
- Genre
- Production value

You are free to decide on the number of characters, but you must show their individual character traits. For example, one of them may be a risk-taker, one or more may be heroic, one villainous, etc.

You need to include at least:
- 3 close ups of characters
- 3 location shots
- 6 of your choice, which demonstrate any of the above criteria.

Technical quality

Your shots should be of acceptable technical quality otherwise you will need to re-shoot them. The following elements should be considered:

- Framing
- Focus
- Lighting
- Sharpness

Figure 11.3 Spy project (1) storyboard

Remember: your pre-production and production task may be linked. The pre-production task must be devised and completed individually, but may share up to six shots with other members of your group. The production task will be shot on video and may be in collaboration with up to three other people.

- **Do** consider your audience carefully. Plan the sequence from the perspective of what they will think. Audiences won't be interested in your plot unless you give them some aspect of the narrative to invest in. Emotionally, this is likely to be a character with whom they can identify. Intellectually, it's likely to be some kind of puzzle or intriguing situation.
- **Do** remember that television drama needs to be primarily entertaining. Two people just walking down a corridor is **not** entertaining, unless there is some purpose and point to it. Remember **every** shot should be there for a reason.
- **Don't** involve weapons of any kind in your project. This includes prop guns, knives etc. This is particularly the case if filming on location.

    There are good reasons for this. The first is most important and concerns health and safety. You should do nothing that involves risk to yourself or others, for example, no real knives. At a time of increased terrorist alert, it is foolhardy to behave in any way in public that might cause genuine alarm. There are documented cases of media students being arrested for filming with fake weapons without having first sought police clearance. So unless you have professional aspirations and are prepared to obtain proper local authority permission – with a supervising adult present – **do not** attempt this. Use your common sense when filming on location and remember you are representatives of the school/college.
- **Don't** plan fights or attempt pyrotechnics or explosions.

    Similar reasons underpin this advice. Without specialist help, fight sequences are difficult to shoot convincingly and in any case, physical violence is surprisingly rare in the contemporary spy series where suspense and intrigue are more common. Explosions can be added in post-production but you may find it more effective to plan an off-screen incident and to bear in mind the point on post-production below.

Devise your sequence with the following in mind:
- **Do** emulate the narrative devices most commonly used in the television spy genre. See Figure 11.5 for some ideas here.
- **Don't** plan effects that you intend to create in post-production (editing) unless you have some experience at this already. Sophisticated software can produce computer-generated imagery (CGI) such as explosions etc. but this takes time and expertise. So **don't** consider this unless:
  - you already know how to achieve what you want;
  - have access to (and know how to use) the appropriate software; and
  - are prepared to commit time and energy to the task.

Figure 11.4 Spy project (2) dos and don'ts

GUIDANCE FOR REVISING YOUR STORYBOARD

- Ensure your story information is clear. Get somebody else to read your storyboard and listen to their feedback. Is the story information clear? Can they follow it? Is it too complicated? Or too simple?
- Present each shot in a uniform way. A standard storyboard in which the shots are presented using guidelines on a grid will look better than a one in which they are not.
- You can use a program such as Publisher or PowerPoint to present your images. (Both are part of the Microsoft Office suite of programs.)
- Use consistent framing for each shot. The standard ratio for television is 16:9. This is (not unsurprisingly) the shape of your television set (unless you have an older 4:3 set!).
- Framing your shot is an art in itself and there is credit available for consideration of how your subject is framed and how you position objects (etc.) within the frame.
- If you have taken photographs with the camera held in the portrait position, you need to *crop* these to the right shape.
- If you have a shot with dialogue. Write it out so we know exactly what the audience will hear.
- Don't forget that film and television are not solely visual media. The soundtrack can and does carry crucial story information. This may be primarily dramatic, such as a sound effect. Go back through your project and find the opportunities to exploit the possibilities of sound. Add this to your shot information.
- If there is to be music in the background, describe the kind of music we would be hearing. Where it starts and stops, or fades up and down.
- If you haven't been able to photograph the shot you need, draw it out instead.
- If you have a photo but no characters in shot, draw them over the top.
- Type out accompanying shot info rather than handwrite it.
- Check it all through again. Are you happy that the story/plot makes sense? What info could you add now to make it easier to follow?

Figure 11.5 Spy project (3) revising storyboard

Production

There is an argument that the production phase should be the shortest of all the three stages of production work and certainly *if* it is possible to guide students to strictly time-limit the time they spend recording, taking photographs or shooting video, then there are distinct advantages in both the learning process and the organisation of the curriculum. Almost inevitably, the sacrifice is one of quality and if the exercise is exam coursework then students will almost certainly want more time. Limiting their production phase through tight deadlines, such as shooting in one day, but then permitting students further reshoots after evaluation and the onset of post-production has a further advantage of mirroring much of what happens within the media industries. Further, this practice helps students to understand the significance of deadlines (along with how to manage them, understand them and, *naturally*, how to stretch them).

However, it is also the case, as is hopefully apparent from the previous discussion, that the acquisition of practical skills ideally should be a continuous and recursive process, whereby students can build on skills by a constant 'drip-drip' reinforcement of media concepts. This should mean that the media classroom opens out into other areas, both physically, in the case of photographic, audio recording or video work, and analytically and reflectively in students' own time.

The examples of production activities in this chapter range from those intended to take place within a single lesson such as the video exercise *A Rendezvous* (1) Figure 11.1 above, plus a reflective homework task, see *A Rendevous* (2) Figure 11.10 below; those that require a visit such as the location *recce* Figure 11.8 (planning it, organising and managing resources); and those that require a series of lessons, such as the magazine cover Figures 11.2 and 11.6, and web page Figure 11.7. Clearly, one of the issues with production work is the time required to complete more complex tasks.

Whereas working on web design and desktop publishing projects can be facilitated across a series of single lessons, it is often difficult to manage more ambitious photographic and video recording work in blocks of less than an hour, and these kinds of projects typically benefit from the kind of flexibility a sixth-form or more flexible use of the timetable can offer. Again, there are several benefits from treating a location shoot as professionals would: meticulously planning the shoot; having students take responsibility for equipment and documentation, and teasing out reflective and evaluative comments in semi-formal or ad-hoc presentations of their material. Exercises such as the Location Recce below also foreground the importance of appropriate and tellingly framed mise-en-scene. The Location Recce may be used as a stand-alone exercise, as part of the *A Rendezvous* skills development task, or the *Spy* storyboard and/or production.

Post-production

Like all these terms, the post-production phase is perhaps less clearly delineated when it comes to the construction of certain kinds of media product such as web pages, desktop publishing and audio recording. The later stages of production work in class are particularly demanding, as the dynamics of a media group, in which a number of students are managing projects, mean that it is possible that all three phases of production are in process simultaneously.

Typically, post-production refers to mixing, remixing and editing in the film, television and recording industries. But the term can loosely incorporate many other processes in every medium, from mastering (the overseeing of recordings to their finished file formats or recordable media) to colour correction of video material, to the 'pre-flight' and 'package' facilities of a professional desktop publishing application. The dominance of digital distribution means that students will never have to engage with the elaborate analogue technologies of darkrooms or printing presses (from which practically all modern terms originate) as modern software offers many of these processes as part of its tool palette. In some ways this is regrettable, as using the more traditional analogue technologies can offer worthwhile experiences in the craft of making media; inevitably, they are now destined to

Task 2 Production

Resources – *For this task you will need:*
* *a digital camera*
* *to collaborate to plan a small-scale photo-shoot*
* *access to photo-manipulation software and desk-top publishing software.*

Step 1
Using a digital camera, and working with a partner or in a group, take a series of shots based on your pre-production sketches. Make sure the camera is suitably close enough to your subject to enable you to emulate your original plans. Shoot at the highest quality setting available for the best image quality (this will depend on the camera you are using). If possible, experiment with lighting and different camera settings. Try to log your shots on a notepad so you can see the difference that specific settings make to the shot.

Step 2
Download your images to a computer using a card-reader or the connecting lead for the camera.

Step 3
Select from the preview menu or thumbnails, the 'best' shot to use for your cover. In Adobe Photoshop select 'adjustments' from the image menu and experiment with contrast, colour etc. to see if you can improve the image. Crop to fit the size of your cover. Is there space for the magazine title and splashes?

Step 4
When you save your work use 'save as' so you do not overwrite the original image. Go to 'image size' to ensure the image is the right 'physical' size for your page. Measure it if you're not sure. When you're working in print, you'll need more pixels in your image to obtain a high quality 'finish'.

Step 5
Now it's time to assemble your elements as a front cover. You can do this is Photoshop but if possible use a dedicated application such as Adobe InDesign. Microsoft Publisher will do the same job, however. Open a blank publication and in 'page setup' check the paper size matches that of your printer (A4 is usually the most convenient to use and is close to the size of many of today's magazines). Make text boxes for your title and increase the font size, choosing the font (or typeface) carefully to suit the style you want. Refer to your original plans for guidance and to other magazines for inspiration (copy strategically!).

Step 6
Import your image using the 'place' function. Position it carefully and crop back to the paper/page size if necessary. Other text, such as your splashes can be written in separate text boxes or copied and pasted from a word-processing document. Change font colours etc. as required. Check your spelling, and paste and rearrange essential elements such as a barcode and issue number. Submit for feedback!

Figure 11.6 Creating a magazine front cover: 'Faces' (2)

Aim: You are assessed on your ability to plan and construct a media product, using appropriate technical and creative skills. These involve your ability to produce appropriate content for a web page or series of web pages and to design the look of the pages including background and graphic elements, typefaces and photographs, video and sound.

The production brief – Create *either* viral marketing web pages *or* an interactive website for a new television espionage drama series.

Step One

Research other viral marketing campaigns. Many television programmes have used them to generate viewer interest. Viral marketing uses a variety of techniques to engage potential viewers. One common strategy is to take a tangential view on the programme, with seemingly unrelated characters or the appearance of advertising a different product. Fake news reports or humorous behind-the-scenes footage can be utilised and, for fans of the programme, can provide 'added value' in the same way as 'special features' on DVDs. TV series such as *House, Flash Forward* (C5) and *Doctor Who* (BBC) have all used viral marketing.

Explore the interactive portion of the archived *Spooks* (BBC) website to see how plot and character elements can be 'discovered' by a potential viewer of the series.

Step Two

Plan your web pages by modeling on similar campaigns. Design the look of your site, considering your use of colour, background textures and sound samples with care. Remember you will be credited for the creation of *original* (not 'off-the-shelf') elements and your creative use of the medium and understanding of its codes and conventions.

Step Three

Create your site using appropriate software. You may need to shoot some video and take some photographs. The creation of images is time-consuming and requires planning and attention to detail. You will need to prepare your images for web use with Adobe Photoshop (or an equivalent software application). Typefaces (fonts) should be chosen carefully and manipulated if possible to obtain a unique 'look'. Type can be created from scratch using an application such as Illustrator.

Step Four

Once you have produced your web pages, test them to ensure they load and work on different computers and browsers and to ensure that the video runs correctly etc. If you choose the interactive option, test all links and embedded elements to ensure they work.

Important
Avoid generic templates for web pages unless you are able to sufficiently manipulate the look and design elements. Use templates – but create your own!

Figure 11.7 Web pages

Aims

- to improve organisational and production management skills;
- to learn how to document production planning;
- to produce coursework / portfolio evidence;
- to work both collaboratively and independently.

Task

To produce a series of (no less than 12) still images. These will be used as reference shots for your own project.

This task should be carried out in pairs or groups of up to four.

You should carefully consider the particular brief to which you are responding (or devising). You should also ensure that you are clear about the assessment criteria for your course. You may seek guidance or clarification wherever necessary.

You will need to plan, agree and document the following:

- Choose the **location** to visit – give brief reasons for choice.
- Plan public transport **route** to and from the location (include map and instructions). Check timings to ensure you can get to the location at (or before) the agreed time. (You should **not** be late!)
- Calculate costs and produce a **budget**.
- Have **contingency plan** (alternative route).
- Consider **health and safety** precautions and requirements. List these and produce a **risk assessment**.
- Produce a **kit list** (to include camera, etc.).
- Produce a **contact sheet** (with mobile phone numbers etc. – all group members should have this).
- Produce a **display of shots** with descriptive detail, and evaluation of their usefulness.
- Pay attention to **framing and composition**. Used creatively, you might indicate through accompanying notes how one location might 'stand-in' for another with careful consideration and selection of elements within the frame. (This might also involve leaving things out or covering them up!)

This activity should be seen as part of the process of overall production management. You should use this as a model for future pre-production documentation and should evaluate each stage of the pre-production process. You may find it useful to keep a production diary.

Figure 11.8 Location recce

be learned only by a small minority, on specialist courses, although there are revelatory moments to be gained from showing students 'how things used to be done'.

It is arguably the post-production phase that has benefited most from low-budget (or even free) software applications. Many of these are so simple that they can happily form part of a media-focused curriculum at almost any phase. There are several highly usable sound editing programs available and programs such as Microsoft's Windows Movie Maker and Apple's iMovie can produce perfectly respectable finished pieces of work without the need for extensive tutoring in how to use them. As pointed out above, however, it is important to maintain critical intervention during the process, through formal and informal feedback (written and verbal), and to allow sufficient time for re-editing, etc.

Evaluation and assessment (building reflective practitioners)

Although students might see evaluation as the final part of the production process, in many respects this *should not be* the case. Production activities should be fully and firmly embedded within a theoretical framework, and as McDougall (2006) argues, the 'practical' is to all intents and purposes 'theoretical' – if it is done properly – reflective interventions should take place at every stage. Projects and assignment briefs such as those used to illustrate this chapter all require a conceptual understanding to be developed along with the practical work itself. Figure 11.9 illustrates how media concepts are located in the *Spy* project; the worksheet, which is given to students following their independent product research reinforces their learning and focuses their narrative and genre planning.

Undoubtedly, as McDougall (2006) maintains, in many ways any distinction between the theoretical and practical might be seen as artificial. However, although this could lead to an argument that suggests reflective writing is irrelevant or unnecessary, for most examination courses evaluation is a crucial part of the assessment process and part of the various ways a student is required to demonstrate knowledge and understanding of what they have learned. Few courses now demand the traditional 'essay' format as the sole evidence of a student's learning, so reports, diaries, blogs, DVD commentaries, PowerPoint notes all now routinely appear as suggestions for the delivery of appropriate reflective comment.

It may seem obvious advice, but it is important for students to understand upon what criteria precisely they are being assessed, together with how and why they are being assessed on it – throughout the entirety of the production process. Therefore, the media teacher should engage in the routine sharing and dissection of those related concepts together with assignment aims and mark schemes. Such an approach also helps students to direct their efforts throughout the entire production period to where it will make the most difference. There may be little point, for instance, in them spending two weeks of evenings on an elaborate Flash animation, or recording a complex piece of soundtrack music with their band if it will contribute only a tiny amount to their overall grade. Having said that, it is invariably the most dedicated student *prepared to do just that*, who will gain the highest marks. Therefore, it is not to suggest that teachers should guide students towards a utilitarian work ethic, merely that it is advantageous to understand how the media industries work (particularly with regards to skill levels and employment) and that discriminating between important and minor details and learning how and where compromises may be made are in themselves useful skills. The irony here of course is that it is often those students

Here are some suggestions for scenarios that you might use as the basis for planning. Remember, as with every other aspect of your production, there is no substitute for individual research into the genre and its common features and iconography:

- **Subterfuge** – elaborate schemes designed to deceive or fool a character. This could involve actions which remain enigmatic until their purpose is revealed and which the audience may (or may not) be 'in on'. Most commonly however, information is revealed to the audience but not the character/victim.
- **Misdirection** – when you actually intend to fool the audience. You might consider ending your sequence with new information that changes the way they see what has gone before.
- **Following/being followed** – a very common spy genre activity. This can be straightforward to film and can focus on **either** the character being followed **or** the character that is following as a focus for audience identification. The trick is to make it interesting and to involve the audience as without character information the danger here is that your sequence will simply be boring. Can you bring anything original to your version?
- **A clandestine meeting** between a spy and her/his secret contact. Usually in a very public place to avoid being overheard (and to add a little production value!). As with several of the other scenarios here it is important to consider the audience and offer them reasons to be interested in the action.
- **Covert surveillance** – another very common device. This can involve CCTV or other gadgets (easily faked with a little imagination).
- **The stake-out** – e.g. bored security officers physically monitor their suspects, but something unexpected is about to take place. Show how agents (enemy or friendly) evade detection.
- **Suspense** – the events and apprehension leading up to (e.g.) an explosion. This might involve the countdown of an explosive device, but does not have to show the explosion itself. Once again, consider carefully how you will involve the audience – for instance it is important to show them what is going to happen. Ideally, they should know more than one (or more) of the characters. Watch the opening sequence of the opening episode of series two of *Spooks* for an example.
- **The silent heist** – an elaborate break-in, while the clock is ticking. The trick here (as taught by Alfred Hitchcock) is that audiences appear predisposed to feel anxiety on behalf of the thief, particularly if s/he appears to be under imminent threat of discovery. Watch the opening of *Entrapment* (dir. J. Amiel, 1999), or the late-night office robbery sequence in *Marnie* (dir. A. Hitchcock, 1964) for good examples. The use of props (such as screwdrivers, gloves, coloured-water spray etc.) is worth investigating here and it is a good way to learn how to use the insert shot.

Figure 11.9 Spy project (4) advice and guidance

who have achieved a high level of ability by working obsessively on minor details who become most successful in the craft side of the creative and media industries.

The guidance in Figure 11.10 supports students in evaluating the practical video exercise *A Rendevous* (1), see Figure 11.1. As the exercise is undertaken at the early stages of a course or production, the evaluation is similarly designed to initiate continuing reflection on practice. Students can later apply the same types of technical evaluation questions to assessing how successfully the theoretical considerations, such as those in Figure 11.9 above, have been conveyed.

Summary

This chapter identified the three main phases of practical work as pre-production, production and post-production and offered suggestions of activities suitable for a range of exam-based courses. The chapter also highlighted some of the debates that have influenced the development of practical work over the last few decades, the most significant being the binary opposition of practical work as either craft skill or as part of an evidential base for conceptual understanding.

In recent years, production work has tended to be accompanied by increasing demands on students to make links with research into the forms and content of similar media and their audiences. As a result, pre-production activities have expanded and can increasingly resemble production tasks. This tendency is exemplified by the shifting status of the storyboard, which for assessment in some courses requires a considerable amount of actual production activity (such as still photography). While technology has improved and continues to improve rapidly, it can also lead to a deadening of genuine creative engagement that should be guarded against.

Finally, evaluative work remains an important opportunity for students to consider the value of their work – in relation to both professional practice and the core concepts of media study. For practical work to be most effective it should be, as far as possible, routinely integrated with reflection and analysis.

Further reading

Buckingham, D. (2003) *Media Education: Literacy, Learning and Contemporary Culture*, London: Polity Press. David Buckingham's book provides beginning and experienced media teachers with a comprehensive overview of the debates, theories and principles underpinning the teaching of media. The book also develops a detailed and compelling rationale for a form of media education that is theoretically rigorous and manageable in practice. It includes a chapter on practical media work entitled 'Getting Creative'.

Buckingham, D. (2007) *Beyond Technology: Children's Learning in the age of Digital Culture*, Cambridge: Polity Press. The book is based on a cross–national study of the emerging digital divide between children's and young people's experience in and out of school. Through an exploration of the hidden structures that shape technology and schooling in a market-driven society and of young people's engagement with diverse media forms, David Buckingham proposes a form of digital media literacy. Essential reading.

Burn, A. and Durran, J. (2007) *Media Literacy in Schools*, London: Paul Chapman Publishing. The book (and accompanying CD ROM) includes a range of case studies that show how, through drawing on children's own cultural knowledge, digital media work – from video editing to computer game authoring – can be developed in schools. The book also presents a model of progression that shows how learning can be developed from Year 7 through to GCSE level.

Reflecting on and evaluating your work

The aim is to help you consider what you have learned about constructing film/television drama.

The camera exercise was designed to help you prepare for your coursework production and to help you develop your camera skills. You will have needed to consider:

- how the camera could be used to frame and compose shots;
- the range of shots that were necessary to record in order to construct a sequence in which meaning was apparent to the viewer.

Now reflect on and evaluate the stages of the exercise:

A) Pre-production

Think carefully about your planning:

- How closely did you stick to your planned sequence of shots?
- What reasons can you think of to support the (commonly held) view that the pre-production stage is the most important part of the entire filming process?

B) Production – filming/recording of shots

Consider the technical competencies listed below. What difference can these make to the overall effectiveness of the sequence?

1. Holding a shot steady.
2. Framing a shot.
3. Using a variety of shot distances.
4. Controlling the 'look' of shots through management of the mise-en-scène.
5. Choice of colours, shades, tones and graphic elements in the shot.
6. Control of lighting.
7. Direction of performers.

C) Post-production – editing a completed sequence

For this exercise you were asked to edit 'in-camera' although you may have also had the opportunity to edit the sequence onto a 'timeline'. In modern film and television, editing is considered essential, so give your views on the following:

- What are the key advantages offered by editing?
- What reasons can you think of to support the view that the post-production stage is the most important part of the entire filming process?
- What can editing 'fix' and what can it not fix?

Overall – success, disaster or . . . ?

Finally, consider these points:

- Sum up what went well or badly. What elements (if any) let the effectiveness of the sequence down most? What could have improved it?
- How important is it to be in control of what you are doing? How important is effective collaboration?
- Remember – it is a media crime to bore your audience. Did your sequence engage the viewer?
- What elements do you need to add tension or drama to your project?

Figure 11.10 A rendezvous (2) evaluation

Fraser, P and Oram, B. (2006) *Teaching Digital Production*, London: BFI Education/Palgrave Macmillan. This guide provides an account of developments in digital production together with an introduction to teaching digital video production. It highlights the importance of effective pre-production practice and gives advice on how practical work can be used to engage with the Media Studies curriculum.

Recommended resources

Practical work support

Cineclub: scripting, shooting and editing films in schools supported by professional filmmakers; annual awards at BFI, http://cineclub.org.uk/.

English & Media Centre: *Picture Power 3* still image editing program, either site licence or single user CD ROM. *MediaMagazine Student Films* CD ROM – of Long Road Sixth Form student work, www.englishandmedia.co.uk/publications/index.php.

First Light: http://www.firstlightonline.co.uk/ community-based filmmaking for young people.

The Guardian Newsroom: range of workshops for KS3, 4, 5 including real-time production of a front page using the day's news feed; also has teacher events, www.guardian.co.uk/gnmeducationcentre.

Media Education Wales: very useful video equipment advice updated periodically www.mediaedwales. org.uk/videokit.htm; products include *editsense* DVD ROM with short films to edit on iMovie or Final Cut.

Our Video: licensed guidance for community group filming using 'professional' practice suitable for students; excellent advice in 'Your Video Toolkit' section, and planning templates in the 'Appendix', http://ourvideo.org/.

The Parkside Federation: guidance for using webcams, capturing moving images, animation, making websites, and video techniques, www.parksidemedia.net/parkside_media/.

British Film Institute

The BFI/Palgrave Macmillan *Teaching Film and Media Studies* series has excellent practical guides from experienced teachers, www.palgrave.com/bfieducation:

Fraser, P. (2005) *Teaching Music Video*.

Readman, M. (2003) *Teaching Scriptwriting, Screenplays and Storyboards for Film and TV Production*.

White, M.L. (2007) *Teaching Digital Video Production at GCSE*.

DVD-ROMs

English & Media Centre – www.englishandmedia.co.uk/publications/index.php.

Movie Power – Scripting with the Moving Image (2010) resources for creating a range of audio-visual forms.

Picture Power 3 (2010), still image editing program with five stories and editing activities for all key stages.

Media Education Wales (2009) *Edit Sense*, films to edit in iMovie or Final Cut www.mediaedwales. org.uk/products/what-is-editsense/editsense/.

Training

Hands-on training opportunities are limited, but the following annual conferences are a starting pc
Awarding Bodies – WJEC/Media Education Wales, and OCR conferences include practical worksh
   (the latter also has online tutorials).
www.mediaedwales.org.uk/training_and_consultancy/teachers-and-schools/.
www.ocr.org.uk/qualifications/type/gce/amlw/media_studies/documents/index.html.
Film Education CP3 conference – www.filmeducation.org/training/.
Media Education Association – www.meaedassociation.org.uk.

Note about equipment

Given the rapid changes in technology any advice about hardware and software is mai
indicative. In addition to the programs noted in this chapter, Chapters 6 and 7 have furth
suggestions for equipment, and Awarding Bodies have advice in their teacher supp
documents, WJEC GCSE Media Studies Teachers' Guide is particularly good for softwa
programs.

Career development

Chapter 12

Setting up, resourcing and managing a media department

Christine Bell

Introduction

This aim of this chapter is to offer support and advice for any media teacher setting up or already managing a Media Studies department. The main aim is not only to support teachers, but also ultimately to ensure that students have a positive experience when choosing Media Studies. As Chapter 1 showed, the subject has enjoyed a rapid growth in popularity at both GCSE and Post-16 levels and the need for specialised Media Studies teachers is great. Chapter 1 also exemplified how it is also the case that, at times, Media Studies receives a negative press; it is therefore likely that the Media Studies teacher will often need to fight numerous battles within their education establishments. While there are well-resourced stable media departments, this chapter does not underestimate the struggles of many inadequately trained 'department' leaders struggling with yearly lack of continuity. The suggestions here are made predominantly for those working in more challenging situations, but the general principles should also be more broadly applicable.

Establishing and maintaining a high profile for the subject

Whether setting up a new Media Studies department, or managing an existing one, maintaining a high profile for the subject is essential if the subject is to survive and flourish. This is of particular importance where several 'new' subjects are offered at GCSE and AS/A level. The profile created from the subject's establishment and how it is marketed to recruit students are likely to be key to the subject's success.

There are several ways in which Media Studies is delivered in schools and colleges. Very often it is part of the English department/faculty. However autonomous Media Studies curriculum leaders seek to be in running the subject, they will usually need staffing hours from the English department. The subject can also be offered as an option subject in its own right, taught by English teachers with one person having responsibility for management of the subject.

In some schools, however, Media Studies is a largely autonomous department staffed mainly by media/film specialists who only teach that subject, and are supported by part-time staff, or staff from other subject areas. Such an organisational structure, with a head of Media/Film Studies who is in charge of a budget, planning schemes of work and the timetable, puts the department in a strong position within the school. If this independent management model can be established from the start it will be advantageous to the subject, whereas a management model with another curriculum leader responsible for the Media Studies budget and staff allocation in the timetable can problematic.

It is also often the case that Media Studies is a one-person 'department', which often constitutes a personal as well as professional challenge. Further, many teachers new to teaching and to the subject are asked to set up a Media Studies department and so have the added burden of quickly acquiring middle management as well as subject skills. INSETs and conferences are full of young staff eager for help in managing a new department. Such events are useful for networking and gaining practical support; some Awarding Bodies have support systems such as AQA's local coursework advisers and Teacher Network Group for GCSE. Local colleagues are often willing to help and more support can be found via Awarding Body online forums.

Even in successful departments with Media Studies a popular option in the school, staff may be largely nomadic and transient. They 'dip into' the subject for experience but tend to gravitate back to their first subject, particularly if they are from a priority core subject such as English. Where possible, it is vital to persuade the headteacher to appoint someone who, from the outset, is officially employed to teach at least half Media Studies. An additional partially dedicated member of staff will strengthen the department's position and greatly support the department's range of work.

Promoting the subject

It is likely that students will not encounter Media Studies as a discrete subject until Year 9 or 10, although they are likely to have had some experience of media education in English. If lower school pupils have positive experiences of the subject before they make their option choices it will help the popularity and profile of the subject. Some experiences will be extra-curricular, such as *Film Club*, but more high profile, school-time cross-curricular projects such as *BBC School Report* can do a lot to raise awareness with students and senior management. Further ideas are suggested below in 'Curriculum Management'.

It is important to be pro-active for GCSE and AS recruitment. Option talks by the subject teacher will give students accurate course information, dispel the myth that all they do is watch television, and create more chance of attracting a good ability range. It can be a mistake to leave such delivery to uninformed non-specialists, but if it is unavoidable it is worth briefing them. Option talks can be organised in several ways (note that it is important to assume that students have little knowledge of the subject content):

- Visit English classes so the whole year can be addressed. Keep it brief and focus on key information such as the percentage of controlled assessment, topics, the range of skills, and highlight how useful the subject is and how it complements other subjects. This is also an opportunity to assert the equal status of Media Studies where it is set up as an alternative to GCSE English Literature.
- Invite seriously interested students to the subject area: pre-arrange permissions for them to be out of lessons, or run the event at lunchtime/after school if this is not possible. The advantage is that students see the teaching area, equipment and examples of work. Experienced media students could offer short demonstrations or hands-on activities, and have a Q&A session about their experiences of the course.
- Assembly presentation: use PowerPoint and/or a DVD promotion that students have made or contributed to. Key information can be interspersed with student work, extracts or stills of topics to be studied, etc. Year 11 Media students could co-present, and it is likely that a senior management member will be present to support it.

• Produce a take home leaflet for parents: they are often unsure about the subject and such information will help them to support informed option choices. Other parent/public communications such as school websites are useful for informative presentations.

Marketing for Post-16 recruitment is also important, particularly where group size may determine whether a subject runs or not. Again, the key is to start early – organise 'taster sessions' in Year 11 for prospective students to get a clear idea of the AS level structure, standards and expectations of commitment. Students are too frequently advised to take up Media Studies as an 'easy' fourth academic, or mainly practical subject, particularly when it is clustered with Arts rather than say Humanities. Some then struggle with the critical analysis, or the practical skills and time demands of production work. Post-16 open evenings are opportunities to address misguided prejudices about Media Studies A level and promote its range of transferable skills through display work, looped PowerPoint presentations, and current students giving information in ways that appeal to younger students and their parents.

Managing a Media Studies department

Running a department is of course much more than just ensuring quality subject delivery; any new Head of Department (HoD) should have access to middle management training courses. There are now a wealth of publications relating to effective middle management and subject leadership: see for example Field *et al.* (1999) and Williams (2001). Departmental management entails being on top of school and subject issues; knowing how to garner help and find guidance; sound organisation, setting up clear structures within which staff can operate in informed and supported ways, financial management, person management, negotiation skills and being determined. While HODs are responsible for disseminating senior management policies, their role is also to protect and support their staff, and to communicate and fight for their departmental vision.

This section focuses on two key aims of leading a department: as curriculum leader to work with media teachers to develop the quality and range of media education provision; as a department manager to set up the appropriate structures and conditions to support media staff development and promote and protect Media Studies in the school's institutional context.

Timetabling staff

It is essential for the well being of colleagues and students to have continuity of staff for the (usually) two years of a GCSE, or A level Media Studies course. It is difficult for students to settle with a new teacher, a particular problem for the two-term 'dash' of the A2 year. Even if there are thorough schemes of work in place with detailed sequences of learning for each lesson, it takes time to ascertain the learning foundations set up in the course's first year, and to attune to students' individual capabilities and learning styles. Where staff have teaching commitments in other departments it is important for the curriculum leader to have responsibility for allocating staff to teaching groups, and to liaise with those departments at an early stage to ensure that Media Studies priorities are met. Early contact is also advisable with the school timetable manager to avoid blocking clashes with subjects that may attract similar students.

Course delivery and staff development

As curriculum leader it is important to have an overview and be aware of work across the subject; this section identifies some key areas to monitor. Sustaining awareness can be done formally through department meetings, though this is difficult if Media Studies teachers' primary departmental or management meeting commitments are elsewhere. Regular informal conversations monitor course delivery just as effectively and indeed are an advantage of small Media Studies departments.

Try to engineer as few split classes as possible. Where this is unavoidable ensure each teacher has responsibility for specific units, understands the specification requirements, and prepares students appropriately for assessment. Teachers sharing classes should communicate weekly to ensure continuity of approach, share strategies, and monitor student progress. Staff should be supported in playing to their strengths but it is a pedagogical issue if students perceive practical and theoretical work as separate learning and makes meeting course requirements problematic for specifications such as AQA GCSE and OCR A level where production work is schematically integrated with theory learning. Some non-specialist teachers may be reluctant to engage with less familiar forms such as video games and social networking sites, or use 'writing' forms other than essays. Subject competence and knowledge development can be supported through jointly planned, trialled and reviewed teaching and learning strategies and, where timetables allow, short-term team teaching.

Department meetings contribute to staff development as a form of mentoring. More structured staff development such as performance reviews can be used to discuss and agree subject knowledge and skills development – and may engender more subject commitment. It is the curriculum leader's responsibility to keep abreast of CPD opportunities. Judgments will have to be made about colleague priority for courses especially given challenging financial circumstances and rarely cover policies. However, this is an area to be strongly fought for in terms of quality assurance and student achievement. Managements tend to favour 'essential' CPD such as Awarding Body training days, rightly so as they are highly informative.

However, students will achieve more if they are taught by staff, who have gained secure subject knowledge and are stimulated by enjoyment and their own rich learning experiences. Conferences run by specialist media education organisations such as the Media Education Association (MEA), British Film Institute (BFI) and Film Education, provide engagement with leading media educators, researchers and industry practitioners. There is a directly functional argument here; media technology and the ways it is used are evolving so rapidly that the content and pedagogy of media education is under urgent review (see Chapters 3 and 9). It is incumbent on schools to ensure their media teachers have the means to update their professional practice and at least come close to the familiarity with which the students they teach operate in today's digital world.

Managing a media curriculum

The daily demands of delivering Media Studies can be pressing, but it is important to have longer term and broader strategies for media education. Short-term promotion of the subject can raise its profile, but its status will be sustained through course quality and serious student engagement. Working on, say, a five-year structure with the English Department so students have systematic, varied and well-resourced experiences of media education at Key Stage 3 will benefit informed choices and achievement at KS4, and beyond, (see Chapter 5 for strategies in English).

Cross-curricular and extra-curricular links

Links with other departments

Developing and maintaining links with other departments are useful ways of sharing expertise and raising media education awareness across the school. Several departments have media related projects in their specifications, and a project with them could add a different dimension to a media work, for example:

- ICT departments often have animation packages in their software and expertise in this area.
- A marketing project could be set up in which media students create an advertising campaign for products designed by Technology students.
- A project with PSHE or Citizenship to raise awareness about a social or health issue can include campaign advertising.
- Film Education produces free cross-curricular resources and screenings, including National Schools Film Week, around which cross-curricular projects can be developed.
- Other departments often need filming expertise and this can be good skills and evaluation practice for media students.

Links with outside agencies

Local television companies have education departments and are keen to target young people. Most of the programmes are news based and they are usually willing to send reporters to speak to students, students can visit them, or be used as a topic of a short film.

Similarly, many local newspapers have a 'Newspaper in Education' department. There may be the opportunity to produce a page for it, or a 'contract print' paper written and designed by students, and delivered with the local paper in the school's catchment area. Again editors or journalists are amenable to visiting schools.

Extra-curricular opportunities

Producing a school newspaper or magazine is often successful and has the added bonus of attracting all ages and abilities. If it is classed as enrichment it is likely to attract senior management funding, as would attendance by Gifted and Talented students. However printing is expensive so it is worth trying parent contacts or raising money by persuading local businesses to place adverts. Many 'Newspapers in Education' initiatives organise competitions among schools, which can be highly motivating.

Digital technology has made audio/visual projects such as school radio or television stations easier to set up, e.g. www.thomastallis.co.uk/www/tallistv/ep6.html. *Cineclub* trains professional filmmakers and teachers to run filmmaking projects culminating in screenings at local cinemas. Partnerships can be established with community-based organisations such as First Light Movies; and many independent regional cinemas have excellent education programmes – a full list of cinemas is available via the 'Organisations' page on the MediaEd website. Filmclub is a national organisation providing free (for state schools) support for weekly after school screenings of films to broaden students' viewing experiences, and they can participate in online reviewing, and industry events. Filmclub could be run by Media Studies students, which in turn would be useful for developing their industry and audience understanding. Murray (2009) has an account of setting up his school's Filmclub.

Writing a Scheme of Work (SoW)

Choice of specifications should be decided by the department following various considerations: school ethos; the students; department resources; staff skills, interests and teaching styles; preferred modes of assessment; Awarding Body support, efficiency and openness to discussion; the examination papers; and Chief Examiners' requirements as detailed in their reports.

An effective SoW should be of use to staff in interpreting the Awarding Bodies' specifications into a series of topic areas and tasks. The tasks and assignments should offer students a broad and balanced range of opportunities in which to develop and demonstrate their skills, knowledge and understanding. The advantage of Media Studies is that SoWs can be treated as working documents that can be adapted to the strengths and interests of staff so they can have a sense of ownership, and new texts and issues can be incorporated.

As with any curricular subject, there are three key elements to a flexible scheme of media work:

1   A long-term plan.
    An overview of each half term in each year group is a useful planning tool – it clearly maps topics covered in the year and when to work in and around other departmental and school activities such as visits, mock exams, work experience, the January exam period, end of year school events and the start of A2. Where there are several media courses production work can be mapped out so equipment is kept available. Consider whether January examination is appropriate – will students' understanding and exam technique be developed enough; will it be a means of reducing the end of course burden; or a used as a mock exam for re-entry in June?
2   A topic Scheme of Work (SoW).
    A topic SoW contains the elements to be covered in a particular topic are addressed in more specific detail with ideas for a 'way through' the topic and for specific lessons. It is useful to plan 'backwards' so that the knowledge, understanding and skills needed in the second year of assessment can be mapped into the 'foundation' year units.
3   A more detailed SoW.
    Contains headings covering areas such as aims and objectives, key concepts, learning and skills, resources, Assessment for Learning (AfL) activities, and activities covering specification (or National Curriculum) areas.

The AQA and OCR Awarding Bodies' websites have useful model course plans and schemes of work in their 'Teacher Resource Bank' and 'Key Documents' sections respectively. At the time of writing WJEC is developing similar support. (See Chapters 6 and 7 for examples of GCSE course planning.)

Homework

While homework strategies should be discussed and agreed with colleagues, ensuring their implementation is the HoD's responsibility. Homework planning will have to accommodate both the school's policy and, for GCSE, controlled restrictions on unsupervised work. Well-planned and relevant homework is an important part of the learning process and one way of assessing students' ability to engage in independent learning. Homework must supplement and support work in lessons and encourage students to progress in their achievements.

However, raising the profile and importance of homework can be difficult in many schools where there is not an ethos that involves the completion and submission of homework. In such cases giving students a choice of tasks can be encouraging, particularly when the choices encompass the range of learning styles. Figure 12.1 below has six different types of task related to a current topic from which students choose two and complete over a set timescale.

Introduction to the Media

Below is a grid of homework tasks related to the current coursework topic of 'Introduction to the Media'. **Select 2 of the tasks to complete.** Your teacher will give you the deadline dates for this work.

TASK ONE   Write a review of a media text that you like. This could be a film, a television programme, a magazine etc. Try to explain with detail from the text **why** you like it and try to avoid description. There is a help sheet for this task.

TASK TWO   Write a media diary. This should cover a day in your life and record all the aspects of the Media you use or 'consume'. Try to give as much detail as possible.

TASK THREE   Write an article for a magazine about a media issue. This could be related to violence in the Media, representation, internet control, the press and privacy, or anything else that interests you. Remember to set it out like a magazine article.

TASK FOUR   Design a poster or a leaflet to provide a specific target audience with information about the media. This could be for younger children, for students deciding on their options or for a broad audience.

TASK FIVE   Make your own spider diagram or mind map around the topic of 'The Media'. Find examples from specific media texts to illustrate your points. You can include drawings and found images.

TASK SIX   Interview someone from your family about their media habits. Ask them questions about what they watch, read and listen to and why. Write up your findings as a report and try to draw some conclusions about your findings.

Figure 12.1 Homework grid

This model can be easily adapted for different topics and purposes. One additional feature could be to accommodate differentiation by allocating task points and setting each student an end of term target number. This allows students some control through choice but also means that they have to complete some more challenging tasks to reach their target points. Another refinement is to colour code tasks according to specification requirements so students cover the range of skills required.

Monitoring, standardising and assessing student work

Teachers have to be clear from the outset what work the students need to produce and when.

The curriculum leader is ultimately responsible for monitoring the appropriateness and quality of departmental work and the subsequent examination results. New members of staff will need support, especially if they are new to the subject and it is important to ensure that for the first half term they have access to resources to help them through the initial topics. New colleagues can also be a great asset with fresh ideas, and younger ones are likely to be more at ease with new media. Once settled in they can be responsible for producing and trialling a unit of work. Media Studies is very adaptable and has scope for them to choose a topic and write a SoW with confidence.

It is the curriculum leader's responsibility to ensure the SoW is adhered to and that students are being prepared for their examination and coursework/controlled assessments. This monitoring can be done informally at department meetings where samples of a range of student work can discussed. These are opportunities to ensure that where options are not prescribed the combination of say pre-production and production tasks allows sufficient student progression, and that (for A level), there is a clear difference between AS and A2 production media. Producing well-focused evaluations linking research and/or theory with practical work is challenging for students so this is an area to monitor closely too.

These sampling sessions can also be used to support the new teacher in developing productive formative assessment, for instance by identifying achievable targets related to media concepts and specification requirements. Broader considerations such as AfL can be concurrently mapped since much of the Media Studies curriculum offers opportunities for formative assessment where 'the learner is responsible for the learning and the construction of knowledge, through cooperative situations, open-ended questioning, discussion and meaningful contexts' (Clarke 2005). The 'successful learner' characteristics identified by QCA – independent enquirers, effective participators, reflective learners, self managers, creative thinkers, team workers – have much in common with Media Studies learning aims, processes and outcomes.

As Media Studies is one of the subjects with high percentages of controlled assessment/coursework (GCSE and A level are 60 per cent and 50 per cent respectively) department meeting sampling can also be used to periodically standardise marking. Focusing on assessment criteria and marking positively for 'best fit' to the levels is another way to aid staff development for formal marking. It is essential for the curriculum leader to be informed at early stages about students falling behind so there are chances to rectify problems well before coursework deadlines and examinations. Use the institutional systems for alerting parents, heads of year, progress coaches etc. who can give support; a pro-forma for classroom teachers to send home is useful and time saving. These procedures also ensure that there is a 'paper' trail should evidence of action be necessary. Deadlines for students must be set and adhered to by staff and students alike; problems will occur if one class is allowed extra time. Production work is particularly prey to missing deadlines; students knowing from the start how marks will be allocated, including deductions for missing the final coursework deadline, is one strategy to encourage responsibility for time management.

The controlled assessment/coursework weightings, and the necessity for procedures to be carried out accurately and fully (such as annotating folders to explain mark allocations) mean that senior management must be made aware of essential formal assessment processes and allocate time for them. Factor in time before standardisation for teachers to check folders have appropriate amounts of documentation (e.g. restrictions on research and planning evidence), to make DVD compilations of productions, check URLs, blogs, etc. are live; and after standardisation to complete the administration tasks before folders are sent to Awarding Body moderators.

Once the department has achieved a good match of predicted and achieved grades, and controlled assessment/coursework marks are validated overall, then it is well worth applying to become an assistant examiner as a form of staff development. The Awarding Body standardising sessions are good networking opportunities, marking focuses awareness of required learning, and provides insights into other approaches to the specifications – in addition to sharpening marking skills examining then is very useful for reviewing courses and improving planning.

Managing a budget

If the department is just being established it is important to have a clear idea of the equipment and resources needed for effective curriculum delivery. Consider the size of the school and classes; and levels, range and types of choices offered. Consult colleagues in other school departments to get advice about DTP resources, and visit a local school where the subject is more established to get further information about equipment, resources and strategies, and some indication of setup outlay; also see 'Equipment' section below.

Budgets are where Media Studies teachers often have to put up a fight. Prepare a draft budget following the school visit. Additionally, research current prices for hardware and software, e.g. www.reviewscnet.co.uk; *Which? Magazine* and specialist journals such as *Stuff* also have informative comparisons. As they are collectively expensive, budget for consumables such as DVDs, memory cards, tapes, printing, batteries (go for lithium-ion if possible as they last longer and will be cheaper in the long run), cash for magazines, a day's set of newspapers.

Department capitation can differ wildly with good reason, instead of making quantitative comparisons make a qualitative case in relation to key areas such as:

- National competition: while centres are marked individually against Awarding Body assessment criteria, candidates' work will be assessed alongside well-resourced and leading centres such as specialist media arts colleges.
- Quality assurance: Awarding Body specifications have statements about the necessity for adequate equipment to meet examination requirements; anything less will jeopardise candidate achievement, especially given the amount of production work.
- Comparisons with other subjects can be made in terms of adequate subject delivery.
- PE, Science, ICT, Art, Photography, etc. cannot be taught without specialist equipment, and neither can Media Studies.

- Value added aspects: media equipment is characteristic of the digital society for which education is preparing future citizens; it can also be highly visible and impressive for public occasions and school visitors – and available for other school curriculum uses.

Refuse to be put off by members of the school management team pleading that there is no money: if they have committed to the subject as a curriculum offer then they should fund it. Level 3 courses/students attract considerable funding to the school/college, and the department should get a fair share. New courses should also have start-up funding. Two additional financial and qualitative points to be borne in mind are:

- Include a commitment for CPD – preferably the year before Media Studies is set up. This is a quality assurance issue as well as kind support; as Chapter 13 demonstrates, subject knowledge is a basic requirement for gaining a professional qualification to teach a subject. Practical skills training is harder to come by if it cannot be offered by colleagues or the local City Learning Centre (CLC); however there are hands on workshops in media conferences run by the MEA, OCR, WJEC/Media Education Wales, CP3 (Film Education). Departments with Mac set-ups can benefit from Mac Training courses www.apple.com/uk/training/.

Making the case for enhanced online access is essential for course delivery, and it has financial advantages. The wealth of free texts on YouTube such as music videos, adverts and television programmes greatly reduces expenditure.

The Bursar or Finance Officer in school can be invaluable as a guide through the trickier aspects of managing a budget. Check whether money can be carried over from one academic year to the next or disbursed by the academic financial year's end. Establish whether it is possible to purchase consumables from cheaper retailers and then reclaim the money rather than using an official order. It is important to be thoroughly organised in filing orders, receipts etc. as a matter of habit: not least in case of an unexpected audit. Finance officers can also suggest other funding sources such as Gifted and Talented, budgets for visits, Creative Partnerships, cross-curricular projects and so on.

Over-spending in the first year of the subject will not go down well. Once funding is agreed then it must be adhered to. If the budget is tight liaise with other departments to see whether there could be joint outlays, e.g. on English and Media Centre resources with the English department, or to share resources with departments like ICT and Technology – this may also be a way into developing cross-curricular projects. Learning Resource Centres in schools often have budgets for purchasing equipment and programs that will benefit several subjects.

CLCs are free and they often have state-of-the-art equipment, but book early as these are popular, particularly around the coursework deadline. Decisions will have to be made about prioritising how the media budget will be allocated, e.g. are GCSE results institutionally important? Will investing in A level first raise the subject status and have a knock-on effect lower down the school?

Equipment

The vexed question of the type and amount of equipment for any media department is never easily addressed and subject to institutional considerations and teacher preferences.

The OCR Awarding Body online message board has very helpful advice, but it is not currently archived. Awarding Body online documents however include recommendations for resources – see 'Useful websites'. At the time of writing, Media Education Wales is compiling technical guidance on strategies, spaces and equipment for filming and, though dated 2006, the online *School Video Equipment* kit and price guide is a very useful starting point in the meantime. (Also see Chapter 6 for suggested GCSE course equipment.)

Plan courses around available resources and teacher expertise and if necessary limit the range of options in line with available equipment. Perhaps choose to specialise in print, audio or video, or offer the range, if possible, to stagger the use of equipment. Argue to keep class sizes below 25 to facilitate practical work. If media is being delivered at Key Stages 3 and 4, perhaps with one or two GCSE groups, then regular access to technology will be required. If money does not stretch to video cameras it is possible to focus initially on print, though printing can be costly. The bottom line here probably means regularly booking a network room with applications such as the Microsoft Office suite, and Publisher for (very) basic print and web design. Image manipulation software, such as the industry standard Photoshop from Adobe, is ideal but if that is too pricey, there are cheaper alternatives (some are free and open-source such as GIMP) but Photoshop Elements is almost as good as its big sister and much cheaper.

Access to decent digital cameras is also essential. Media Education Wales and *Which?* recommend Panasonic as the most reliable brand; Canon and Sony are also dependable. Video and still digital cameras can be very affordable but the usual warnings about kit always apply: the cheaper the equipment the quicker it is likely to fail (especially tripods). Another dilemma is the fact that the more expensive versions are possibly going to attract those people in school (not only students) with light fingers. With good organisation, one class of 24 students can just about get away with four cameras but six is obviously best. In 2010 many still cameras, such as the Panasonic Lumix DMC-TZ7, offer high definition video recording at around £200–£250. Students invariably find these easy to use and capable of producing very high quality work.

More extensive video work requires purpose built video cameras, and connectivity is a key consideration for choice, such as DV in/out and an external microphone socket. However, unless absolutely necessary, it is worth working with forms that need little location sound recording or small amounts that can be dubbed later, such as music video, film trailers, TV opening credits. There is always a trade off in price. Cheap camcorders can be bought in more numbers – but in the hands of students they will inevitably never last long. If the budget stretches, a £1000+ well-built *prosumer* camera will almost certainly outlast the cheap ones. Many people still use tape-based devices, which have advantages but are becoming less available and affordable. If solid-state recording (such as memory cards) is used, then ensure the editing hardware and software can cope with the file format used by the camera. The Panasonic HDC-HS300 (c. £750 in 2010) is a hard disk camera with a card option and works well with iMovie and Final Cut Express. Reliable camcorder reviews can be found at www.simplydv.co.uk/. If the budget cannot yet run to decent camcorders, Media Education Wales suggests using digital cameras that record video such as the Panasonic TZ7. The same considerations apply to audio recording, where few devices match the flexibility of the Roland Edirol R-09HR at 2010 price of around £250. Here again there is a range of audio editing software from free to more fully featured applications such as Pro-Tools (M-Audio/Digidesign).

For doing audio/visual work at Level 3 it is advisable to move away from network machines to stand-alone suites or laptops. Either Apple Macs or high specification PCs will serve and will reflect what is paid for in terms of processor speed, reliability, graphics capability and so on. Apple's iMovie software is better and more flexible than Windows Moviemaker as an entry-level – and free – solution to video editing, but both are much easier to manage as standalone machines to store video files, unless there is very good and amenable school network technical support. Dedicated editing software packages such as Adobe Premiere or Apple's Final Cut Studio offer industry-standard features and results, and it is worth shopping around for deals on site licences.

Increasingly the convergence of design, print, web and a/v software means that all-in-one solutions (such as the Adobe Creative Suite 5 Master Collection) can be bought, but training time and money will be needed if they are unfamiliar. To offer print and web-based work at Level 3, it's similarly best to go for industry standard applications such as Adobe InDesign and Dreamweaver (which are also part of the Adobe Suite).

As well as buying good essential equipment, more serious commitment to quality of (for example) photographic or video work entails buying lighting kits, external mics, colour (including greenscreen) backdrops and reflectors. Some kind of secure storage is vital. Student access to all this technology needs careful management; check out strategies at the local school visit or online forums. A booking/loan system is essential to ensure equipment availability. Responsible use contracts and returnable deposits for off-site loans help careful handling and prompt returns.

Managing a technician

If there are enough courses delivered to enough students, then there is a good case for dedicated technical support. It can significantly ease teachers' workloads, improve security and equipment longevity and help raise attainment. They can support student recording and editing, prepare equipment for lessons, upload footage and burn DVDs for moderators, and offer advice on equipment and software. Like any teaching staff, a media technician needs to have a timetable and to be managed effectively. When he/she is working with a class he/she needs to know exactly what the end product will be and the timespan in which they are working. There may also be a willing school network technician, but overall their availability tends to be very limited and unpredictable. Or, it may be possible to share a technician with other subjects such as Performing Arts, Music, or ICT. It will be essential to plan ahead and liaise with the other departments particularly for crucial times like coursework deadlines. Skilled former A level students familiar with course requirements who are say taking a gap year can be very supportive, great technicians and work well with students.

Resources and materials

One of the most challenging aspects of running a Media Studies department is ensuring that resources are up to date and relevant; there are very few other subjects for which many resources have such a short life. Most Awarding Bodies require focus on 'recent' and/or 'contemporary' texts and current media issues, as well as having regular prescribed topic changes, especially for GCSE. Although a broad topic such as 'television' may be taught year after year, the way in which it is taught and the case studies used must reflect industry changes. The English and Media Centre's quarterly *Media Magazine,* which targets A level students and teachers, has stimulating articles with fresh ideas and approaches; a departmental subscription to its print version and online archive is an excellent investment. Additional specialist magazines such as *Sight & Sound* (BFI) are useful, especially if Film Studies is part of the department offer. Subscribing (free) to the subject association Media Education Association (MEA) is a sound way to keep up to date with developments in the field of media education for example through its online discussions, *PoV* magazine, and annual conferences.

Specification focused books have useful classroom materials as they have very high production values, and Awarding Body endorsed books indicate approaches that are likely to be 'approved'. However, books are also likely to be out of date a few years after publication and best bought as several copies for departmental and library use, and recommended to students for wider and independent reading. Attendant online applications can be very useful and timesaving classroom resources, but also expensive so consider long-term value for money. Choices of TV programmes and films for classroom screenings should be led by curriculum considerations; age certifications and scheduling concerns can be pre-empted by informing senior management and sending letters to parents/carers inviting notification of any objections.

Media Studies teachers need to keep aware of current media issues and to be constant collectors of materials and resources, for instance by scanning online newspapers, the BBC News website, TV listings, YouTube and other online sites, and accumulating more tangible texts – the burden can be shared by teachers focusing on preferred areas. A Smartboard linked to the classroom computers will save a lot of money in photocopying, and encourages interactivity in lessons. The school may have someone responsible for its website/VLE who is willing to find resources and place them on the school web.

There are several online media education sites that host teacher donated resources, though they will need to be critically assessed in the same way as any such resource, e.g. the MEA, MediaEdu and Teachit. http://itpworld.wordpress.com/ has informative global film materials, hotlinks to several media sources, and the online dimension of Branston and Stafford (2010, 5th edition) an essential text for media teachers. Publications, including those from media education specialists such as Auteur, BFI Publishing, English and Media Centre, Film Education are reviewed in, for example, *PoV*. Awarding Body websites are well stocked with regularly updated resources and offer regular training; OCR and WJEC/Media Education Wales additionally have annual conferences that provide excellent ideas and resources.

Summary

Running a department can be an early career boost to some Media Studies teachers, though exceptionally challenging for those new to the subject. The advantages of relative independence and freedom to develop schemes of work that engage students and enables them to achieve can be highly stimulating. The opportunities to work co-operatively with colleagues across the curriculum and to cultivate mutual support should not be overlooked, and can be very fruitful. Working with school management structures and critically implementing school policies means developing the skills that provide broader perspectives to supplement departmental activities, funding and outlook while simultaneously protecting the department's own vision, staff and strategies.

Developing management skills at any career stage takes many teachers into unfamiliar territory, and formal middle management career development should be sought if it is not offered. Media Studies by its nature is a complex field and has a concomitant exceptional range of demands, not least to establish and sustain its academic value in sometimes less than empathetic contexts. Keeping on top of the job and up to date means rigorous application of specification requirements; knowledge and understanding of new and evolving media texts, organisations and issues in society; replenishing an unusually high turnover of materials; and keeping track of fast changing hardware and software.

Sustaining links with the high quality media education organisations and resources will refresh and extend subject expertise and resources. In larger more established departments there are great rewards to be found in developing and supporting the careers of a team of independent creative teachers actively committed to the media curriculum, and successfully preparing students to be competent, creative and critical in the world of modern media communications.

Further reading

Clarke, S. (2005) *Formative Assessment in the Secondary Classroom*, London: Hodder Education. Clearly structure approaches to assessment, including Assessment for Learning, strategies that blend well with the active pedagogy of media education.

Field, K., Holden, P. and Lawlor, H. (1999) *Effective Subject Leadership*, London: Routledge. A key text for all teachers undertaking leadership of any subject.

McDougall, J. and Potamitis, N. (2010) *The Media Teacher's Book*, London: Hodder Education. A broad overview of approaches to teaching Media Studies GCSE, A level and Creative and Media Diploma, includes website access.

Murray, S. (2009) Film Club Induction, in *PoV: The Journal of the Media Education Association*, vol. 1, issue 2, Spring 2009 www.themea.org.

Williams, J. (2001) *Professional Leadership: Effective Middle Management and Subject Leadership*, London: Routledge. A comprehensive guide to the principles and practices of middle management in schools.

Recommended resources

Websites

London Centre for Leadership in Learning – www.ioe.ac.uk/study/departments/365.html – Based at the world-renowned Institute of Education, University of London, the Centre offers research, qualifications at all levels, professional development opportunities and consultancy in leadership and learning.

National College of School Leadership – www.nationalcollege.org.uk – Unsurprisingly, the website is an extremely comprehensive resource of professional development. NSCL has introduced a free membership scheme. Once registered, teachers have access to news, information and services, extensive leadership resources, opportunities to network and collaborate with peers, consultation events, and access to advice on leadership development from the College's professional support service. As a member, teachers also receive a monthly e-newsletter, personalised to their role and region.

Chapter 13

The professional preparation, progression and development of media teachers

Kate Domaille

Introduction

> Anyone else applied for Media PGCE at CSSD [Central School for Speech and Drama] or Institute of Education? I have just sent my application, and was feeling fine until I read this board! The fact that there are only 14 places at CSSD is terrifying, and now I am preparing myself for rejection.
>
> (*TES noticeboard*, 28 November 2008)

This prospective candidate received some reassuring responses from other eager candidates following the same path as her on the *Times Educational Supplement Noticeboard*. The plea captured here is a familiar one for anyone having attempted to find a direct training route into media teaching – places are few and far between.

Some things have changed in teacher education but not as much as one might imagine. The overwhelming majority of places in Initial Teacher Education (ITE) that offer a media teaching pathway do so subsumed within an English subject route. Many Postgraduate Certificate in Education (PGCE) English tutors would like to extend their course title but it is a surprisingly difficult bureaucratic battle to win. This has not prevented tutors being creative about who is admitted, trained and supported to achieve in media teaching but it is nevertheless an official barrier that influences what is taught in a course, how the placements are managed and how student teachers' achievements are described. Becoming a teacher of media is not common through ITE routes.

Despite the lack of a clear route to media teaching through training, many careers show that there are multiple ways in which the network of media teachers has grown and there is a vast, *virtual university* of support created collectively and voluntarily by media teachers themselves and supplemented now through the endeavours of a subject association – the Media Education Association (MEA). Generally, media educators have been optimistic about the viral spread of media education: there are many very good courses, networks, resources and publishing that have made the self-taught approach to becoming a media teacher more manageable. Nevertheless it is rueful that though media education has gained more ground on wider policy agendas, such as Ofcom's push for media literacy, it remains low down the ITE agenda as an area for action.

This chapter will explore the professional preparation of teachers for teaching media drawing on approaches in ITE as well as exploring post-qualification and continued professional development (CPD) avenues. It is aimed at new teachers thinking of media teaching, teacher tutors and mentors, and for existing teachers looking to extend their knowledge further.

Initial teacher education and teaching media

In 2010 the Training and Development Agency's (TDA) rationale for student numbers on PGCE programmes (the most common route into school teaching) is primarily focused on the need for teachers to teach National Curriculum subjects. Once statutory elements of the curriculum have been met by schools, there is some room to diversify and extend the curriculum offer, marking themselves out as distinct or unique from others in what children can study and learn. This is most notably seen in schools in post-14 provision. These differences in schools' curricula, which have long been encouraged since local management of schools was introduced in the Education Reform Act in 1988, mark out the unique selling points of one school from another. Developments since the early breakaways from local government control have now amounted to more than 40 schools in England being designated as specialist media arts colleges where the work of those schools has a steer around media education across the curriculum as well as in specialised courses. Media education has grown most notably in schools in specialised courses of Media Studies – at GCSE and A level and a proliferation of other vocationally based courses over the years such as GNVQ, BTEC and now the Creative and Media Diploma.

My biography is familiar for those teaching media. First I trained as an English teacher with an excitement about a live and relevant English for the late twentieth century – it was 1988 – and an interest in multi-literacies. My enthusiasm took me to a school where opening up the options in media education was high on the agenda.

My media teaching began with GCSE, then A level, then joining an army of informal trainers, spreading the word and passing the message on. This informal knowledge was augmented through continued professional development opportunities and through joining a network of in-service training providers, delivering workshops, producing resources for the classroom, and writing chapters in books. Later in my career I worked in a media industry and eventually undertook a Masters in Media Studies. I became an English teacher through an initial qualification and a media teacher through an apprenticeship route.

The increased demand for media teachers does beg a question about training. But persuading the funding of different routes into teacher training rather depends upon making a case for the difference in teaching or subject knowledge that demands. There are instances of Business Studies or Citizenship or Classics as identified areas of ITE courses. These courses would attract funding and bursaries and demonstrate the esteem in which they are held. Notably, the numbers are few and equally importantly these very specialised subject courses are often located either by a new initiative, e.g. 14–19 Diplomas, or by specific local need for teachers in a given area, for example in schools running School-Centred Initial Teacher Training (SCITT). Graduate Training Programme (GTP) routes, such as the one organised by St Paul's Catholic College validated by Sussex University (see Domaille 2009) can have the advantage of placements in media rich departments, but low numbers make them vulnerable to being short-lived. These options do not fill the gaps in media teaching: vacancies advertised in the teaching press demonstrate a growing demand for knowledgeable media teachers.

If prospective teacher training candidates begin their homework at the Graduate Teacher Training Registry (GTTR) website, www.gttr.org.uk, they will find 12 media courses listed for entry in 2009/10. This is an increase on previous years because seven of these courses are newly developed to provide for the 14–19 Creative and Media Diploma. This step forward might be celebrated if it was not equally important to acknowledge the despair of the candidate on the message board concerned about gaining a place in a small market of media training places.

Does being trained matter?

Histories of media education summarised by Buckingham (2003) show that this area of teaching and learning has had a long evolution. Buckingham summarises the phases of media education as congealed around broader considerations about children. These are summarised as defending children from cultural corruption; saving children from harmful exposure to dangerous messages or ideas; or from the pernicious effects of political ideology (see also Chapter 1). In these three distinct phases of evolution Buckingham argues children are essentially viewed as passive individuals susceptible to the craven effects of media viewing and use. He rejects all these positions in favour of a genuine acknowledgement of young people's engagement with media, their uses and gratifications of media, and debates with media including a distinct and celebratory sense of children's creativity through media production.

Despite the attention of official curriculum makers to devising a media curriculum, a framework for media teaching has emerged and largely been adopted, as evidence in how learning objectives are organised in official exam specifications. In the framework for teaching about the Media, learning about media is not consigned to a series of nominated texts or processes but rather built around key conceptual areas that have remained relatively consistent and fairly longstanding as: *Media Language, Representation, Institution and Audience.*

The essential question is – how does this framework become known to teachers? How do teachers get to know that media teaching is not so much about textual choice as it is about conceptual analysis of the media if they are not trained? What is to stop a novice media teacher opting for teaching *through* media rather than *about* it? The use of media to support learning across the curriculum is ubiquitous across subjects but this is not what is meant by *media education* (see Chapter 2). An outcome of media education would be media literacy, something vaunted by government departments beyond education through the Department of Culture, Media and Sport for example, and promoted through the work of Ofcom stretching beyond regulation of the Media to education about the Media. In fact this whole complex area steeped in debates about the nature of childhood, protection, empowerment, choice and use is, for those of us working in and around it, an area in its own right. These debates are theoretical, cross-disciplinary, political and personal. Learning about media education is about learning the language of meaning making; it is about how media is produced and circulated, and it is about how media is consumed and used. Adding Web 2.0 applications also means considering interactivity and media literacy as a live and vital set of practices (see Chapter 3). Learning about media education indeed might be about extending definitions of what it means to read and write in the twenty-first century. After all, covering language as a skill in the curriculum speaks to but a fraction of the skills children actually need to make meaning in the world (Pahl and Rowsell 2005).

The tensions that exist between government departments mark out the battle lines about training in media teaching more broadly, for while there is some educational policy acknowledgement of children growing up in a rapidly changing world, this is not developed without recourse to anxieties to protect them from it. In short, educational policy on reading and writing has begun to acknowledge a wider definition of reading and writing but not yet a wider pedagogy for teaching and assessing literacy practices beyond the page. Essentially these gaps left in official policy become the areas requiring specific training for teachers new to media teaching. They need to know about subject content, about practices and about pedagogy.

Teaching media and Qualifying to Teach Standards

The *Qualifying to Teach* (QTT) Standards (TDA 2007) identify very clearly that in order to be competent to teach, students must demonstrate a 'secure knowledge and understanding of their subjects/curriculum areas and related pedagogy to enable them to teach effectively across the age and ability range for which they are trained' (QTT, 14).

Guidance from the TDA on meeting this standard states that students' curriculum and subject knowledge:

> should be such that they demonstrate a sufficiently secure grasp of the concepts, ideas and principles in their subject(s) to be able to teach the relevant school curriculum in the age ranges they are trained to teach.

The exemplification of these standards continues with this list related to assessing competence. Does the student demonstrate that they:

a) Have secure subject-related pedagogical knowledge and understanding of the relevant subject?
b) Can plan and set subject-related targets for individuals and groups of learners?
c) Can break down ideas and concepts and sequence them logically to support the development of learners' knowledge and understanding?

As there are few ITE courses specifically about training media teachers, these subject knowledge descriptors might be applied best in ITE where some media education and training might take place, principally within English PGCE courses. The chapter will now consider them in turn.

a) Have secure subject-related pedagogical knowledge and understanding of the relevant subject?

A survey of initial teacher educators conducted in 2004 to inform the QCA publication *Media Matters* (2005) revealed that those ITE providers covering the areas of media within English took time out to cover the conceptual differences between the two subject areas and provided opportunities through outside speakers or in-house activities to practise approaches to media reading. Few institutions felt they had the time and resources to address media practical work. Nevertheless the processes of reading the Media, through specific reference to media language, are a relatively stable part of what teaching English in ITE might entail. Here there is a convergence of theoretical interest in English and media – the shared areas of semiotics, structuralism and post-structuralism have informed study in both subject areas. But the subjects diverge when it comes to thinking about revising the definition of writing or when media study reaches out to look at texts and practices that have, in public discourse, been considered to exist at the lower end of the cultural spectrum, like computer games, for example.

Burn and Durran (2007) observed that one of the most significant challenges to training in media education is the 'bagginess' of the media curriculum. This has become ever more apparent when trying to consider how a media curriculum might be written and therefore what a trained teacher in media education might be trying to teach. What would be in a media curriculum? How does learning about the Media progress across ages and stages of education? Should all Media be studied or is some media more worthwhile than other media? What, ultimately, will be taught and learned?

Figure 13.1 suggests one way to enable student teachers to consider their own attitudes to the media.

Use the outcomes of these discussions to explore the similarities and differences between the two curriculum areas. Commonly, English is talked about in terms of processes: Reading, Writing, and Speaking and Listening. Media study is discussed in terms of concepts:

- Who is communicating what and why? (Institutions)
- What kind of text is it? (Genre, category)
- How are texts produced, distributed, regulated? (Institutions)
- How do we know what the text means? (Language)
- Who is consuming? What do they make of it? How are audiences targeted or shaped by texts? (Audiences)
- What messages or values does this text represent? How? (Representations)

Student teacher knowledge can be supplemented through reference to wider reading, summaries of the media conceptual framework exist in a wide range of theoretical and practical books or articles – some of which are listed at the end of this chapter, and Chapter 2.

With student teachers use the questions to explore attitudes, values and beliefs about media study.

- Why study the Media?
- What should be studied?
- What is it you want students to learn?
- What kinds of activities will students undertake in studying media?
- What challenges does teaching a media text make on your subject knowledge?
- What overlaps can you see between teaching English and teaching media?
- If studying *Shrek* in KS2 and again at KS4 – what are the differences in what will be taught and learned?

Figure 13.1 Attitudes to the Media

b) Can plan and set subject-related targets for individuals and groups of learners?

In thinking about media study through English this target presents many challenges. It is well-established to draw upon media to illustrate aspects of study being undertaken in other forms, the film of the book, for example. Having students think explicitly about the learning that they expect to take place when teaching a media unit in English might focus their minds on the processes and understanding required. Most often, as McDougall (2006) notes, the highest form of outcome of media study is the traditional, discursive essay so that the study of the media itself becomes secondary to the output of an essay achieved through the use of predominantly English-based skills in writing. In essence much media work in English is not really media study at all. Consequently for training purposes the *modelling* of what is media work may intervene in some of the assumptions about the outcomes, and focus more attention on the processes.

The Year 8 activity below could be used with student teachers to demonstrate an example of work in English that combines media education processes with English learning. Figure 13.2 explores the overlaps and distinctions they may discover.

Year 8: Create an outline for a computer game based on a Greek myth you have studied. As a group, prepare to deliver a verbal presentation of the game to an imaginary media company outlining who the target audience is. You should create the artwork for the game and the blurb describing how the game works.

It is possible to explore other relatively traditional aspects of English curriculum work through the ways in which these might draw on areas of media analysis. A recent example from AQA trial marking at GCSE showed pupils engaged in a cross-analysis between Baz Luhrman's *Romeo and Juliet* (1996) and the original text to explore how character had been developed through filmic techniques. Such cross-over comparisons might be termed *multiliterate* activity.

Theories of multiliteracies have developed out of research into the modes of reading and writing undertaken by children. Here the work of Lankshear and Knobel (2003), Kress (2003) and Pahl and Rowsell (2005) draw attention to the different ways of understanding

English skills	Media study
Discussion, shared understanding, collaboration and presentation (S&L)	Understanding audience for the game and for the presentation (audience)
Reading skills (on screen and paper) – extending the notion of reading	Reading skills on screen and paper (media language)
Analysis of genre, presentational features and narrative on screen and on paper	Understanding of genre, conventions and narrative
Writing at the level of notes and outline	Understanding of institution – who to pitch to, why and how

Figure 13.2 Cross-referencing English and media study

language in relation to other presentational features of texts including images, pictures, fonts, etc. Theories of multiliteracies put technological changes and audience interactions with texts at the forefront of thinking about what literacy might mean. While teaching about media study in English doesn't do a lot to address the specifics of media study, it can go a long way towards thinking about the connections between the two areas. This is well exemplified by Walsh's (2008) example analysing the literacy processes involved in creating an eight-minute podcast using an information text format. Here Walsh demonstrates the processes involved in the task combining traditional literacy skills with new literacy processes to create an altogether different kind of 'written' text. What the pupils produced was a podcast – to be listened to – but built from a combined set of literate actions:

> Reading: researching, understanding and selecting information.
> Writing: constructing different text types with appropriate knowledge of structure, grammar, spelling and conventions.
> Talking: use of voice for recording (tone, pitch, pace, etc.), collaborative.
> Listening: to 'radio genre', to self and others for recording, editing, selection and editing of sound and music.
> Viewing: text and image arrangements on page and on screen.
> Designing: planning, arranging, producing and interacting.
> Use and manipulation: of screen and software.
>
> (Walsh 2008)

c) Can break down ideas and concepts and sequence them logically to support the development of learners' knowledge and understanding?

Demonstrating subject knowledge understanding in a lesson plan specifically requires attention to the same kinds of categories that exist in all lessons. Presenting an outline plan and having students identify what is happening on the plan is a way into thinking about specific knowledge required to teach media. The next activity models the ways in which knowledge of the media curriculum is shown under some objectives and encourages student teachers to take the ideas further by planning the lesson themselves. They are encouraged to annotate the plan first to identify the specific aspects of media teaching and learning before developing the sequence of learning for the lesson.

Continued work to develop subject knowledge expertise with student teachers around media teaching then might focus on whether teachers:

- can answer learners' questions confidently and fully? (set targets for subject knowledge gaps);
- know and can respond to learners' common misconceptions? (again, about continued learning);
- are able to make effective interventions to construct and scaffold learning?
- can analyse learners' progress and make accurate assessments of their learning and achievement?

Training in media teaching requires many of the same kinds of target-setting and progress opportunities as learning to teach in other subject areas.

Name:	Date:	Year Group: Year 12
School:	Time: 11.00am–11.55am	Set: (if not mixed ability)
Subject: Media Studies		Mixed Ability
		ATG for Year 12
		2 @ A Grade
		4 @ B Grade
		1 @ C Grade

Teaching objectives

(*The Curricular area being taught,* e.g. National Curriculum, programmes of study, Awarding Body specification) WJEC AS MS1 Media Representations and Responses – Genre – Repertoire of Elements within Genre Theory.

Learning intentions

The students will today learn about one of the most recent academic approaches to genre theory, which identifies each genre as a Repertoire of Elements. They will be introduced to an analogy to help their learning and understanding of this theory. They will be able to identify the elements that make up the repertoire for any genre and transfer their learning through the familiar genre of action adventure. This is in preparation for the AS exam where they are required to identify generic elements in an unseen text and apply contemporary theories (AO1).

BIG PICTURE – Students will need to have a confident understanding of genre theory and explore it in detail in the A2 MS3 Media investigations and Production should they choose the Genre option. Their arguments will be informed by this particular way of thinking about genre. They will also need to draw on their knowledge of this critical theory to show how they have applied it to their production (AO2).

Differentiation

During the lessons the students will be working in pairs and groups before finishing off the lesson as an individual. The higher level students will be encouraged to work on the more difficult elements while the lower level students will be supported by myself in coming up with new 'sweets' for the 'jars'. The lesson is quite kinaesthetically strong as this group of students are by majority kinaesthetic learners. Questioning will be used to challenge the higher level students.

Assessment opportunities

(*Check if learning intentions have been achieved, by formative or summative assessment, by self or peer assessment and questioning e.g. in the plenary by written work in the lesson or homework.*)

Students will be informally assessed by myself as I circulate the class, but will be required to write their conclusions down in the plenary, which should be a demonstration of their learning. I will be using their Independent Learning Task on an alternative genre as formative assessment of their grasp of the 'repertoire of elements' theory.

Figure 13.3a Lesson plan

Write the lesson plan that you think will come out of the notes in Figure 13.3a above. You must cover a starter, main development and plenary – the timings and arrangements for activities are up to you.

Time	Task	Students	Resources	Learning style
	STARTER			
	MAIN ACTIVITY			
	PLENARY			

Figure 13.3b Lesson structure

Increasing knowledge across the teaching career

What does it mean to be widely read as a media teacher? Chastisement would be rife if English teachers arrived in the classroom without due preparation for literary study or a clear understanding of the linguistic features of a text. In addition to knowing and understanding the conceptual framework for media, the checklist of knowledge development in ITE and beyond can focus on formal and less formal processes.

A good media teacher is a media consumer without a doubt. There needs to be a way of drawing connections across media and across texts and this in part comes from sharing some experiences with students as audience for media. Undoubtedly, however, there are age differences between teacher and pupil groups that mark out clear distinctions. If a teacher were to draw on her/his own experiences, it may well be that she/he has strengths in 'old' media above 'new media': she/he does not play computer games and is not entirely convinced by the pleasures of Facebook. But ongoing knowledge building relies on gaining some understanding of these new media: the teacher does not have to become a user but the importance of Facebook cannot be ruled out.

English teachers are likely to be comfortable with textual analysis and may struggle more with sociological analysis evident in some aspects of studying media institutions or audiences. Further training in media studies is available so it is best for teachers to draw up and maintain an action plan for development, listing the action point for the developmental need, the time-scale and deadline and the ways in which the need will be met, for example.

Media pedagogy

If understanding the demands of the subject content is one area requiring training, then understanding pedagogy is another connected area. David Buckingham asks pertinently, 'What *kind* of theory of learning do we need in media education?' (2003, p. 139). On ITE courses student teachers are inducted into a variety of learning theories, and media students would benefit from the same induction here. Certainly, the work of Gardner (1983) on multiple intelligences is valuable in thinking about the variety of ways in which pupils will demonstrate their learning in media education settings through production as well as in more familiar models of assessment. Equally, the notion that children will gain a stronger or deeper understanding of concepts as forwarded in a developmental model like Piaget's, or through the spiralling of learning as detailed by Vygotsky or Bruner, are all important

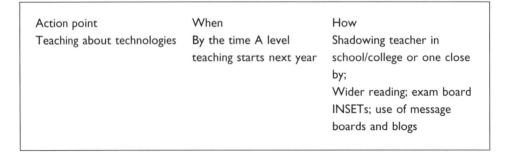

Action point	When	How
Teaching about technologies	By the time A level teaching starts next year	Shadowing teacher in school/college or one close by; Wider reading; exam board INSETs; use of message boards and blogs

Figure 13.4 Action plan template

in encouraging beginner teachers to engage with *how* children learn not just with *what* they will learn (see also Chapter 9).

One area of learning that seems vital and specific to media teacher education and training, however, is the almost unique phenomena that many students will already be very knowledgeable about the subject matter in media and in many cases exceed the knowledge of their teachers. By being very experienced media users, children have a great deal of what Vygotsky (in Daniels 2001) has termed 'spontaneous' knowledge. Being media users from a young age has enabled children to be very conversant in media conventions, forms of representation, means of production and varieties of reception. They already possess a strong and wide-reaching understanding of the Media before they take to studying it. They may not talk in the language of how media is theorised but there is evidence, Buckingham (2003) argues, that their implicit knowledge can be made explicit through certain social processes.

Buckingham (2003, Chapter 9) puts forth a dynamic model of media learning drawn out of discussions of the work of Vygotsky and Bahktin building on the social constructivist approach. He argues that media learning is not simply a stepped progression between spontaneous knowledge and 'scientific' knowledge – the scientific knowledge put in by a teacher. Rather, he claims it is a more varied and socially situated range of negotiations between knowledge and identity that may be taking place. Consequently, the model suggested here is staged and Buckingham privileges the first stage of this model as focused on the school students' own media practices and knowledge:

Stage 1: Students need opportunities to show what they know already.
Stage 2: In showing that knowledge first they have an opportunity to render that knowledge as systematic and to generalise from it.
Stage 3: They can then question that knowledge and extend and move beyond it with input from teachers, research, reading and practice.

Buckingham's Stage 1 is an advance on Vygotsky's presumption that spontaneous knowledge is less secure than scientific knowledge. Buckingham contends that the spontaneous knowledge in media learning may indeed be crucial to extending any further knowledge. It is not a lesser form of knowledge but a building block on the way to greater understanding.

The staged model emphasises that the learning is a social process involving reflection and discussion opportunities and negotiation of ideas with peers and teachers. In classroom terms this means that learning activities are predominantly socially organised and a media classroom would be expected to be organised around reflective tasks, socially produced steps for development, further reflection and evaluation.

> The aim of media education, then, is not merely to enable children to 'read' – or to make sense of – media texts, or to enable them to 'write' their own. It must also enable them to reflect systematically on the processes of reading and writing, to understand and to analyse their own experience as readers and writers.
>
> (Buckingham 2003, p. 141)

Figures 13.5 and 13.6 suggest ways in which to organise teaching and learning based upon Buckingham's staged model.

Identify the first set of activities you might want to prepare for using Buckingham's dynamic model of media learning.

What systematic knowledge are you expecting to emerge from these activities and generalisable outcomes?

How will you use this process to begin to plan to extend their knowledge and move beyond it?

Write a sequence of learning activities related to this task.

Figure 13.5 Organising teaching from the staged model

Use a class list of students you are already teaching. Design a seating plan for the class that you think best suits achieving learning through the dynamic model of media learning:

- Where and how are pupils sitting?
- Where is the teacher in the room?
- What resources do you provide to assist in Stage 1 of the learning?
- How you will support any pupils with specific needs?

Figure 13.6 Organising classroom use of the staged model

If not through training, then how do we teach each other?

Neil Mercer's (2000) assertion that we learn best through explaining to others is characterised fully by the emergence of events and training through individuals, websites, agencies and Awarding Bodies. The following section of the chapter highlights some key specialist media organisations and indispensable events that support media teachers at any stage in developing their skills, knowledge and understanding of the media education field. Organisation websites are at the end of the chapter, and more media education resources are listed in Chapter 2.

The media specialist subject association, MEA noted above, has free membership. Benefits include an online journal, *PoV*, with articles on classroom practice, media issues, media cultural organisations, and reviews of media education resources. The MEA was re-launched in 2010 with an extended website for an online interactive community of support, networking and discussion, including an ITE section with resources linked to the TDA's online Teacher Training Resource Bank (which also has media education pages in the English ITE area). The MEA's annual conferences progamme, jointly organised with the Centre for the Study of Children, Youth and Media (Institute of Education) in partnership with Ofcom, was also re-launched in 2010. The workshops, seminars and panel discussions offer opportunities to explore cutting edge media education practice, both academic and practical, and to debate current media education issues with experienced teachers, researchers, leaders in policy making and industry practitioners.

The British Film Institute (BFI) annual summer A level conference is a well-established three-day event that draws media teachers from across the country. Keynote speakers include leading media academics and industry practitioners; others in the same fields lead research seminars and 'Inside Industry Sessions' respectively. 'Teacher-led Sessions' draw on the expertise of media teachers who share classroom approaches and materials for teaching media topics, theory and curriculum areas. The BFI runs INSETs and education events throughout the year, and has a series of classroom targeted publications, *Teaching Media and Films Studies,* written by experienced teachers and examiners, now owned by Palgrave MacMillan.

The main MEA and BFI conferences are in London, but regional activities have included MEA South's *Teaching James Bond* event, which attracted 60 teachers from across the south-east, and an MEA North day conference in Bradford that debated Web 2.0 and its impact on media theory and learning. West Sussex Local Authority runs an annual two-day media conference where Graduate Teachers demonstrate part of their learning and share their practice.

The English and Media Centre in London runs excellent CPD courses and publishes award-winning classroom resources focused on active learning. Film Education has a stimulating annual conference (*CP3*) and online resources including free film case studies. Auteur Publishing has a wide range of media topic books targeting classroom practice, a quarterly film magazine *Splice*, and the media education research journal *MERJ*.

The Awarding Bodies also provide high quality extensive, but also inevitably specification-focused online resources and INSETs; OCR and WJEC additionally run annual conferences that provide useful materials and academic and practical workshops.

Media teachers are avid teachers of other media teachers. Certainly, the work of media teachers and the associations built up around media teaching fit a description provided by Wenger where 'communities of practice develop around things that matter to people . . . their practices reflect the members' own understanding of what is important' (Wenger 1998).

Masters in Teaching and Learning (MTL)

In the December 2007 *Children's Plan* (DCSF 2007), the government announced its intention that teaching should, over time, become a Masters' level profession. The new qualification was to be introduced in a staged way during 2009–2010 with the TDA coordinating implementation of support. The MTL is driven by aims to improve 'teacher quality, to raise standards and narrow the achievement gap'.

Features of the MTL are that it is:

* primarily a school-based programme;
* jointly delivered by schools and Higher Education Institutes;
* supported by trained coaches and tutors;
* undertaken through some independent study;
* *personalised to meet the participants' learning needs.* (This is author's emphasis.)

This last point has the potential to enable media educators to focus additional learning needs on their own teaching loads. Work that has been established in other areas of Masters level study in media education, for example, the BFI's collaborations with both the Open University and the Institute of Education's distance learning models have worked through action-research based approaches. Here relatively new media teachers have had an opportunity to join in an educational experience that they may not have had when training initially: that is sharing ideas, views and practices among themselves; engaging with reading and meeting media educators from the Higher Education sector. Connecting media teachers with the research community in media education, principally through the Centre for the Study of Children, Youth and Media or the work of *Futurelab* and *Becta* (closed in 2010 but its website is extant) opens doors to wider understanding, which will both inform and develop media teaching further. While it is too early in this publication to comment on how effective the MTL will be in enabling media teachers to collaborate on, and to overcome, their problems with their professional development in media education, it is, nevertheless, a significant step forward for the lone self educator in media teaching.

Summary

While media teacher education is not systematic, or likely to become so in the near future, resources do exist within teacher education courses and more widely through networks, training events and CPD for the community of media educators to continue to grow. The spread of courses in support of the 14–19 Creative and Media Diploma will be worth exploring to see how the pedagogies and frameworks are taught and who comes onto those courses and where they go (see Chapter 9). This is future work. In the meantime, the case for formalising ITE in media is one still worth making, not least to ensure the quality of media education experience for pupils being taught in schools. Only when really engaging with the passion of the arguments from media education advocates does it become clear just how important it remains to develop the argument further for media training. A *YouTube* video *Shift Happens* tells how education is changing in a world of rapid flux and shifts. Such apocalyptic storytelling of the speed of change in children's lives indicates just how vital keeping up with all of this is in educational terms and a systematic programme of media education taught by trained and enthusiastic teachers might be the means to address that need.

Further reading

Domaille, K. (2009) 'Preparing the media teachers of the future: materials for ITE', in *PoV: The Journal of the Media Education Association*, Summer 2009, vol. 1, no. 3, pp. 11–15. The article includes an example of a student teacher's action plan (see Figure 13.4).
(See also Further reading at the end of Chapter 12.)

Recommended resources

Publishers

Auteur Publishing – www.auteur.co.uk – publishes *MERJ – the Media Education Research Journal* – www.auteur.co.uk/index.php?main_section=8&textentryid=39.
BECTA ('innovative use of technology in learning') www.becta.org.uk.
British Film Institute – www.bfi.org.uk/education.

BFI Publishing – www.palgrave.com/bfi/indes.asp.
Centre for the Study of Children, Youth and Media (Institute of Education, University of London) – www.childrenyouthandmediacentre.co.uk.
English and Media Centre – www.englishandmedia.co.uk.
Futurelab ('innovation in education') – www.futurelab.org.uk.
Media Education Association – www.themea.org.
The Teacher Training Resource Bank – www.ttrb.ac.uk – includes English ITE media education pages at www.ite.org.uk/ite_topics/media/001.html.

Websites

Graduate Teacher Training Registry – www.gttr.org.uk.
Shift Happens – www.youtube.com/watch?v=ljbI-363A2Q.
Times Educational Supplement Noticeboard – www.tes.co.uk/noticeboard.aspx.

Bibliography

Aarseth, E.J. (1997) *Cybertext: Perspectives on Ergodic Literature*, Baltimore: John Hopkins University Press.

Alvarado, M. and Boyd-Barrett, O. (eds) (1992) *Media Education: An Introduction*, London: British Film Institute.

Alvarado, M., Gutch, R. and Wollen, T. (1987) *Learning the Media: An Introduction*, London: Palgrave Macmillan.

Anderson, B. (2002) 'National identity and the media', in Briggs, A. and Cobley, P. (eds) *The Media: An Introduction* (2nd edition), Harlow: Pearson Education.

Anderson, C.A. and Bushman, B.J. (2001) 'Effects of violent video games on aggressive behaviour, aggressive cognition, aggressive affect, physiological arousal, and prosocial behaviour: A meta-analytic review of the scientific literature', in *Psychological Science*, 12, pp. 353–359.

Anderson, P. (2007) *What is Web 2.0? Ideas, Technologies and Implications for Education*, JISC www.jisc.ac.uk/publications/publications/twWeb2.asp (accessed 7 September 2011).

Andrews, J. and Clark, J. (2009) *The World in the Movies*, BFI, www.bfi.org.uk/education/teaching/pdfonlyresource/world_in_the_movies.pdf (accessed 2 April 2010).

Ang, I. (1985) *Watching Dallas: Soap Opera and the Melodramatic Imagination*, London: Methuen.

Arthur, J. (2007) *International Handbook in Citizenship and Democracy*, London: Sage.

Baker, J. (2003) *Teaching TV Sitcom*, London: BFI/Palgrave Macmillan.

Baker, J. and Toland, P. (2007) *Teaching Film at GCSE*, Leighton Buzzard: Auteur.

Barker, M. and Petley, J. (2001) *Ill Effects: The Media/Violence Debate*, London: Routledge.

Barratt, A.J.B. (1998) *Audit of Media in English: A BFI Education Research Report*, London: BFI Publishing.

Barthes, R. (1973) *Mythologies*, London: Paladin.

Bateman, A., Peter Bennett, Sarah Case Benyahia and Peter Wall (2010) *A2 Media Studies: The Essential Introduction for WJEC*, London: Routledge.

Baudrillard, J. (1972) *The Consumer Society: Myths and Structures*, London: SAGE/in association with TCS.

Bazalgette, C. (1991) *Media Education (Teaching English in the National Curriculum)*, London: Arnold Hodder & Stoughton.

Bazalgette, C. (2008/9) 'Literacy in time and space', in *PoV: The Journal of the Media Education Association*, Winter 2008/9, vol. 1, no. 1, pp. 12–16.

Bazalgette, C. (2009) *Impacts of Moving Image Education: A Summary of Research*, Scottish Screen, www.scottishscreen.com/images/documents/mie_research_summary.pdf (accessed 11 May 2010).

Bazalgette, C. (ed.) (2010) *Teaching Media in Primary Schools*, London: Sage.

Bazalgette, C., Bevort, E. and Savino, J. (1993a) *New Directions: Media Education Worldwide*, London and Paris: BFI, CLEMI, UNESCO.

BBC (2009) *BBC Six o'Clock News*, 23 January 2009.

BBC (2010) 'Should schools teach *The Simpsons?*', *Today*, 21 July 2010, BBC Radio 4, http://news.bbc.co.uk/today/hi/today/newsid_8840000/8840618.stm (accessed 7 September 2011).

BBC (2011a) *Editorial Guidelines*, www.bbc.co.uk/guidelines/editorialguidelines/edguide/impartiality/ (accessed 7 September 2011)

BBC (2011b) *School Report*, www.bbc.co.uk/schoolreport/ (accessed 7 September 2011).

BBC Radio 4 (2009) *The World at One*, 27 May 2009.

Bentham, S. (2002) *Psychology and Education*, London and New York: Routledge.

Benyahia, S.C. (2008) *Teaching Film and TV Documentary*, London: BFI/Palgrave Macmillan.

Berens, K. and Howard, G. (2001) *The Rough Guide to Videogaming*, London: Rough Guides.

BFI (2000) *Moving Images in the Classroom*, 'Citizenship/PSHE', pp. 32–33, www.bfi.org.uk/education/teaching/miic/pdf/bfi_edu_miic_teachers-guide.pdf (accessed 5 April 2010).

Blumler, J.G. and Katz, E. (1974) *The Uses of Mass Communications: Current Perspectives on Gratifications Research*, Beverly Hills, CA: Sage.

Board of Education (1910) *Circular 753*, London: HMSO.

Board of Education (1921) *The Teaching of English in England* (The Newbolt Report), London: HMSO.

Board of Education (1938) *Report on Secondary Education* (The Spens Report), London: HMSO.

Bolas, T. (2009) *Screen Education: From Film Appreciation to Media Studies*, London: Intellect.

Boles, D. (2011) *Language of Media Literacy: A Glossary of Terms*, Center for Media Literacy, Canada www.medialit.org/reading-room/language-media-literacy-glossary-terms (accessed 8 March 2011).

Boorstein, D. (1971) *L'Image – A Guide to Pseudo-events in America*, New York: Athenæum.

Bordwell, D. and Thompson, K. (2008) *Film Art: An Introduction* (8th edition), New York: McGraw-Hill (includes text-specific CD ROM of film extracts).

Bouissac, P. (2010) *Saussure: A Guide for the Perplexed*, London: Continuum.

Branston, G. and Stafford, R. (1999) *The Media Student's Book*, London: Routledge.

Branston, G. and Stafford, R. (2006) *The Media Student's Book* (4th edition), London: Routledge.

Branston, G. and Stafford, R. (2010) *The Media Student's Book* (5th edition), London: Routledge.

Brett, P. (ed.) (2002) *GCSE Citizenship Studies*, London: Folens Ltd.

British Film Institute (1999) *Making Movies Matter: Report of the Film Education Working Group*, London: BFI.

British Film Institute (2000) *Moving Images in the Classroom: A Secondary Teachers' Guide to Using Film & Television*, www.bfi.org.uk/education/teaching/miic/pdf/bfi_edu_miic_teachers-guide.pdf (accessed 11 March 2011).

Bryant, J. and Davies, J. (2006) 'Selective exposure processes', in J. Bryant and P. Vorderer (eds), *Psychology of Entertainment* (pp. 19–33), Mahwah, NJ: Lawrence Erlbaum Associates.

Buckingham, D. (1995) *Learning Media and Technology*, London: Routledge.

Buckingham, D. (2000) *The Making of Citizens: Young People, News and Politics*, London: Routledge.

Buckingham, D. (2000) *After the Death of Childhood: Growing Up in the Age of Electronic Media*, Cambridge: Polity.

Buckingham, D. (2003) *Media Education: Literacy, Learning and Contemporary Culture*, London: Polity Press.

Buckingham, D. (2007a) *Beyond Technology: Children's Learning, in the Age of Digital Culture*, London: Polity.

Buckingham, D. (2007b) 'Battle in print: beyond technology: rethinking learning in the age of digital culture', www.battleofideas.org.uk/index.php/site/battles/886 (accessed 11 February 2011).

Buckingham, D. (2011) *The Material Child*, London: Polity Press.

Buckingham, D., Grahame, J. and Sefton-Green, J. (1995) *Making Media: Practical Production in Media Education*, London: English and Media Centre.

Burn, A. (2010) 'From Beowulf to Batman: connecting English and media education', in Davison, J. *et al.* (eds) *Debates in English Teaching*, London: Routledge.

Burn, A. and Durran, J. (2007) *Media Literacy in Schools*, London: Paul Chapman Publishing.

Burn, A. and Durrant, C. (eds) (2008) *Media Teaching*, Wakefield Press: NATE.

Byron Review (2008) *The Impact of the Media on Children and Young People*, London: DCSF.

Calleja, G. (2007a) 'Digital game involvement: a conceptual model', *Games and Culture* 2007, vol. 2, p. 236.

Calleja, G. (2007b) *Digital Games as Designed Environment*, Ph.D. thesis Victoria University, Wellington: New Zealand.

Campbell, J. (1949) *The Hero's Journey: Joseph Campbell on His Life and Work* (2003 edition, Cousineau, P. ed.), Novato, CA: New World Library.

Carr, D., Buckingham, D., Burn, A. and Schott, G. (2006) *Computer Games: Text, Narrative and Play*, Cambridge: Polity.

Carr, D. (2008) *Un-Situated Play? Textual Analysis and Digital Games*, DiGRA Hardcore Column 18, www.gameology.org (accessed 7 September 2011).

Chanda, S. (2010) *My Beautiful Laundrette*, BFI Screenonline, www.screenonline.org.uk/film/id/443819/index.html (accessed 22 March 2010).

Channel 4 (2010) *Breaking the News*, www.channel4.com/learning/breakingthenews/ (accessed 20 March 2010).

Clark, V. (2007) *Media and Film Studies Handbook*, London: Hodder Arnold.

Clark, V., Baker, J. and Lewis, E. (2002) *Key Concepts and Skills for Media Studies*, London: Hodder and Stoughton.

Clark, V., Jones, P., Malyszko, B. and Wharton, D. (2007) *Complete A–Z Media and Film Studies Handbook*, London: Routledge.

Clarke, S. (2005) *Formative Assessment in the Secondary Classroom*, London: Hodder.

Claxton, G. (2002) *Building Learning Power*, Bristol: TLO Limited.

Collins, R. (1992) 'Media studies: alternative or oppositional practice', in Alvarado, M. and Boyd-Barrett, O. (eds) *Media Education: An Introduction*, London: British Film Institute.

Connell, B. (ed.) (2010) *Exploring the Media: Text, Industry, Audience* (2nd edition), Leighton Buzzard: Auteur.

Connolly, S. (2011) 'Pulling the pin: media education as a tool for social inclusion', www.manifesto formediaeducation.co.uk/2011/01/steve-connolly/ (accessed 11 March 2011).

Considine, P. (1997) in Kubey, R. (ed.) *Media Literacy in the Information Age*, New Brunswick, NJ: Transaction Publishers.

Cope, B. and Kalantzis, M. (eds) (2000) *Multiliteracies: Literacy Learning and the Design of Social Futures*, London: Routledge.

Crick, B. (1989) *Essays on Politics and Literature*, Edinburgh: Edinburgh University Press.

Crick, B. (2008) 'Citizenship, diversity, and national identity', in *London Review of Education*, vol. 6, no. 1, March.

Daniels, H. (2001) *Vygotsky and Pedagogy*, London: Routledge Falmer.

Davison, J. (1997) 'Battles for English 1: 1870–1980', in Davison, J. and Dowson, J. (1997) *Learning to Teach English in the Secondary School*, London: Routledge.

Davison, J. (1997) 'Battles for English 2: English and the National Curriculum', in Davison, J. and Dowson, J. (ed.) *Learning to Teach English in the Secondary School*, London: Routledge.

Davison, J. (2009) 'Battles for English', in Davison, J. and Dowson, J. (2009) *Learning to Teach English in the Secondary School* (3rd edition), London: Routledge.

Davison, J. and Dowson, J. (2009) *Learning to Teach English in the Secondary School* (3rd edition), London: Routledge.

Deleuze, G. and Guattari, F. (2004) *A Thousand Plateaus: Capitalism and Schizophrenia*, London: Continuum.

Department for Children, Schools and Families (2007) *Children's Plan*, London: DCSF.

Department for Children, Schools and Families (2008) *Safer Children in a Digital World*, London: DCSF.

Department for Children, Schools and Families (2009) *The Impact of the Commercial World on Children's Wellbeing*, London: DCSF.

Department of Education and Science (1963) *Half Our Future* (Newsom Report), London: HMSO.

Department of Education and Science (1975) *A Language for Life* (Bullock Report), London: HMSO.

Department of Education and Science (1983) *Popular Television and Schoolchildren: The Report of a Group of Teachers*, London: HMSO.

Department of Education and Science & Welsh Office (1989) *English for Ages 5–16* (Cox Report), London: HMSO.

Department for Education and Skills (2004) *14–19 Curriculum and Qualifications Reform Final Report of the Working Group on 14–19 Reform* (The Tomlinson Report), London: Stationery Office.

Department for Education and Skills (2007) *Diversity and Citizenship Curriculum Review*, Sir Keith Ajegbo, http://publications.education.gov.uk (accessed 20 June 2010).

Domaille, K. (2009) 'Preparing the media teachers of the future: materials for ITE', in *PoV: The Journal of the Media Education Association*, Summer 2009, vol. 1, no. 3, pp. 11–15.

Domaille, K. and Grahame, J. (2001) *The Media Book*, London: English and Media Centre.

Dovey, J. and Kennedy, H.W. (2007) *Game Cultures: Computer Games as New Media*, London: Open University Press.

Duffy, J. (2008) 'Media studies: the next generation' in *BBC Online News Magazine*, 30 January 2001, http://news.bbc.co.uk/1/hi/magazine/3444499.stm (accessed 9 September 2011).

Eco, U. (1997) *The Future of the Book* (edited by Geoffrey Nunberg), Berkeley, CA: University of California Press.

English and Media Centre (2008) *Doing Ads*, London: EMC Publishing.

Esseen, M., Phillips, M. and Riley, A. (2009) *GCSE Media Studies for WJEC*, London: Heinemann.

EuroMediaLiteracy (2009) *European Charter for Media Literacy*, www.euromedialiteracy.eu/charter.php (accessed 11 March 2011).

Field, K., Holden, P. and Lawlor, H. (1999) *Effective Subject Leadership*, London: Routledge.

Film Education Working Group (1999) *Making Movies Matter*, London: BFI.

Fiske, J. (1987) *Television Culture*, London: Methuen.

Fraser, P. (2005) *Teaching Music Video*, London: BFI Publishing.

Fraser, P. and Oram, B. (2006) *Teaching Digital Production*, London: BFI Education/Palgrave Macmillan.

Fraser, P. and Wardle, J. (2011) *A Manifesto for Media Education*, www.manifestoformediaeducation. co.uk/why-a-manifesto/ (accessed 13 September 2011).

Freire, P. (1972) *Cultural Action for Freedom*, Harmondsworth: Penguin.

Freire, P. (1976) *Education, the Practice of Freedom*, London: Writers and Readers Publishing Co-operative.

Freire, P. (1985) *The Politics of Education: Culture, Power and Liberation*, South Hadley, MA: Bergin & Garvey.

Friedman, L.T. (2005) *The World is Flat*, New York: Farrar, Strauss and Giroux.

Gardner, H. (1983) *Frames of Mind: The Theory of Multiple Intelligences*, New York: Basic Books Inc.

Gauntlett, D. (1998) 'Ten things wrong with the "effects model"', in Dickinson, R., Harindranath, R. and Linné, O. (eds) (1998) *Approaches to Audiences – A Reader*, Arnold: London.

Gauntlett, D. (2004) *Introduction to Web Studies* (2nd edition) (2000), www.newmediastudies. com/intro200.htm (accessed 7 September 2011).

Gauntlett. D. (2006) 'Ten things wrong with media effects studies', in Weaver, K. and Carter, C. (eds), *Critical Readings: Violence and the Media*, Maidenhead and New York: Open University Press.

Gauntlett, D. (2007a) *Creative Explorations – New Approaches to Identities and Audiences*, London and New York: Routledge.

Gauntlett, D. (2007b) *Media Studies 2.0: A New Approach to Today's Media Landscapes*, www. theory.org.uk/mediastudies2.htm (accessed 7 September 2011).

Geraghty, C. (2005) *My Beautiful Laundrette*, London: I.B. Tauris.

Gibson, W. (1984) *Neuromancer*, London: Harper Collins.

Goodwin, A. (1992) *Dancing in the Distraction Factory: Music, Television and Popular Culture*, Minneapolis, MN: University of Minnesota Press.

Grahame, J. (1991) *The English Curriculum: Media 1 – Years 7–9*, London: English & Media Centre.

Grahame, J. (1996) *Picture Power*, London: English & Media Centre.

Grahame, J. (2003) *The Media Pack: Units for GCSE Media and English*, London: English & Media Centre.

Grahame, J. (2006) *Doing News*, London: English & Media Centre.

Grahame, J. (2008/9) 'Media literacy CPD: exactly what it says on the tin', in *PoV: The Journal of the Media Education Association*, Winter 2008/9, vol. 1, no. 1.

Grahame, J. (2009) *Doing TV Drama*, London: English & Media Centre.

Grodal, T. (2000) 'Video games and the pleasure of control', in *Media Entertainment: The Psychology of its Appeal*, Zillmann, D. and Voderer, P. (eds), pp. 197–246.

Habermas, J. (1989) *The Structural Transformation of the Public Sphere* (1st paperback edition, 1991), Cambridge, MA: The MIT Press.

Hall, S. (1981) 'The whites of their eyes, racist ideologies and the media', in Bridges, G. and Brunt, R. (eds) *Silver Linings*, London: Lawrence & Wishart.

Hall, S. (1994) 'Cultural identity and diaspora', in Williams, P. and Chrisman, L. (eds), *Colonial Discourse and Post Colonial Theory: A Reader*, London: Longman.

Hall, S. (1996) 'Cultural studies: two paradigms', in Bennett, T. *et al.* (eds) *Culture, Ideology and Social Progress*, London: Batsford.

Hall, S. (ed.) (1997) *Representation: Cultural Representations and Signifying Practices*, London: Sage Publications.

Haraway, D. (1991) 'A cyborg manifesto: science, technology, and socialist-feminism in the late twentieth century', in Haraway, D. *Simians, Cyborgs and Women: The Reinvention of Nature*, New York: Routledge.

Harindranath, R. and Linné, O. (eds) (1998) *Approaches to Audiences – A Reader*, London: Hodder Arnold.

Hart, A. and Hicks, A. (2002) *Teaching Media in the English Curriculum*, London: Trentham Books.

Hendry, S. (2008a) 'A monster of a marketing campaign!' in *Media Magazine*, issue 24, April 2008.

Hendry, S. (2008b) 'Analysing media texts: how to use media concepts and avoid simple description' in *Media Magazine*, issue 25, September 2008.

Hendry, S. (2009) 'Cross-media platforms: an overview', in *Media Magazine*, issue 28, April 2009.

Hewlett, M. (2008) *Educating People for the 21st Century*, the Nuffield Review of 14–19 Education and Training, Nuffield Review Working Paper 47, www.nuffield14-19review.org.uk/files/documents205-1.pdf (accessed 20 June 2009).

Hill, J. (1999) *British Cinema in the 1980s*, Oxford: Clarendon Press.

Hills, M. (2005) *How To Do Things with Cultural Theory*, London: Hodder Arnold.

Homer, E. (2008) 'Who's got the power, cult fans versus the film industry', in *Media Magazine*, EMC Publishing, issue 25, September.

Homer, E. (2008) '10 tips for making the most of online research', in *Media Magazine*, EMC Publishing, issue 24, April.

Huizinga, J. (1970) *Homo Ludens: A Study in the Play Element in Culture*, London: Paladin.

Ipsos MORI (2007) *Young People and British Identity*, Camelot Foundation.

Jamal, M. (1985) 'Dirty linen', in Mercer, K. (1987) *Black Film, British Cinema*, London: ICA Documents.

Jenkins, H. (2004) 'Game design as narrative architecture', in N. Wardrip-Fruin, N. and Harrigan, P. (eds), *First Person; New Media as Story, Performance and Game*, Cambridge, MA: MIT Press, pp. 118–130.

Jenkins, H. (2008) *Convergence Culture* (Revised edition), New York and London: New York University Press.

Jenkins, P. (1986) *Definitions and Re-defining Media Studies in Further Education: The New Curricula, Media Studies and State Control*, paper presented to the 1986 International Television Studies Conference.

Jones, N. (2000) *Sultans of Spin: The Media and the New Labour Government*, London: Gollancz.

Juul, J. (2003) 'The game, the player, the world: looking for the heart of gameness', in Copier, M. and Raessens, J. (eds) *Level Up: Digital Games Research Conference Proceedings*, University of Utrecht, pp. 30–47.

Kirwan, T., Learmonth, J., Sayre, M. and Williams, R. (2003) *Approaches to Instruction and Teacher Education in Media Literacy*, http://academic.mediachina.net/article.php?id=5530 (accessed 7 September 2011).

Kress, G. (2003) *Literacy in the New Media Age*, London: Routledge.

Kubey, R. (1997) *Media Literacy in the Information Age*, New Brunswick, NJ: Transaction Publishers.

Lankshear, C. (1997) *Changing Literacies*, Buckingham: OUP.

Lankshear, C. and Knobel, M. (2003) *New Literacies: Changing Knowledge and Classroom Learning*, Buckingham and Philadelphia, PA: Open University Press.

Lewis, E. (2003) *Teaching TV News*, London: BFI Publishing/Palgrave MacMillan.

Lewis, E. (2008) *Teaching Television at GCSE*, Leighton Buzzard: Auteur.

Lewis, E., Rodgers, M., Morris R. and Goddard, J. (2009) *OCR Media Studies for GCSE*, London: Hodder Education.

Lister, M., Kelly, K., Dovey, J., Giddings, S. and Grant, I. (2003) *New Media: A Critical Introduction*, London: Routledge.

Little, A. (2010) *The Daily Express* 25, June, www.express.co.uk/posts/view/182947/Britain-s-population-soars-to-62m (accessed 7 September 2011).

Lurhs, G. (2008) 'AS coursework – charity ads', in *Media Magazine*, EMC Publishing, issue 23.

Lusted, D. (1991) *The Media Studies Book: A Guide for Teachers*, Abingdon: Routledge.

Lyng, T. (2008) Headteacher, Brockhill School of Performing Arts, panel member, Culture Trip? Conference, Channel 4, 22 April 2008.

Marsh, J. (2005) *Popular Culture, New Media and Digital Literacy in Early Childhood*, London: Routledge.

Masterman, L. (1980) *Teaching About Television*, London: Macmillan.

Masterman, L. (1985) *Teaching the Media*, London: Comedia.

Masterman, L. (1989) *Media Awareness Education: Eighteen Basic Principles*, www.medialit.org/reading-room/media-awareness-education-eighteen-basic-principles (accessed 7 September 2011).

Masterman, L. (1995) 'Media awareness education: eighteen basic principles', in *Mediacy*, vol. 17, no. 3, Summer.

McCluhan, M. (2001) *Understanding Media: The Extension of Man*, London: Routledge.

McDougall, J. (2006) *The Media Teacher's Book*, London: Hodder Education.

McDougalll, J. (2008) 'Media 2.0 critical perspectives', in *Media Magazine*, issue 24, April.

McDougall, J. (2009) *OCR Media Studies for A2* (3rd edition), London: Hodder Education.

McDougall, J. and Potamitis, N. (2010) *The Media Teacher's Book* (2nd edition), London: Routledge.

McInnes, R. (2003) *Action/Adventure Films: A Teacher's Guide*, Leighton Buzzard: Auteur Publishing.

McLaren, P. (1988) 'Essay review of *Literacy: Reading the Word and the World* by Freire and Macedo 1987', *Harvard Education Review*, vol. 58, Winter.

Mercer, N. (1995) *The Guided Construction of Knowledge: Talk Among Teachers and Learners*, Oxford: Multilingual Matters.

Mercer, N. (2000) *Words and Minds: How We Use Language to Think Together*, London: Routledge.

Merrin, W. (2009) http://twopointzeroforum.blogspot.com (accessed 7 September 2011).

Mirza, M. (2005) 'Yasmin, Kenny Gleenan', in *Culture Wars*, Institute of Ideas, www.culturewars. org.uk/2005-01/yasmin.htm (accessed 5 May 2010).

Morris, R., Varkey, D., Robinson, K. and McInerney, J. (2009) *GCSE AQA Media Studies*, London: Nelson Thornes.

Mottershead, C. (2009) 'Out of the Past', in *PoV: The Journal of the Media Education Association*, Summer 2009, vol. 1, no. 3.

Murray, S. (2009) Film Club Induction, in *PoV: The Journal of the Media Education Association*, vol. 1, issue 2, Spring 2009 www.themea.org.

Murray Copier, M. and Raessens, J. (eds) (2003) *Level Up: Digital Games Research Conference Proceedings*, University of Utrecht, pp. 30–47.

Newman, J. (2004) *Videogames*, London: Routledge.

Ofcom (2010) *UK Children's Media Literacy*, http://stakeholders.ofcom.org.uk/market-data-research/media-literacy/medlitpub/medlitpubrss/ukchildrensml/ (accessed 8 March 2011).

O'Reilly, T. (2005) *What Is Web 2.0?: Design Patterns and Business Models for the Next Generation of Software*, www.oreillynet.com (accessed 7 September 2011).

O'Sullivan, T., Dutton, B., and Rayner, P. (2003) *Studying the Media* (3rd edition), London: Arnold.

Pahl, K. and Rowsell, J. (2005) *Literacy and Education*, London: Paul Chapman Publishing.

Phillips, D. (2001) *Online Public Relations*, London: Kogan Page.

Points, J. (2006) *Teaching TV Drama*, London: British Film Institute.

QCA (1998) *Education for Citizenship and the Teaching of Democracy in Schools: Final Report of the Advisory Group on Citizenship 22 September 1998* (The Crick Report) London: QCA.

QCA (2005) *Media Matters: A Review of Media Studies in Schools and Colleges*, order online only www.qcda.gov.uk/resources/search-results.aspx?keys=&page=21&phase=&topic=48&format=&for=&sortby=1&sortdir=0 (accessed 7 September 2011).

QCA (2007) *Citizenship Specification*, http://curriculum.qcda.gov.uk/key-stages-3-and-4/subjects/key-stage-3/citizenship/index.aspx (accessed 19 March 2010).

QCA (2007a) The National Curriculum, www.qcda.gov.uk/13575.aspx (accessed 7 September 2011).

QCA (2007b) *The Global Dimension in Action: A Curriculum Planning Guide for Schools*, www.qcda. gov.uk/15333.aspx (accessed 7 September 2011).

QCA (2007c) *NC Guidance: Identity and Diversity*, curriculum.qca.org.uk/key-stages-3-and-4/cross-curriculum dimensions/culturaldiversityidentity/index.aspx (accessed 7 September 2011).

Quart, A. (2005) 'Networked: Don Roos and *Happy Endings*', in *Film Comment*, vol. 41, no. 4, July/August, pp. 48–50.

Quin, R. and McMahon, B. (1997) 'Living with the tiger: media curriculum issues for the future', in Kubey, R., *Media Literacy in the Information Age*, New Brunswick, NJ: Transaction Publishers.

Quy, S. (2001) *Teaching Short Film*, London: BFI/Palgrave Macmillan.

Ranson, S. (1984) 'Towards a tertiary tripartism: new codes of social control and the 17 plus', in Broadfoot, P. (ed.) (1984) *Selection, Certification and Control: Social Issues in Educational Assessment*, Lewes: Falmer Press.

Readman, M. (2009) *Making Sense of Creativity*, Presentation OCR Annual Conference www. slideshare.net/rikhudson/cemp-mark-readman-ocr-media-conference-2009 (accessed 11 March 2011).

Roberts, P. (2006) *Nurturing Creativity in Young People: A Report to Government to Inform Future Policy*, DCSF/DfES, www.idea.gov.uk/idk/aio/5720952 (accessed 19 May 2009).

Rodriguez, R. (1996) *Rebel Without a Crew; Or How a 23 Year old Film-maker with $7000 Became a Hollywood Player*, London: Faber and Faber.

Rogers, C. R. (1977) *Carl Rogers on Personal Power: Inner Strength and its Revolutionary Impact*, Oxford: Delacorte Press.

Rothschild, N. (2008) 'Immigration should not be a political football', in *Spiked*, 2 April, www.spiked-online.com/index.php/site/article/4943/ (accessed 7 September 2011).

Scholz, T. (2008) *Market Ideology and the Myths of Web 2.0, First Monday*, 13, 3 http://firstmonday. org/htbin/cgiwrap/bin/ojs/index.php/fm/article/viewArticle/2138/1945 (accessed 7 September 2011).

Sefton Green, J. (1999) *Young People, Creativity and the New Technologies: The Challenge of Digital Arts*, London: Routledge.

Stafford, R. (1990) 'Re-defining creativity: extended project work in GCSE media studies', in Buckingham, D. (ed.) *Watching Media Learning: Making Sense of Media Education*, London: The Falmer Press.

Stafford, R. (2001) *Media Education in the UK*, www.mediaed.org.uk/posted_documents/media eduk.html (accessed 6 July 2011).

Stafford, R. (2009) '"Look for the money!" How new media pays its way and what we should teach in media studies', in *PoV: The Journal of the Media Education Association*, Winter 2009, vol. 2, no. 1.

Tapscott, D. (1997) *Growing Up Digital: Rise of the Net Generation*, New York: McGraw-Hill.

Thompson, K. (1999) *Storytelling in the New Hollywood: Understanding Classical Narrative Technique*, London: Harvard University Press.

Telegraph.co.uk, www.telegraph.co.uk/culture/tvandradio/4329701/BBC-attacked-by-Ben-Bradshaw-for-refusal-to-broadcast-emergency-fund-appeal-for-Gaza.html (accessed 24 January 2010).

Times Educational Supplement (1915) 'Children and the cinematograph', 5 January, London: Times Newspapers.

UK Film Council (2009) *Film: 21st Century Literacy. A Strategy for Film Education Across the UK*, www.21stcenturyliteracy.org.uk (accessed 11 March 2011).

Vogler, C. (2007) *The Writer's Journey: Mythic Structure for Writers* (3rd edition), Studio City, CA: Michael Wiese Productions.

Wallis, C. (2006) 'How to bring our schools out of the 20th century', in *Time*, www.time.com/time/magazine/article/0,9171,1568480,00.html (accessed 24 May 2009).

Walsh, M. (2008) 'Worlds have collided and modes have merged: classroom evidence of changed literacy practices', in *Literacy*, vol. 42, no. 2, pp. 101–108.

Walters, B. (2010) 'Film of the month: *Four Lions*', *Sight and Sound*, June, www.bfi.org.uk/sightandsound/review/5471 (accessed 6 July 2011).

Weaver, K. and Carter, C. (eds) (2006) *Critical Readings: Violence and the Media*, Maidenhead and New York: Open University Press.

Wenger, E. (1998) 'Communities of practice: learning as a social system Systems Thinker', www.open. ac.uk/ldc08/sites/www.open.ac.uk.ldc08/files/Learningasasocialsystem.pdf (accessed 11 March 2011).

Williams, J. (2001) *Professional Leadership: Effective Middle Management and Subject Leadership*, London: Routledge.

Williams, R. (1958) *Culture and Society 1780–1950*, Columbia: Columbia University Press.

Williams, R. (1974) *Television, Technology and Cultural Form*, London: Fontana.

Woodhead, C. (2000) 'Teenage culture is harming pupils', *Church Times*, 11 February.

Index

Please note that page references in *italics* refer to Figures and Tables. Page numbers followed by the letter 'n' refer to notes.